JULIUS CAESAR

ASPECTS OF GREEK AND ROMAN LIFE

General Editor: Professor H. H. Scullard

JULIUS CAESAR

and his Public Image

Zwi Yavetz

THAMES AND HUDSON

For my friends at Queen's College, New York, N.Y.

Translated from the German

© 1983 THAMES AND HUDSON LTD, LONDON

© 1979 DROSTE VERLAG GMBH, DÜSSELDORF

Typeset in Linoterm Bembo by Keyset Composition, Colchester
Printed and bound in Great Britain
by The Pitman Press, Bath

CONTENTS

PREFACE

In 1945 I attended a course on the Late Roman Republic at the Hebrew University of Jerusalem. My teacher, Victor Tcherikover, was a graduate of the University of Berlin, a pupil of Eduard Meyer and Ulrich Wilcken. When he spoke about Caesar's aims, his words left scarcely any room for doubt: in his opinion, Caesar was endeavouring to found an absolute monarchy based on divine kingship. He was aware that Sir Ronald Syme's book, *The Roman Revolution*, had been published in 1939, but regretted that a copy was unobtainable because of the war.

In 1955, while participating in Syme's seminars at Oxford, I realized that none of my English tutors shared Meyer's views. At that time, I was not particularly interested in Caesar, and in my early days as a university teacher I recommended that my students read Matthias Gelzer's carefully written book, but did not take sides in this particular argument. I was more interested in the social and economic problems of ancient Rome than in Caesar's ambitions. But, in the course of time, it proved impossible to avoid fundamental issues when teaching ancient history. In 1970 I gave a seminar on Caesar at Queen's College in New York, and in 1973 I returned to the subject at the University of Tel-Aviv. However, it was not until I read Hermann Strasburger's fascinating book, *Caesar im Urteil der Zeitgenossen*, that I felt compelled to study the sources from A to Z. I present my conclusions to the reader but a few words of explanation must be added.

I am not of the school that considers it unnecessary to immerse oneself in the modern literature on the subject, and which holds that we should be exclusively concerned with primary sources. To disregard the modern literature of the nineteenth and twentieth centuries is to make the study of ancient history intellectually unprofitable, whereas it is precisely the interplay of modern controversies that helps one to read the same source from new and fresh points of view.

Unfortunately, the number of students of the subject who read
German is continually dwindling in Great Britain and the
United States as well as in Israel. The problem of Caesar's final
aims cannot be fully understood without an understanding of
the German scholarly literature. That is why a historio-
graphical survey forms the first chapter of this book.

I do not want to go into the question of divine kingship in
detail once again; this subject has been explored and treated out
of all proportion to its real significance. In my opinion, no one
can make a substantial contribution to the present state of the
argument. Everyone can form his own judgment on the basis
of material published in the comprehensive works of Alföldi,
Weinstock, Dobesch, Gesche and Rawson. But the question
arises: is it possible to understand the Ides of March without
providing a definitive answer to the problem of divine kingship: I have attempted to do so by means of a thorough analysis
of the sources concerned with Caesar's legislation, and have
taken pains, in the last chapter, to make a general judgment
of Caesar's public image, pointing out that this image might
have been of greater political importance than Caesar's
true character, which bewildered not only modern scholars
but also Caesar's contemporaries: Caecina once expressed
his doubts and said that he was far from knowing Caesar
('. . . totum enim Caesarem non novi', Cic., *ad fam*. VI, 7, 4).

For practical reasons I have avoided lengthy Greek and Latin
quotations, and made use of them only in the appendix, which
constitutes the first part of an article published in *Harvard
Studies in Classical Philology* in 1974. I am grateful to the
editorial board of that journal for permission to reproduce it
here.

It only remains for me to thank the friends and institutions
without whose help this book would not have appeared.
Above all, I am grateful to Fred and Helen Lessing, donors of
the Chair of Roman History at the University of Tel-Aviv,
who made it possible for me to spend some months in the
libraries of Oxford and Pavia, since I could not have accom-
plished the work in my own university library. I am indebted
to the personal intervention of Dr Wolfgang Treue, of the
Deutsche Forschungsgemeinschaft, for smoothing out
financial difficulties.

I am much appreciative of the hospitality of Queen's
College in New York, N.Y., where I twice stayed as Visiting

Professor, and owe much to its former President, Joseph Murphy, its former Rector, Nathan Siegel, and its Dean, Al Levinson and, above all, to my colleagues in the history faculty. Professors Keith Eubank, Paul Avrich and Stuart Prall, who made my stay so pleasant, and who produced such good students for my seminars.

My relationship with Queen's College continued even after giving my seminar on Caesar there, as did the friendships established with the faculty of that institution. Indeed, only rarely are such close personal relationships created between colleagues and friends, as those which I have enjoyed there.

I would like to thank Saul Cohen, the new President of Queen's College; William Hamovitch, the new Provost; Dean Charles Hoffman; and many other friends outside of the Department of History there. I would especially like to express my gratitude to my old friends Professors R. W. Hartle, Harry Greenfield, Henry Morton and Ernest Schwartz.

I am obliged to the Institute for Advanced Study at Princeton, N.J., where I wrote the first draft of this book, and for the frequent opportunities to discuss questions of particular interest to me with Professors Frank J. Gilliam, Christian Habicht and Andreas Alföldi. It was an enormous pleasure to have discussions with scholars of such stature. I am deeply indebted to Sir Henry Fisher of Wolfson College, Oxford, and Sir Ronald Syme, who made Oxford a second home for me.

I owe much to my friends and former pupils at the Department of History, Tel-Aviv University, Mrs R. Vishnia, Mr Y. Zlattner, and Professor Z. Rubin, who not only read the proofs and prepared the index for the English edition, but also gave their time to discuss with me matters of form and substance. For translations of ancient authors I have gratefully made use of the Loeb Classical Library with some minor adjustments.

Finally, I record my gratitude to three good friends, whose support was ever ready, who read the manuscript in its different stages, drew my attention to important points of interpretation, and who have been a continual source of inspiration and encouragement to me since I began my studies in ancient history. I refer to Christian Meier of Munich, Fergus Millar of London and Emilio Gabba of Pavia. To all of them, my thanks.

Z.Y.

CAESAR AND CAESARISM IN THE HISTORICAL WRITING OF THE NINETEENTH AND TWENTIETH CENTURIES[1]

THE PROBLEM

In 1953 Hermann Strasburger startled a group of German teachers when he stated briefly and persuasively,[2] that Julius Caesar, despite his image of great popularity,[3] was nothing more than a lonely dictator: not a single Roman senator supported his fateful decision to cross the Rubicon.

Before he took this risk, Caesar addressed his companions, 'My friends, if I do not cross this stream, there will be manifold distress for me; if I do cross it, it will be for all mankind.'[4] This warning left his friends unmoved. Some of them, including Calpurnius Piso (his father-in-law), Publius Dolabella, Scribonius Curio, Sulpicius Rufus and Trebatius Testa, absolutely refused to cross the Rubicon; others, like Oppius, Balbus and Matius (who were reckoned in Rome to be Caesar's most trusted associates), had their own views about it. According to Strasburger, one factor was crucial: at no point did Caesar command the total devotion of his followers.

Strasburger did not concern himself with Caesar's plans, his final aims, or his place in history. He agreed with Jakob Burckhardt that, 'so far-reaching a view, implying that Caesar's plans were on a world-wide scale, must, since it is based on false assumptions, lead to wrong conclusions.'

At the beginning of his career Caesar was merely a Roman senator,[5] and it is highly debatable whether he was at that time capable of thinking of himself as an absolute monarch. Most modern historians[6] reject as unhistorical Suetonius' assertion in the name of Cicero,[7] 'Caesar in his consulship established the despotism which he had already in mind when he was aedile.'

It was only after the conquest of Gaul that Caesar decided on war as the means of raising his own *dignitas* to a level with that of Pompey.[8] Viewed from this angle, Caesar was not for one moment planning for monarchy in the year 49 BC, he was not attempting to undermine the Republic, and he was not yet thinking of transforming it into an empire by means of a 'new order'. Caesar declared that his aims in waging war were 'the tranquillity of Italy, the peace of the provinces, the safety of the Empire',[9] but Strasburger dismissed these as words of propaganda, and having nothing in common with the pronouncements of a manifesto. Actually, Caesar was anything but a revolutionary; it was he who suggested a spirit of co-operation in the Senate, and challenged senators to share with him the burden of leading the state.[10]

In assessing Caesar, Strasburger asserted that Caesar was no Augustus, no Trajan and no Hadrian: he was the last patrician of the old school.

Caesar's isolation grew from day to day. While his soldiers and the masses worshipped him like an idol, his peers, and even his closest friends, accused him of tyranny. His murderers had no alternative plans of any kind. They wanted quite simply nothing more than to be rid of the hated dictator. The fact that some of Caesar's laws remained in force even after his death proves only that there was a practical necessity for them. In the last analysis no one regretted his murder.

Thus far Strasburger.

The German teachers were shocked.[11] In their view, Strasburger had 'assassinated' one of their great heroes, and some of them even wondered whether they were justified in continuing to teach the works of Caesar in their schools. In their perplexity, they sought advice from the great Matthias Gelzer,[12] so that they could bolster their belief in the view expressed in all the editions of his book[13] that Caesar was, in fact, a great statesman.

Gelzer (rightly) praised Strasburger's article as brilliant. He agreed that Caesar was, perhaps, unloved by his contemporaries, but categorically disputed the conclusion that he was nothing but an average Roman politician. To wage war on a well-established oligarchy – and a victorious one – was the act of a great statesman. In contrast to Augustus, whose motto was *festina lente*, Caesar was a great improviser. In his latter days he acted like a monarch, but that is not the decisive factor for an assessment of his achievement. Caesar had a plan. Tranquillity for Italy, peace for the provinces and safety for the Empire, was more than a mere slogan. It constituted a programme, 'in so far as one should expect a programme from Roman statesmen at all'.[14] Finally, Caesar's legislation was proof of his statesmanlike insight and energy.

It is to be hoped that Gelzer succeeded in allaying the fears of those teachers who felt deprived of an heroic figure. Yet, even if the 'Gallic War' is again being taught in those high schools that have not so far totally abolished the teaching of Latin, the controversy over Caesar has nevertheless not reached a con-clusion – and never will.[15]

In the sixth edition of his biography of Caesar (1960),[16] Gelzer was more sceptical in his assessments of the aims of the dictator than in his earlier writings. Two decades previously he had argued against Eduard Meyer, who emphasized Caesar's personal power rather than his political intentions. 'Living ourselves at a time when the political order is in a state of evolution, we are better able to comprehend some aspects of Caesar than former generations . . . Caesar founded the Roman *Kaisertum* designated by his name,' he wrote in 1942.[17]

After the war, Gelzer changed his mind,

He published no programme; a practical politician through and through, he recognized the problems in every situation and set about mastering them with a will. Our sources . . . give us an insight into individual cases but no certain information about his innermost thoughts. We may go so far as to assert that eventually the dictator-ship for life corresponded to his wishes. But it remains obscure when . . . he decided on this form for his principatus. For it is not possible to determine how far the extravagant senatorial decrees which granted him this vast power were inspired by himself. We must guard against ascribing to him actions, plans and motives for which there is no authority.[18]

We do not know what provoked the change in Gelzer's point of view. Possibly the impact of Syme's research drove him closer to Strasburger's argument. It is also possible that his experiences under a dictatorship in World War II moved the scholar, who never overlooked a source, to take more seriously the judgment of Cicero, who remarked after Caesar's murder, 'So great was his passion for wrong-doing that the very doing of wrong was a joy to him for its own sake even when there was no motive for it.'[19] Finally, it is also possible that he was influenced by a seldom-quoted passage of Pliny, who not only praised Caesar's intellectual vitality, the extent of his benefactions and his military genius, but also pointed out that his wars cost 1,192,000 lives, which is why Caesar neglected to mention the casualty figures in his writings.[20] In the last edition of the most comprehensive and important biography of Caesar written in the twentieth century, Gelzer stated that Caesar did not shrink from corruption or acts of violence to further his purposes, and that he was a man who simply had no moral scruples where politics were concerned.

Although Gelzer never questioned Caesar's greatness as a statesman, his hesitation in making a total assessment of the man was criticized by Otto Seel,[21] who risked a more acute formulation of the question, namely whether Caesar was merely a successful scoundrel, or whether he should be regarded with awe, respect, enthusiasm and affection – a prototype worthy of imitation. To dismiss this question would be to debase history itself. One can understand Seel's aversion to scholars parading patient wisdom, ironic scepticism and cheerful resignation in their books, yet this appears to be caused by the fact that the days are long since gone when Theodor Mommsen could believe that Caesar's personality might be sketched either superficially or more profoundly, but not differently.[22] (See also p. 37.)

Cicero was of a different opinion. In 46 BC he addressed Caesar,

Among those yet unborn there shall arise, as there has arisen among us, sharp division; some shall laud your achievements to the skies, and others shall ignore them.

(Cic., *pro Marc.*, 29)

The problem was clearly recognized by Tacitus, 'the killing of the dictator Caesar had seemed to some the worst, and to others the fairest, of high exploits (*Ann.* I, 8, 6). And Seneca found it difficult to answer Livy's question, whether it would have been better for the Republic or not if Caesar had not been born at all (Sen., *Nat. Quaest.* V, 18, 4).[23]

Historiography followed the same path. It was not enough to describe Caesar as a man with 'two souls in but one breast'. He was no Jekyll and Hyde, but rather a phenomenon of many facets which are confirmed in iconographic studies. Likenesses of Caesar show every possible character trait: majesty, pride, disdain, audacity, reflectiveness, elegance, wit, corruption and affection.[24] For two thousand years Caesar's personality has intrigued the heart of Europe.[25] In time, a 'Caesar myth' developed, and eventually an 'ism' was attached to his name. This last complication makes it necessary to define this controversial concept before returning to the investigation of Caesar the man.

CAESARISM

Historians and political scientists of the nineteenth century made more frequent use of the expression 'Caesarism' than their twentieth-century counterparts. W. Roscher provides a good example.[26] He knew, as did numerous political scientists before him, that democracy can degenerate into military despotism. The two Napoleons come to mind: Caesarism was frequently used as a synonym for Bonapartism. What expression would Roscher have used, had he written his book after World War I can only be guessed. Fascism, perhaps. His interest lay not so much in the personality of the ruler as in his attitude to the various groupings and strata of society. Everything was promised to everyone, and only the leader's genius could preserve a certain unity. No rational acts could bridge the contradictions in his programme; it depended simply and solely on blind belief in the superhuman capabilities of the ruler.

When Napoleon created his new nobility, he said to some, 'I guarantee revolution; this caste is highly democratic, for all the time everyone is being summoned to it.' To the great proprietors he said, 'It will secure the throne'; to the friends of moderate monarchy, 'It will be opposed to the abuse of absolute power, for it is becoming influential in the country'; to the Jacobins, 'Exult, for, the ancient nobility is completely destroyed', and to the old aristocracy, 'In decking yourselves with fresh honours you are reviving your own again.'[27]

Roscher was, in fact, talking about Napoleon I, but a similar account could easily be given of Napoleon III. Did not the latter promise, 'l'Empire c'est la paix', only to entangle France a few months later in the hopeless Crimean War? Did he not promise the Italian nationalists and likewise the Pope his support, only to disappoint both ultimately? Did he not promise free trade and protective tariffs, but when his position shifted was he not obliged to vindicate French prestige by a Mexican adventure? A. J. P. Taylor expresses it admirably,

The more we strip off the disguises, the more the disguises appear. Such was Louis Napoleon, the man of mystery: conspirator and statesman, dreamer and realist, despot and democrat, maker of wars and peace, creator and muddler. You can go on indefinitely.[28]

Was Caesar's fate any different? Did he not also enter into fateful connections with a very mixed collection of advisers, then being compelled to satisfy the desires of a motley group of dependants (see pp. 168 ff.)?[29]

Pompey, his great adversary, was not so clever. Cicero assessed one of Pompey's speeches as being 'of no comfort to the poor or interest to the rascals; the rich were not pleased and the honest men were not edified' (Cic., *ad Att.* I, 14). Caesar would not have let such an opportunity slip away. He would have obliged everyone, at least for a short time. And it was precisely this gift that led some political scientists to regard him as the father of modern Caesarism.

Gleichschaltung is the dictator's ideal and goal – or, in Heinrich von Treitschke's words, 'Before the Emperor's divine blood all subjects are fundamentally alike.'[30] So must Roman Caesarism have also appeared: slaves ruled their owners, freedmen their *patroni*, the upper classes succumbed to the strictest control and the masses were entertained with sport and the circus. One of the emperors is alleged to have said to his people, 'Devote your leisure to games and to the races in the circus. Let me be concerned with the needs of the state, and busy yourselves with your pleasures' (*SHA, Firmus* 5).[31] In a letter ascribed to Sallust, we read his advice to Caesar that the common people (corrupted by the corn dole and other hand-outs) must be occupied with their own concerns, to prevent them from causing any political damage.

That was Caesarism, a form of rule, which, under the cloak of a legitimate monarchy, was in reality based on military power. The old institutions remained unchanged. The magistracies kept their former names, and the real situation was concealed under a camouflage of artful legal fictions. Government was based on an association of heterogeneous groups, often opposed to one another, from which the key position of the leader necessarily emerged, for only he could oblige everyone. Tacitus described the situation clearly: Augustus 'conciliated the army by gratuities, the populace by cheapened corn, the world by the amenities of peace' (*Ann.* I, 2).

The concept of Caesarism, however, was not yet known to Tacitus. It was used for the first time in 1850 (!) by an enthusiastic Bonapartist, François Auguste Romieu (in *Ere des Césars*). Burckhardt did not take exception to this usage. In his opinion, Caesarism, as a concept, was nonetheless very well defined.[32] Mommsen, too, made use of the concept of Caesarism in his *History of Rome*, although, in contrast to Romieu, he loathed Bonapartism. His readers misunderstood him, however, in so far as they believed he (Mommsen) supported absolute monarchy even in his own day. In the second edition of his book the celebrated historian then clarified his view by being sharply critical of autocracy. He made clear his distinction between Julius Caesar the man, on the one hand, and Caesarism as a form of government on the other.[33] Some of his arguments are worth quoting:

At this point, however, it is proper expressly once and for all to postulate what the historian everywhere tacitly presumes, and to protest against the custom – common to simplicity and perfidy – of using historical praise and historical censure, dissociated from the given circumstances, as phrases of general application, and in the present case of construing the judgment respecting Caesar into a judgment concerning what is called Caesarism.

It is true that the history of past centuries ought to be the teacher of the present; but not in the vulgar sense, as if one could simply by turning over the leaves discover the conjunctures for the present from in records of the past, and collect from these the symptoms for a political diagnosis and the specifics for a prescription;[34] it is instructive only in so far as the observation of older forms of culture reveals the organic conditions of civilization generally – the fundamental forces everywhere alike, and the manner of their combination everywhere different – and leads and encourages men, not to unreflecting imitation, but to independent reproduction. *In this sense the history of Caesar and of Roman Imperialism, with all the unsurpassed greatness of the master-worker, with all the historical necessity of the work, is in truth a more bitter censure of modern autocracy than could be written by the hand of man* (my italics, Z.Y.).

According to the same law of nature, in virtue of which the smallest organism infinitely surpasses the most artistic machine, every constitution, however defective, which gives play to the free self-determination of a majority of citizens infinitely surpasses the most brilliant and humane absolutism; for the former is capable of development and therefore living, the latter is what it is and therefore dead. This law of nature has been verified in the Roman absolute military monarchy and all the more completely verified, that, under the impulse of its creator's genius and in the absence of all extraneous material complications, that monarchy developed itself more purely and freely than any similar state.

From Caesar's time, as the sequel will show and Gibbon showed long ago, the Roman system had only an external coherence and received only a mechanical extension, while internally it became even with him utterly withered and dead. If, in the early stages of the autocracy and, above all, in Caesar's own soul, the hopeful dream of a combination of free popular development and absolute rule was still cherished, the government of the highly gifted emperors of the Julian house soon taught men in a terrible way how far it was possible to hold fire and water in the same vessel.

Caesar's work was necessary and salutary, not because it was or could be fraught with blessing in itself, but because – with the national organization of antiquity, which was based on slavery and was an utter stranger to republican-constitutional representation, and in presence of the legitimate civic constitution which in the course of five hundred years had ripened into oligarchic absolutism – absolute military monarchy was the copestone logically necessary and the least of evils.

When once the slave-holding aristocracy in Virginia and the Carolinas shall have carried matters as far as their counterparts in Sullan Rome, Caesarism will there too be legitimized at the bar of history; where it appears under other conditions of development, it is at once a caricature and a usurpation. But history will not submit to curtail the true Caesar of his due honour, because the verdict may lead simplicity astray in the presence of bad Caesars, and may give to roguery occasion for lying and fraud. She too is a Bible, and if she cannot any more than the Bible hinder the fool from misunderstanding and the devil from quoting her, she too will be able to bear with, and to requite, them both.[35]

After Mommsen only a few historians made use of the concept of Caesarism, although political scientists still refer to it. Roscher has already been mentioned, F. Ruestow constitutes a further example,[36] as does Robert von Pöhlmann: the latter applied concepts such as communism and socialism to the classical world, and also used the concept of Caesarism where appropriate. In fact, in 1895 Pöhlmann published *Die Entstehung des Caesarismus*,[37] which added something to the contribution of his predecessors. He was not satisfied with Roscher's statement that it is possible to find prototypes of Caesarism in Roman history (such as, for example, Scipio, Marius, Sulla and Pompey). In his view Roman Caesarism had its origin in the late Greek tyrannies. Dionysius of Syracuse, Agathocles, Euphron of Sicyon, Chaeron of Pellene, Clearchus of Heraclea and Nabis of Sparta were the models for Caesarism. As far as these rulers were concerned, Pöhlmann maintained, they were indifferent to the concepts of morality, justice and law. Therefore, it was not difficult for them to be two-faced by appearing to be absolute monarchs to some and extreme democrats to others.

In general, nineteenth-century scholars were agreed that Caesarism was the outcome of a degenerate democracy, and that the rise of a dictator is usually facilitated by unavoidable conflict between the love of freedom – characteristic of the wealthy and educated classes – and the desire for equality among the masses. These objectives are mutually exclusive, and incompatible in the long run. The appetite of the mob may be contained for a while, but in the course of time its greed grows, for, as Pöhlmann said, 'the communist idea of sharing one another's victuals for these proletarians has become second nature'.

In these circumstances, the most able withdraw from state service and leave the field to professional politicians, the gulf between the social classes deepens and the demagogues intensify their efforts. Unrest breaks out, and eventually people begin to yearn for the benefactor as sole ruler. Of course, they desire a prudent and moderate ruler, but that does not always turn out to be the case. Usually they put up with one who is not so good, for 'in the last resort they prefer to permit person and property to be consumed by a single lion rather than by a hundred jackals or even a thousand rats' (Roscher).

Pöhlmann identified this type of Caesarism as being already present in fourth-century Greece, and thought that the beginnings of a Sultanism can even be traced in Alexander of Macedon and in Julius Caesar (p. 105). Therefore, Roscher's complaint in 1888 that the word Caesarism was used in an unscholarly fashion is readily understandable, as was his unwillingness to accept a definition such as that of Littré, 'Princes brought to government by democracy, but clad with absolute power.'

And yet, the concept of Caesarism still appears in the literature of the twentieth century. Spengler believed that democracy was doomed and predicted the approach of Caesarism with firm and measured steps. Antonio Gramsci[38] made use of the concepts of progressive and regressive Caesarism, and maintained that 'Caesar and Napoleon are examples of progressive Caesarism' because, under their regimes, the revolutionary element put the conservative in the shade.

Even if we grant that the elements sketched above are common to all Caesarisms, that every 'Caesar' seeks to attach himself to his predecessors, and that every sole ruler must declare, like Napoleon 'I must remain great, glorious, and admired'; does that bring us any closer to a better understanding of this specific phenomenon?

The use of the word Caesarism, however, does not lead to a real understanding of the problem. Karl Marx had no doubt about that. In his essay, 'Der 18. Brumaire des Louis Bonaparte', he characterized Caesarism as a schoolboy expression and its use as a superficial analogizing of history. N. A. Maškin, one of the Soviet Union's most important historians, agrees with Marx in this respect, because he finds that an analogy between Fascism, Bonapartism, and a proletarian regime has no historical value of any kind. For all that, Maškin is unable to dismiss the question of Caesarism easily, for the expression 'Roman Caesarism' (whatever its worth) occurs in the works of Lenin, an authority with whom a Soviet historian will not lightly venture to argue.[39]

A. Momigliano could not be restrained by such inhibitions. He based his criticism of those contemporary historians who employed the concept of Caesarism on the proposition that this kind of terminology was utterly unintelligible to the man of antiquity, while at the same time it is too inexact for the modern man.[40]

Caesarism is a typically nineteenth-century concept, which was necessary to help explain the emotional and demagogic factors in the government of the two Napoleons. In the twentieth century, however, Caesarism is of as little use as Fascism in helping us understand Caesar.

Detailed elaborations of the differences between the world

of antiquity and the modern world are superfluous. Roman equites were not capitalists and the plebs were not proletarians. The Senate was no parliament, and the Roman popular assemblies have no counterpart in the modern world. Caesar was first and foremost a Roman senator, and to be able to understand him properly he must be placed within the context of his own time, that of Rome in the last century BC. But even then, many problems remain unsolved. The fact that the concept of Caesarism has developed a diversity of meanings in modern historical writing only proves once again that 'all history is contemporary history' (Croce). The truth of this statement finds its expression in the assessment of Caesar as a man and a ruler.

CAESAR

Mention has already been made of Mommsen's Caesarism as an anti-autocratic manifesto. He did not shed a single tear over the destruction of the old corrupt republican form of government, to which Caesar dealt the *coup de grâce*. Mommsen, the liberal revolutionary of 1848 and arch-enemy of the Prussian aristocrats, wrote history that offered the educated reader as much pleasure as it provided provocative reflection for the scholar. To familiarize the German reader with the Roman personalities, the author of the *Römisches Staatsrecht* even described a Roman magistrate as Burgomaster, and compared Cato with Don Quixote, Sulla with Don Juan and the great Pompey with a sergeant-major. His view of the Roman Republic was to,

Try to imagine London with the slave population of New Orleans, the police of Constantinople, the lack of industry of present-day Rome, and agitated by politics like the Paris of 1848, and an approximate picture will be attained of the grandeur of the Republic whose decline is deplored by Cicero and his friends in their glum letters.[41]

Such a regime could not long endure. Yet, as luck would have it, the man responsible for its downfall was 'a king anointed with the oil of democracy'.[42] Caesar was a monarch, not a deluded dictator. His personality was flawless, he was sincere, adaptable and fair, and appears to have wanted to be nothing other than *primus inter pares*. He understood how to avoid the error of so many who brought the abrupt tone of military command into politics. Caesar was a great statesman and a great realist. Each of his steps was prudently planned. None of his successes should be regarded as an isolated incident because there were none. The outstanding characteristic of his life's work was its complete harmony. Caesar was the last creative genius of the ancient world and the sole one that Rome produced.

Mommsen's view found followers not only in the nineteenth century, but also in the twentieth, who carried it further with minor variations. Many of them agreed that Caesar was a great statesman, a benevolent ruler, of noble distinction, and that it was he who laid the foundation for the Roman Empire.[43] Some condemned the conspiracy against him as the act of mean and envious persons.[44] Others enthusiastically praised his deep understanding of his times and his clear vision of the future.[45] But Hegel, himself a great admirer of Caesar, would not have accepted these paeans for one moment. In his lectures on the history of philosophy, he described him as a man,

who may be cited as a paragon of Roman adaptation of means to ends – who formed his resolves with the most unerring perspicuity, and executed them with the greatest vigor and practical skill, without passion. Caesar, in terms of history, did right, since he furnished a mediating element, and that kind of political bond which men's condition required. Caesar effected two objects; he deterred domestic strife, and at the same time developed a new struggle beyond the limits of the empire. For the conquest of the world had reached hitherto only to the circle of the Alps, but Caesar opened up a new scene of achievement: he founded the theatre which was on the point of becoming the centre of History. He then achieved universal sovereignty by a struggle which was decided not in Rome itself, but by his conquest of the whole Roman World. His position was indeed hostile to the Republic, but, properly speaking, only to its shadow; for all that remained of that Republic was entirely powerless.[46]

But Hegel, too, knew that Caesar, fighting for his honour and esteem, reacted instinctively to the historical constraints of the moment. Not every one of his successes was based on prudent foresight. Hegel, like Mommsen, deplored Caesar's murder and bitterly criticized that small band who did away with the great man from pure envy. For all that, Hegel would probably scarcely approve of Mommsen's view of Caesar as the last great personality of the ancient world. Later scholars too are opposed to Mommsen's view, but unfortunately a complete survey of all the disagreements is impossible in a short work. Instead, there follows a roughly schematized examination of five main theories, organized to show the principal tendencies of each. We must also add the *caveat* that this investigation is restricted to so-called 'professional historians' – and cannot extend to philosophers and littérateurs, although they have made many contributions towards a more penetrating discussion of Caesar. This is why Hegel is alluded to only briefly, and not because we belittle his influence, quite the contrary.

A considerable number of historians have resisted Hegel's philosophy of history. They preferred to concern themselves with Caesar the historic figure as sketched by the sources, and not with a Caesar who served Hegel merely as an example for a paragon of Roman adaptation of means to ends.

F.Gundolf, in considering the views of Caesar from Petrarch to Nietzsche and Wagner, maintained in one of his brilliant synopses (to say it is inexact is pointless, for he had no intention of being exact) that with regard to Caesar 'the French were best at assessing his person, the English his work, and the Germans his mind'. Yet, by means of an excursus that guides his readers from Petrarch and Dante, Montaigne and Voltaire, Klopstock and Goethe, to Mommsen and Burckhardt, Nietzsche and Wagner (to mention only the most important), he proves that European men of letters never intended to tabulate Julius Caesar in a short and narrow column.

They all went back to Petrarch, who again relied on Cicero. A man of letters himself, Cicero understood Caesar's multi-faceted character, but was continually tormented by the discord between Caesar's greatness and his wantonness. Just as Petrarch could grasp that Caesar was Cupid's slave and Glory's fellow-traveller, it was unnecessary for Herder to hate Caesar in order to love Brutus; and, just as Byron tormented himself with the Caesar who wrecked the Republic, Lamartine, too, was torn between his admiration for Caesar's rich gifts and his aversion to their pernicious application.

The theme has been treated exhaustively by Gundolf in two well-known books, and although some topics could be added to the content, or alternative opinions discussed, in their genre they will remain unsurpassed for many years to come.[47] Professional historians, however, were not as sophisticated.

In 1901 G. Ferrero published *Grandezza e Decadenza di Roma*. Caesar was, for him, a great general and a gifted writer, but never developed into a great statesman. Ferrero admired Caesar's practical thinking, well-balanced intelligence, untiring facility for achievement and quick power of decision. On the other hand, he saw in Caesar a spirit of destruction whose mission was principally one of annihilation, and who brought about the decline and break-up of the ancient world. According to Ferrero, Caesar's contemporaries could expect nothing from him, and to succeeding generations in Europe his greatest act was the conquest of Gaul, an achievement to which he himself attached very little importance.[48] After Munda his dictatorship dissolved into an aimless, degenerate opportunism that recalled the fanciful intrigues of the old Republic. Ferrero maintained that Caesar had neither a political nor a legislative programme; he was an adventurer, whose only coherent plan was for the war in the east and the annexation of Parthia. Ferrero concluded, from a bust in the Louvre, that the dictator's face expressed deep physical suffering. In 44 BC Caesar was tired and exhausted.

In 1933 Ferrero wrote a preface to the English translation of his book.[49] Banished from Fascist Italy, he was teaching history at the University of Geneva. He did not alter his views. Rather, he saw his book as an anti-Fascist, or, should the reader prefer it, an anti-Bolshevist history of Julius Caesar. He sharply criticized historians of the nineteenth century who appeared to be swept by waves of enthusiasm for the gifted dictator, and who were not prepared to be satisfied with a single slice of historical greatness at the beginning of the nineteenth century (Napoleon).

After 1830, when the horrors of Napoleon had been forgotten, Caesar found favour in all circles. Conservatives considered him a bulwark against the liberal and democratic tendencies of the middle and lower classes, while liberals thought of him as a weapon against traditional monarchy, the principle of dynasticism and respect for the old classes. Thus, in the historical writing of the nineteenth century, there took shape one who resembled a quasi-elder brother of Napoleon rather than the historic Caesar.

At the beginning of the twentieth century a gradual disengagement from the romanticism of the nineteenth century became apparent, and historians, too, began to see Caesar in another light. However, World War I intervened, and these ideas went awry. Revolution and changes of regime in various European countries permitted the revival once more of the old romantic illusion of the dictator as saviour. Ferrero fits in at this point. He made no secret of his opinion, and is unequivocal,

If the West fails to put an end to the fairy-tale and to introduce some clarity into the confusion of facts, it (the West) will fall victim to usurpers who are swaggering about all over Europe, Asia, and America. The West has nothing to hope for from usurpers, and should be on its guard against bombastic promises, made by people who believe they can alter the course of history.[50]

His hatred of all dictators won Ferrero many followers. In 1942 L. R. Taylor compared Caesar with Mussolini, and in 1948 F. R. Cowell compared him with Hitler, remarking *inter alia*,

Useful and important as were some of his ideas [Caesar's], they did not amount to a New Deal, still less did they offer any hope of enlarging the lives of the masses and so of filling the vacuum of Roman social life with a new moral spirit. We have seen dictators fail in our own day – despite their tremendous propaganda machines – which for a time seemed likely to wield an influence over the minds of their victims. Caesar did not form a political party. He did no more than recruit a gang. He was supported by some respectable figures – but all in all – apart from the solid ranks of his legions – he was supported only by a few personal friends. Most of his supporters came from the disaffected classes, needy debtors, failures and misfits.[51]

Notwithstanding the vast gulf between Mommsen and Ferrero, they do have something in common: both admitted to their political conviction either in the preface or in the body of the work. Thus, their *Zeitgeist* is easily detectable. In any case, it would be unjust to criticize only those who openly acknowledge their prejudice. Every historian of the past is also a man of his age, and nobody is free from bias.

Historians who wrote after World War I disclosed their personal views only rarely. Accordingly, it is not easy to judge their political motivation. Conjecture is possible, not certainty. Tacitus might have maliciously put it: the one who conceals his ways is no better than the others – 'occultior non melior' (*Hist.* II, 38).

Communist and Fascist interpretations of history are the exception. They leave nothing to the reader's imagination. To Fascist historians, Caesar was the great magician of antiquity, who attempted to improve the social position of the provincials in order to achieve a supra-national or imperial homogeneous organism.

A. Ferrabino, in *Cesare* (Turin, 1941) was not as simple-minded. He believed not only in the indestructibility of Romanity and its universality, but also depicted Caesar as an instrument of divine will. In his view Caesar founded a new order, based on the concepts of *clementia, aequitas* and *voluntas* of the nations.

It is not surprising that a reaction set in after World War II. Italian scholars seem to have lost all interest in studying Julius Caesar, the statesman and conqueror, and concentrated instead on a thorough investigation of Caesar's writings and the *Corpus Caesarianum*, as well as on an analysis of his personality as it emerged from the literary stance of the *commentarii*. In this respect, they made a decisive contribution and yet, although there is a wealth of allusions to political and social questions to be found, we cannot concern ourselves more closely with their writings in the present context.[52]

Soviet researchers, on the other hand, stressed Caesar's position as the representative of the slave owners who supported his dictatorship in the hope that through it the old regime, which was being destroyed by slave uprisings and the unrest of the plebs, might be rescued. This kind of historiography is worth a special study.[53]

THE HELLENISTIC MONARCHY

Towards the end of World War I Eduard Meyer published *Caesars Monarchie und das Principat des Pompeius*, one of the most authoritative works written in the first half of the twentieth century. In the first edition he did not even mention Ferrero, but in the third edition (1922) he conceded that Ferrero's work was certainly interesting and even stimulating. However, 'if the author intended to offer us a picture true to history, he [Ferrero] failed in his aim' (p. 330). Even Mommsen, who was Meyer's predecessor as Professor of Ancient History at the University of Berlin, was not spared. A Caesar as sketched by Mommsen had, in Meyer's view, never

existed. It is no coincidence that Mommsen never wrote a
fourth volume of his Roman history to embrace the foundation of the Principate. After the third volume he published a
fifth, on the Roman provinces. The reason, in Meyer's view,
was very simple: after Mommsen's Caesar there was no room
left for Augustus.[54]

Meyer rejected the theory that Caesar occupied himself with
plans for monarchy from the beginning of his career. He also
repudiated the Shakespearean Caesar: 'the vain, pompous,
cantankerous, ageing egotist surrounded by sycophants,
swayed by flatterers, suffering from a fever in Spain and from a
falling sickness'.[55] Meyer's Caesar had no ideals of any sort. He
was fighting for a position of power (p. 468), and one who
intends to achieve it must overcome opposition. After his
victory over Pompey, he could not let power slip from his
grasp. The conferment of royal dignity, therefore, was an
attempt to legitimize usurpation and establish it on a legal
basis. *'Caesar's intentions* and the steps he took *to achieve the final
aim* are as clearly displayed as anything else in his history'
(p. 504), and no inconsistencies or Sultanic whims can be
traced in his conduct (as, for example, Pöhlmann thought
(p. 18)). In his latter days, it was his intention to turn himself
into an absolute monarch in the oriental style and attain once
more the world monarchy of Alexander. The conquest of Dacia
and Parthia, the transfer of the capital from Rome to
Alexandria, and the foundation of a dynasty – all were integral
components of the grand master's plan. Meyer accepted
Caesar's plans as described in Plutarch, *Caes.* 58, as authentic
and concludes that Caesar consciously strove for divine
honours, as reported in Suetonius (*Div. Jul.* 76),

For not only did he accept excessive honours, such as an uninter-
rupted consulship, the dictatorship for life, and the censorship of
public morals, as well as the forenamed Imperator, the surname of
Father of his country, a statue among those of the kings, and a raised
couch in the orchestra; but he also allowed honours to be bestowed
on him which were too great for mortal man: a gold throne in the
House and on the judgment seat; a chariot and litter in the procession
at the circus; temples, altars and statues beside those of the gods; a
special priest, an additional college of the Luperci and the calling of
one of the months by his name.

This passage has been arbitrarily selected to illustrate and sum
up a series of honours. A full account of all such honours might

suggest that Caesar's aim was for royal dignity and deification but would overload this chapter. Countless books and treatises have been written on this subject, and the abundance of material is, in truth, vast, but one striking fact emerges: the reports concerning Caesar's aim of royal dignity and deification have their origin in texts of the imperial period (the few indications in contemporary sources do not suffice to give a comprehensive picture). One cannot fail, however, to be impressed by the persistence with which these stories continue to recur. Meyer fully documented Caesar's presumption and stubborn purpose in order to emphasize the signs of kingship and divinity (p. 447).

Meyer stressed that such conduct could not be considered fortuitous, and that Mommsen was wrong in assuming that the royal title was of secondary importance to Caesar. It is precisely in the case of monarchy that the title is absolutely inseparable from the power.[56] That Julius Caesar valued it highly is mentioned by Plutarch, Dio, Suetonius and Appian, and is emphasized by the historians who preceded Meyer.[57] But Meyer was the first to produce a fully-fledged theory that envisaged as the final aim of Caesar's work a Hellenistic monarchy, and this signifies a state structured with an absolute ruler at its head, who enjoys divine worship.

Is it at all possible to find an explanation for this theory in *Zeitgeist*? Certainty is impossible; we may only hazard conjectures. Meyer, more than any other ancient historian, went to great pains to integrate the history of Greece and Rome with that of other Mediterranean and Near Eastern peoples of the time. In his view the picture of the history of the ancient world is necessarily distorted when the fate of individual nations is examined independently. His *Geschichte des Altertums* was intended to make good such an omission. At the same time, concerned with interpretations of historical methodology, he published various articles on the subject.[58] World War I, however, prevented a visit to the East, and his universal history was never completed. Instead, he published a series of monographs, including the one on Caesar and Pompey. At that time (1918) Oswald Spengler's *Untergang des Abendlandes* fascinated many of the readers who identified Germany's collapse in 1918 with the decline of the West. Only a few historians agreed with Spengler. Meyer, however, while critical of details, sympathized with Spengler more than any other professional historian.[59] Meyer may have been tormented for some time by the weakening of the West. Therefore, Caesar's attempt to unite West and East, to wipe out the dividing line between victors and vanquished, and to found a new regime in Rome might have impressed Meyer so forcefully that he allowed himself to accept without hesitation sources which, under other circumstances, he would have subjected to thorough-going criticism. Thus Meyer made some far-reaching generalizations that he could not document, and expressly mentioned Caesar's tendency to put citizens and non-citizens on an equal plane and to 'subject the empire to a process of levelling down. Before the absolute ruler legal differences between subjects disappear in a subjection that affects all alike' (p. 483).

It is, therefore, quite remarkable that Meyer, a scholar whose knowledge of the sources was unrivalled, made not a single reference to evidence that pointed out that Pompey (who, according to Meyer, was the precursor of the 'Western' Principate) also attempted to imitate Alexander of Macedon. Let an extract from a contemporary text (Sall., *Hist.* III, 88) testify, 'Sed Pompeius a prima adulescentia sermone fautorum similem fore se credens Alexandro regi facta consultaque eius quidem aemulus erat'. Did Meyer perhaps think a 'western' statesman like Pompey was incapable of such an idea?[60]

By and large, Meyer's work was positively received, with only a few objectors to his main ideas.[61] However, under the influence of recent studies of a more fundamental nature such as those of P. A. Brunt and E. Badian, C. Nicolet and C. Meier, there was a retreat from Meyer's obsolete terminology. For example, after Nicolet's monumental work *L'Ordre equestre*, no one would write, like Meyer, 'Brutus belonged to the democratic party, i.e. the party of the equites' (p. 450). The oriental (= Hellenistic, absolute) monarchy, on the other hand, became in Meyer's day one of the accepted 'facts', although with many variants.

J. Carcopino is a case in point. His work[62] is too important and too original to be treated as a parenthesis to that of Meyer, yet in a schematic survey such as this it is not possible to give everyone his due. On the one hand, Carcopino was sharply critical of Meyer, and wrote that his book was 'badly structured, badly written, but illuminated throughout by a splendid intelligence' (p. 592). He decisively rejected the difference between Caesar and Augustus put forward by Meyer, and saw in Caesar the true founder of the Roman Empire, 'Caesar created the fertile elements of this "Empire", to which the ancients owed several centuries of beneficent peace.' On the other hand, Carcopino was in no doubt about Caesar's intention to exercise dominion over Rome as monarch. Caesar isolated himself from the city population so that he could better rule over it; he did not stumble into monarchy, but planned it carefully. Yet Roman monarchy of the eighth to sixth centuries BC was essentially different from Caesar's monarchy. The earlier monarchy was transitory, fortuitous, elective, secular and moderate, in contrast to Caesar's monarchy, which was solidly planned, divine, absolute and based on a plebiscite.

E. Pais, in *Richerche sulla Storia e sul Diritto Romano* (vol. I, 1918), came to similar conclusions independently, and spoke of 'Caesar's aspiration to the throne', but he stressed, more strongly than Meyer, the role of Cleopatra. H. Volkmann maintained that Caesar wished to elevate himself to king and god, and described his relationship with Cleopatra as a union in which affection and political considerations were inseparably amalgamated (*Kleopatra*, 1953, p. 61 and 77). In *Divinity of the Roman Emperor* (1931) L. R. Taylor never doubted Caesar's political intentions. L. Cerfaux and J. Tondriau emphasized that Caesar strove for a 'kingship, oriental and divine in its tendency',[63] and L. Homo, too, in *Les institutions politiques Romaines*, accepted Meyer's thesis completely.

The Soviet scholar N. A. Maškin followed Meyer's arguments and updated them by using Marxist terminology. C. N. Cochrane, the Canadian scholar, insisted that the sources left no room for any doubt that in the latter months of his life Caesar conclusively set his sights on the Alexandrine monarchy,[64] and in 1948 E. Kornemann returned to his view, developed at the end of the nineteenth century, that Caesar's dreams of empire expressed themselves in the grandiose plan to destroy the Parthian kingdom, push forward through the Caucasus to Dacia, and, by a concentrated attack from the east and west, stab the Germans in the back.[65]

These few examples prove only that the attempt to classify views about Caesar according to national points of view must fail. There is no English, German, Italian or American inter-

pretation. Anatole France and C. Jullian attached themselves
to Mommsen. The views of J. Carcopino and L. Homo were
closer to those of Meyer, who, for his part, was criticized by
his countrymen M. Gelzer and P. Strack.[66] Some English
scholars, including F. E. Adcock, R. Syme and J. P. V. D.
Balsdon, roundly rejected Meyer's interpretation, which leads
one to refer to an 'English view'. But the Italian, L. Pareti (just
like the English) does not believe that Caesar wanted to make
himself a king or god.[67] The important fact is that the English
scholars used different arguments from each other. In the
matter of method Syme, from Oxford, was closer to the
German F. Münzer than to Adcock, his Cambridge colleague.

<h3 style="text-align:center">THE MINIMALISTS</h3>

A further wave of criticism – that opposed Mommsen's view –
arose in Britain. This school ought to be designated 'Minimal-
ist' rather than 'British', since W. W. Fowler and C. Merivale
cannot be considered among its members. On the one hand, we
have seen that Meyer was not prepared to concede Caesar's
greatness as portrayed by Mommsen. On the other, for all the
energy Meyer expended in advancing his theory of the Hellenistic monarchy, he nevertheless considered Caesar an interlude.
The real precursor of Augustus' principate was Pompey, and
the future state theory was already sketched in Cicero's *De
Republica* and in his speech on behalf of Marcellus. By and
large, Caesar had no grasp of the historic moment, and
historical development took a path different from the one he
had previously delineated.[68]

H. F. Pelham had quite different objections. He suggested,
however, an open admission: that we have no key of any kind
to the understanding of Caesar's future plans, even if we assume
that he had the fundamental capability of such foresight.[69] Adcock did not consider it necessary to imagine a
Hellenistic monarchy, in order to explain the participation of
several honourable men in the conspiracy against the dictator.[70]
Caesar was murdered for what he was and not for what he
might perhaps have been. Meyer's Caesar was, for Syme, a
mythical Caesar, conceived intellectually.[71] (Actually, Meyer
encountered precisely the same objection that he had levelled
against Mommsen's Caesar.) If one must judge Caesar, that
judgment must be based on facts and not on alleged intentions.

One need not believe that Caesar planned a Hellenistic monarchy, irrespective of how one defines this concept. The simple charge of dictatorship suffices. For Syme, Caesar's final aims are uninteresting. He excluded statements about intentions from the realm of proof and counterproof:[72] Caesar should be left as he is in his time and generation, and one should neither laud him for superhuman vision, nor damn him for his blind haste to pluck unripe fruit.

Syme's *Roman Revolution* is not a book about Caesar and Augustus. It is a study of the metamorphosis of the regime and the administrative hierarchy. Caesar set in motion a process which was to last long after his time. Many of the measures he hit upon were temporary and of limited purpose, which left behind the impression of superficial action. On the other hand, the elevation of the non-political classes[73] had an effect long after his death. Syme is convinced that the history of the end of the Republic and the beginning of the Principate was that of the ruling classes. The fact that he does not mention the lower classes lies not in lack of interest but in lack of evidence. We know more about the upper classes because they had more freedom of action.[74] Rome was always ruled by an oligarchy, open or concealed,[75] and it is precisely this oligarchy which Syme presents to his readers. Caesar's new party is better portrayed by sketching men and their personal connections, hopes and ambitions, than by an investigation of political programmes and ideologies. Thus prosopography is a necessary instrument in Syme's hands, but it never impedes the account of events.

Syme offers technical matter for the specialist in special sections, but the more general reader has no difficulty in understanding the manifold adumbrations of the new Caesarian party. To contrast reviled good-for-nothings on the one hand and noble patriots on the other is schematic and leads to the wrong conclusions. Caesar's party was an amalgam of senators, knights, centurions, businessmen, bankers from the *municipia* and provinces, kings and princes. Caesar's connections with the representatives of business interests were as good as his connections with the landowners. He never preached a radical division of property. The heterogeneousness of his followers was the dictator's strength and made him independent of individual factions. Syme believed that Caesar, without benevolence, would have been a second

Sulla or a Gaius Gracchus, had he not lacked a revolutionary programme. He was a true Roman, more than any other. The sources of his plans for a Hellenistic monarchy are either hostile or posthumous. Concerning his plans for the future, there is room for opinion, but no certainty. No evidence for such plans is to be found in his dictatorship, and, lastly, 'a fabricated concatenation of unrealized intentions may be logical, artistic and persuasive – but it is not history' (p. 271).

On this point Syme agrees with Adcock, who also argues that there is insufficient evidence to prove Caesar's official deification in his lifetime. All the honours he enjoyed can be explained as an exaggerated expression of recognition of what he had achieved.[76]

It is true that contemporary sources are often more valuable than posthumous ones. Nevertheless, one can scarcely imagine that Suetonius, of all people, should have invented the story of the honours offered to Caesar.

At any rate, with reference to Tiberius, he makes it abundantly clear that the princeps refused divine honours,

Of many high honours he accepted only a few of the more modest. He barely consented to allow his birthday . . . to be recognized by the addition of a single two-horse chariot. He forbade the voting of temples, flamens and priests without his permission; and this he gave only with the understanding that they were not to be placed among the likenesses of the gods but among the adornments of the temples. He would not allow an oath to be taken ratifying his acts, nor the name Tiberius to be given to the month of September (Suet., *Tib.* 26).[77]

There is no basis for the assumption that Suetonius was particularly hostile to Caesar;[78] in any case there is room for serious doubt that he is indulging in his own opinions. Had Caesar refused the honours (as Tiberius did) the fact would have been recorded. Indeed, Cassius Dio and Appian frequently reported his refusal to accept certain honours. And yet Suetonius' account is rejected because he was not Caesar's contemporary. But Cicero was.

In a letter of June 45 (*ad Att.* XII, 45), Cicero talked about Caesar as 'Synnaos/contubernalis Quirini'. This letter could be interpreted as a bad joke, had not Cicero's statements in the *Philippics* been even more pointed (II, 110). He listed certain divine honours in particular, and added, 'As Jupiter, as Mars, as

Quirinus has a flamen, so the flamen to divine Julius is Marcus Antonius'. Turning to Antony, he castigated him, 'O detestable man, whether as priest of Caesar or of a dead man!'. This passage, weighty even in Syme's view,[79] caused scholars of the 1950s and 1960s to take up a novel position on Cicero's argument. That brings us to the fourth theory, which may be termed Revisionist.

THE REVISIONISTS

These scholars are all more sharply critical of Syme than of Meyer, and not one of them is prepared to come to terms with any diminution in Caesar's greatness. At first glance, it might be supposed that the Minimalists, who were British, would necessarily have been less enthusiastic about Caesar because they were reared on Shakespeare. They were probably un-decided even in their youth whether the great hero of the drama was Caesar or Brutus.

However, that is not the case. Shakespeare modelled his tragedy on Plutarch, and accepted the latter's notion that Caesar was an ambitious man (Plut., *Caes.* 69). But Shakespeare was equally impressed by the tragedy of the conspirators, in that their work came to nothing even before it came to pass. Yet he did not despise Caesar, and it is no coincidence that these words were given to Antony, 'Caesar was the noblest man that ever lived in the tide of times'. And, as Prince Edward says in Richard III,

> This Julius Caesar was a famous man:
> With what his valour did enrich his wit,
> His wit set down to make his valour live;
> Death makes no conquest of this conqueror,
> For now he lives in fame, though not in life.

W. W. Fowler[80] is right when he stresses that Shakespeare's Brutus never censures Caesar the man. Only lesser intellects refuse to understand clearly Caesar's eruptions of *superbia*, and when Antony's slave, speaking on behalf of his master, says to Brutus, 'Caesar was mighty, bold, royal, and loving', the reader is alerted to the fact that this is not merely Antony's opinion. Shakespeare himself probably leaned toward this view, and, as we now turn to a description of the historians we designate Revisionists, we must count among them all those who, in rejecting Meyer's idea of a Hellenistic monarchy, are nevertheless not prepared to subscribe to the statement that Caesar was no more than a regular Roman dictator and the last Roman patrician, and that his similarities to Sulla were more striking than the differences (Adcock).

In 1953 J. Vogt published a new interpretation of the passage from Cicero's *Philippics*[81] cited above (pp. 32 f.), and came to the conclusion that Caesar really had enjoyed divine honours, and that, although the Romans would not have opposed the idea of such honours for a genius like Caesar, they would have shuddered at the title of king. V. Ehrenberg[82] took Vogt's reflections a stage further. In his opinion it was not the con-stitutional honours and the trappings to which Caesar owed his position – so much higher than that of a regular dictator – but to his personal power which grew from day to day. Ehrenberg accepted Vogt's explanation of the significance of 'bases for sacred statues, an enormous god-like statue in his house and his own priest', and came to the conclusion that, in regard to Caesar's general and religious policy, Roman and non-Roman elements alike characterized his regime. As a result he was the first of the Caesars and not the last of the patricians.

K. Kraft contributed extremely detailed investigations of the coins of that period which led him to recognize that Caesar's aim was to reintroduce the old pattern of Roman kingship and not the Hellenistic – oriental – form.[83] Kraft examined the wreath worn by Caesar on portrait coins and concluded that this was not the triumphator's laurel wreath, which he was permitted to wear continuously after his victory in Spain (Dio XLIII, 43, 1), but was a gold one as represented in Etruscan paintings and on coins and vases. By the time of the Lupercalia (February 15), Caesar is portrayed as wearing this wreath (*coronatus*) for the purpose of making clear to all present that he had in mind a 'royal symbol in the Roman national tradition' (p. 60). Therefore he indignantly refused the diadem offered by Antony, since gold wreath and diadem were incompatible.

Here we have the actual essence of the Revisionist school, which began to flourish after World War II. Yet even in historical research, 'there is nothing new under the sun'. References to kingship of an old Italian style are to be found earlier in Mommsen, and also, many years later, in A.

Ferrabino. As far as the history of ideas is concerned 'Revisionism' goes back to A. Bachofen, but he had no influence of any sort on any historian. He believed in Rome's mission to subdue the sensual materialism of the East, and, by the establishment of the patriarchal state, to replace it by the virile spirit of the West. For him, Caesar was a western hero whose building of Rome was not after a foreign pattern. The argument had come full circle, 'from the son of the oriental Aphrodite had emerged the creator of the Western Empire'.[84] But, as pointed out, Bachofen made no impression on twentieth-century historians, and the immense influence of Meyer's work allowed the theory of a Roman type of kingship to sink into oblivion. Vogt, Ehrenberg and Kraft gave it fresh impetus, and many followed in their footsteps.

L. Wickert[85] positioned himself between the two camps. In his inaugural lecture in the Chair of Ancient History at Cologne, he essentially attached himself to Meyer's school. He remarked that Caesar, for all his greatness, could be considered as an interlude, 'Yielding to a playful impulse, one might, in theory, remove from history the monarchy of the strongest master Rome had ever produced, but never the principate of Augustus.' Likewise, he did not exclude Hellenistic influences on Caesar. But in the last resort Caesar's actual achievement is not to be derived from Hellenism. It is Caesarian and simultaneously Roman. Caesar was the first to embrace the idea of empire in an inspired fashion – he also decided to put it into practice. His most important achievement was the extension of the citizenship of Rome to citizenship of the empire. Rome, formerly head of a commonwealth, expanded to become head of an empire. The process of representation for the empire's population begins with the appointment of provincials to the Senate – in spite of the angry opposition of conservative Roman senators.

F. Vittinghoff[86] proceeded in this direction. In fact, he was concerned only with Caesar's colonization and policy on citizenship, but *inter alia* put forward the view that for Caesar, Italy and Rome signified the fulcrum of the empire. In Strabo (V, 216) we read, 'And at the present time . . . they (sc. the Italians) are all Romans', and in Vellius Pat. (II, 15, 2) they are already 'men of the same race and blood'. That was Caesar's idea of empire. In this respect, it is unproductive to look to the Hellenistic kings as prototypes. Caesar's work was so completely orientated towards the future that his contemporaries could not appraise it (p. 95).

In 1958 H. Oppermann, who had already proved to be a distinguished Caesarian scholar by his earlier work on Caesar as a man of letters, stated that Meyer's evidence for the Hellenistic monarchy did not always stand up to meticulous examination.[87] In his opinion, a sharp distinction should be drawn between Caesar's titulature in Rome and in the Empire. The decision on Caesar's title in the area designated *domi* was postponed until the end of the projected Parthian war. Until 44 BC he was satisfied with the dictatorship, an entirely Roman office, which Sulla had also held. Kingship should apply only in the realm of *militiae*: it would appear natural to the eastern regions. Oppermann pointed out that this new form of world dominion, unlike divine kingship, was not based on the mysterious incarnation of a god in human form – a mystery that man cannot grasp, but before which he can only bend the knee – but on the greatness and majesty of the man in question. That is not a Hellenistic idea but a European one, and Caesar had fought for the leadership of the European part of the empire. His victory over Pompey signified the victory of the West in the historic struggle between Europe and Asia.

Charisma,[88] F. Taeger's two-volume work, appeared two years later. Taeger had no doubts about Caesar's steadfast determination to translate his power into the form of a kingdom to be held by his house in perpetuity and of his equally firm belief in the providential nature of his undertaking. Incarnation was indispensable to his political position, and the connection of the cult of *clementia* with the cult of Caesar presupposed deification as an established component of the new ruling ideology. On the one hand the great Julius resembled Alexander (Taeger remained convinced that Caesar was already *divus* in his lifetime), yet Meyer's view that Caesar intended to introduce a Hellenistic monarchy to Rome is but a half-truth. In an attempt to demonstrate that Caesar's efforts in this direction were a product of the Roman environment rather than an import from the Orient, Taeger remarked, 'Caesar's position aroused in his opponents and adherents attitudes that promoted him to the realm of charisma. This emotion was genuine and had its roots in Roman religion.'

R. Klein also attempted to describe a Caesar whose thought

took root from the irrational and the metaphysical.[89] As a pupil of Seel, he also believed that history cannot be realized without a tincture of the irrational, the tragic and the transcendental. Klein rejected Meyer's notion of a Hellenistic monarchy as well as his observation that Caesar considered religion merely as a tool to be used for political ends.[90] He tended to follow B. E. Giovanetti, who stressed Caesar's attachment to the irrational.[91] Romulus was not a mere model for Caesar, and in this respect the chapters in Book II of Dionysius of Halicarnassus, recognized many years previously by M. Pohlenz as a piece of political pamphleteering of the Caesarian period, served as a useful source for Klein.[92] As *Basileus*, alongside supreme command in war, Caesar was obliged to exercise the supreme religious functions in the state. His *Regnum* was not an office but a sacred duty, and the people were obliged to suffer his performance of it as the rule of a deity.

Finally, J. Dobesch[93] also scrutinized yet once more Caesar's deification in his lifetime and campaign for the royal title. His analysis showed that Caesar did desire royal dignity and divine status. But, in spite of his well-ordered source material and his clear and logical style, Dobesch could not produce any new evidence because it simply does not exist. Thus many readers continued to harbour doubts. As one conservative scholar opposed to the theory of divine kingship put it, 'You cannot build a king out of a golden crown and a pair of red shoes' (Balsdon).[94]

Those who reject Caesar's aims to achieve kingship prove less extreme than the exponents of such a view. It is perhaps interesting to note that the opponents of the kingship theory make use of the same arguments as those employed by Napoleon I when he composed *Précis des Guerres de Jules César* in exile on St Helena. Napoleon concluded that the accounts of Caesar's efforts to become king were a shameless slander on the part of his assassins, 'To justify after the event a murder that was slipshod in its execution and ill-advised, the conspirators and their partisans alleged that Caesar wanted to make himself king, a statement obviously constituting an absurdity and calumny . . .' The French emperor could hardly imagine that Caesar could be capable of seeking 'stability and grandeur' in the crown of a Philip, Perseus, Attalus, Mithridates, Pharnaces or Ptolemy.[95]

A more detailed scrutiny of the 'revisionist' view would unnecessarily inflate this chapter. This brief survey may satisfy the non-specialist and professional historians will turn to the sources anyway. But the exception proves the rule, for the indefatigable studies of two great scholars – A. Alföldi and S. Weinstock, who devoted virtually their whole lives to the subject – can scarcely receive their due in a few lines. They ought to be treated in somewhat greater detail.

The essential significance of Alföldi's contribution lies in the fact that he was not content to evaluate once more the literary and epigraphic material, but took pains to analyse afresh and reinterpret the evidence of the coins. He was the leading exponent in our time of the view that, even if the sole rule of an autocrat had its origins in the Greek east, 'in the last resort this foreign element too became fused with Rome, and was eventually submerged in the political arena as on the battlefields'.

In his work on Caesar's monarchy published in 1952,[96] Alföldi attempted to evaluate the complex evidence of the coinage in relation to the events of the first months of the year 44 BC. He came to the clear conclusion that Caesar did, in fact, want the title of king, but the Senate begrudged it him. All attempts to achieve it also foundered in that year, and Caesar was eventually obliged to be content with the compromise solution that he could employ the title only in the provinces but had to be satisfied with *dictator perpetuo* (never *perpetuus!*) in Rome and Italy. This compromise solution was to be announced at the meeting of the Senate on March 15 on the basis of a Sibylline oracle. This step of Caesar's did away with his obligation to abdicate.

On the basis of his work on the coinage Alföldi established an exact chronology for the events of February and March of 44 BC. Until then it was generally accepted, and, in fact, based on an express assertion in Cicero (*Phil.* II, 87), that Caesar was already dictator for life at the time of the Lupercalia on February 15. Alföldi rejected Cicero's statement. In his assessment of an issue of M. Mettius (with the legend CAES. DICT. QVART.), he found that instead of the *lituus*, which normally appears on the *denarii* of Mettius, there is clearly recognizable the diadem, which Caesar refused at the Lupercalia, and dedicated to Jupiter on the Capitol. Alföldi spotted on the coins a diadem hanging on a hook (Alföldi, *loc. cit.* pls 2, 5, 6), and concluded that Mettius wished to perpetuate this gesture of Caesar's, for he could have struck these coins only immediately after February 15. In fact, Caesar does not appear on these coins as DICT. PERP. (dictator for life), but as DICT. QVART. (dictator for the fourth time).

Consequently, if Alföldi is right with his interpretation of the 'diadem', the exact chronology – with its far-reaching historical implications that literary sources cannot provide – appears to be:

1 January 44: *denarii* of the old style with 'Sulla's dream'
2 Beginning of February until shortly after February 15: issues with Caesar's portrait and legend CAES. DICT. QVART.
3 March 1 CAES. IMP.
4 After March 1 CAESAR DICTATOR PERPETVO
5 All the coins struck by Macer and Maridianus with the legend CAES. DICT. PERPETVO and CAESAR PARENS PATRIAE, portraying Caesar with veiled head, are to be attributed, at the earliest, to the period after the Ides of March

Up to April 10, the coins with DICT. PERP. remained in circulation but after the abolition of the dictatorship the coins with *parens patriae* appeared. At that point Antony needed to show Caesar in priestly garb, to demonstrate to the Roman people that its Pontifex Maximus had been murdered. He himself appears as consul on the denarius struck by Macer, with head covered and beard unshaven as a sign of mourning. No one can still harbour doubts about Caesar's final plans, for 'he assigned the charge of the mint and of the public revenues to his own slaves' (Suet., *Div. Jul.* 76, 3), and that, too, was one of the reasons that led to his murder.

Alföldi pursued the subject further in a series of articles in *Museum Helveticum*, the *Schweizer Münzblätter* and the *Schweizer Numismatische Rundschau*, etc.,[97] and later presented his discoveries to his followers and critics in two impressive volumes (only one of which has been published), entitled *Caesar im Jahre 44.*[98] He remained, apparently, largely true to his former opinions, although he modified certain points in matters of detail.

Alföldi was convinced of Caesar's endeavours towards monarchy, although he attempted to prove that they were not the sudden whim of a confident autocrat. Quite the contrary. In the time of Scipio Africanus a vague vision of a saviour was awakened in the Roman people (*Phoenix* XXIV (1970), p. 166), while since Sulla's time monarchy had been knocking at the gates of Rome. From the turn of the last century of the Republic the saviour theory was proclaimed on the annual issues of *denarii*. The belief in the return of a 'Golden Age' became fused with the yearning of the masses for a new Romulus. Alföldi pointed out that even those in the highest circles in Rome attempted to work out the imminent return of the ideal king of antiquity through the arithmetical tricks of astrology. Prominent politicians from Sulla to Augustus wanted to be considered the new Romulus. The misgivings of lesser persons concerning a rule by a king – so dreaded by the Senate – disappeared over the years. For them the dream come true would be the return of a king, and the hated symbols of sovereignty, such as diadem, sceptre and the ruler's wreath, are concealed by the apparently guiltless garb of a king of remote antiquity. Thus a predisposition for a king's actual return is facilitated by fantasy.

In 67 BC, Pompey was reviled as Romulus by a consul, yet five years later Romulus appeared on the issues of *denarii* struck by M. Plaetorius Cestianus. Pompey's exaltation at the end of the Republic – an alternative to his glorification as saviour – had to be enveloped in the Romulus Allegory.[99] Foundation and establishment of a new order were prized even by Cicero as acts of the highest virtue, and the concepts *conditor, servator, parens* and *deus* are inseparable from the concept of the new Romulus.

The virtues of Romulus as depicted by Dionysius of Halicarnassus are intelligible only through their adaptation to Caesar's political programme. Caesar was reviled as Romulus by Catullus (29, 5; 28, 15; 49, 1), yet Alföldi had no doubt that in the last phase of his life Caesar strove to be compared with Romulus. He wanted to derive his claim to renew Romulus' virtues as ruler from his family tradition: the red shoes, the garb of the former kings, the purple gown and white diadem[100] were symbols of the Caesarian-Romulean monarchy that Caesar so fervently desired. But, since he also knew how much the appellation 'king' in Rome was held in odium, his real aim had to be camouflaged by the catchword *parens patriae*.

The old father-symbol penetrated political life in the first century BC. Even before this it was a stereotyped honour accorded to many, and thus provided an established title for one. The expression *pater patriae* has a different significance

with reference to Cicero than with reference to Caesar, who
was continuously *parens* but never *pater*, and the Brundisium
inscription, 'C. Julio Caesari pont. max. patri patriae' (*ILS*
71), is, in Alföldi's opinion, a scholarly forgery. Further,
Cicero was hailed as *pater patriae* for giving the order for the
execution of the Catilinarians, and his *severitas* was accordingly
represented as the virtue of a saviour. Caesar, on the other
hand, was called *parens patriae* on account of his *clementia*. The
gentle, fatherly quality of the benevolent prince is antithesized
with the tyrant's anger and the *mitissimus parens* with the
crudelis tyrannus (*de dom.* 94). As domestic slaves swore by the
genius of the head of the household, men must now swear by
Caesar's *genius*; and, as, according to tradition, it was a worse
offence to kill a *parens patriae* than to kill one's own father ('est
atrocius patriae parentem quam suum occidere'). Caesar was
foolish enough to discharge his bodyguard in the hope that he
could rely on his legally established *sacrosanctitas*. That was his
undoing, and Rome lost a man of unheard-of tolerance and
magnanimous *clementia*.

Alföldi, it must be granted, never obscured his views in
hazy phraseology. On the contrary, he ruthlessly judged the
republican regime as 'a collective monarchy of the nobles who
were sucking the blood from the Empire like leeches'.[101] It did
not occur to him that Caesar broke the law by crossing the
Rubicon, and he posed the question whether the frenzy of the
gangs in Rome before Caesar's rise to power had been in any
sense constitutional. 'One might describe the event in terms of
an analogy, as the act of conceiving outside the mother's body,
in the case of the Republic – a conception outside the constitution. The emergence of the child into the world spelt
certain death for the mother.'

Likewise, Caesar should not be blamed for trying to become
king. The idea occurred to him only after the Senate had
showered him with honours – initially against his will – which
eventually led him to overstep the limits of the permissible
'only after the chorus of time-servers had led the way'.[102] In an
article, 'La divinisation de César', Alföldi also remarked that 'a
slavish Senate' had pronounced Caesar a god.[103] In his general
eulogy of Caesar he recalls the emotional style of nineteenth-
century scholars, 'He (Caesar) wanted to rule as sovereign, but
preferred to expose his body to his murderers' daggers rather
than go on wasting his life away like a tyrant reliant on a

bodyguard for safety. The *nobile letum Catonis* has its counter-part: the *nobile letum Caesaris*'.[104]

Despite the impressive collection of sources and numismatic evidence Alföldi used to support his thesis, his work attracted little attention in the English-speaking West. In E. S. Gruen's highly interesting and stimulating book, which concludes with an extensive bibliography, Alföldi is not mentioned[105] – whether accidentally or intentionally can only be surmised. Yet it must surely be recognized that Gruen totally disagrees with Alföldi, and rejects as 'hindsight' the theory that, since the time of Sulla, the idea of monarchy hovered like a bird of prey over the gates of Rome. Actually, in speaking of the Romans' longing for a great man, Alföldi reflected to some extent the remarks of Gundolf, written before Hitler's rise to power, 'Today, since the need for a strong man is voiced, since men, weary of critics and carpers, make do with sergeants instead of generals, since, particularly in Germany, the government of the people is entrusted to any especially note-worthy talent displayed by soldiers, economists, civil servants or writers . . .'

Alföldi himself admitted, 'My researches on the year 44 have been rejected without serious argument and have remained ignored.'[106] There are some important reasons why this is so. In the first place, there is no agreement about the significance of *pater patriae*. In Alföldi's view the expression *pater* constitutes a superior concept, embracing the whole essence of the *princeps*. This title, in his opinion, is the immediate prerequisite for one man's rule; it is not merely an honorary title; it puts the whole community under an obli-gation to the one in power.

Most scholars reject Alföldi's position. It was Mommsen's opinion that the title *pater* was not essential to the emperor's position, and that no rights were associated with it.[107] A. von Premerstein took it simply as an honorary title; for A. H. M. Jones it was 'a harmless and ornamental title and office', and even S. Weinstock attributed no decisive importance to it.[108] We cannot attempt a more detailed discussion of all the different opinions on this question, but it is sufficient to say that there is no agreement on the significance of the distinction between *parens* and *pater*, nor, indeed, on the significance of the title *imperator*, which Caesar, in Alföldi's view, adopted after his failure to be proclaimed king on 15 February 44, since only this title remained acceptable to the republicans.[109]

Despite their readiness to make use of Dio, Appian, Suetonius and Plutarch as important sources for Caesar's history, modern scholars are not prepared, without further discussion, to take as gospel every statement of later sources. Alföldi, in turn, was not prepared to recognize this problem, and introduced the coinage as conclusive proof for his fundamental statements about Caesar's honours. But it is precisely here that he encountered the most decisive opposition from his fellow numismatists. Although impressed by his acuteness and originality, they did not agree that the Roman mintmasters would have worked into their coins 'shrewdly conceived combinations of types'.[110] A numismatist as remarkable as M. H. Crawford is strongly critical of Alföldi's work.[111] The latter's basic argument, that it was possible to discover on the coinage of the first century BC the desire for a new Romulus, is rejected as 'obsessed with supposed prophecies of a golden age and full of surprising assertions'.[112]

In a short footnote (n. 108), Weinstock, who was ideologically not far removed from Alföldi, observed that although the latter had devoted a hundred pages to an examination of the concept *pater patriae* only a few of them touch on the problem. Alföldi continued the argument with Weinstock – after the latter's death – and replied in a long article (*Gnomon* XII 1975, 154–79). Non-specialists should steer clear of such debates. Yet, the most important objections raised by experts such as C. M. Kraay and R. A. G. Carson in England, and, independently, by H. Volkmann in Germany, must be briefly mentioned.[113]

All scholars are united in their recognition of Alföldi's pains to work out a precise chronological table of the issues and a detailed sequence of the dictator's intentions. Kraay, however, maintained that most of Alföldi's conclusions were untenable, and that they yielded no key to Caesar's policy. Alföldi was convinced that he could prove which coins were struck before February 15, which were struck in the second half of February, and which were struck at the beginning of March. But on this point there is no agreement. These are weighty questions not to be ignored.

Carson rejected the conclusion that Caesar, convinced of the failure of his attempt to become king on February 15, allowed coins to be struck in the second half of February merely with the legend IMP., and only at the beginning of March issued those with DICT. PERP. It is, however, expressly reported in a contemporary source such as Cicero (*Phil.* II, 34; 87) that Caesar was already *dictator perpetuus* on February 15. Why, then, throw away a reliable literary source in favour of a baseless numismatic theory? Why should the assumption of the title *imperator* be seen as surrender to the republicans? Was even a ten-year dictatorship so acceptable to these republicans?

Furthermore, on what ground should it be supposed that the series with CAES. DICT. (later replaced by PATER PATRIAE) and those with the legend CAES. IMP. were not struck simultaneously (1) as a normal state issue, which Caesar employed to demonstrate the offices on the basis of which he governed, or (2) to supply coinage for the Parthian wars, designed by the commander-in-chief?

Finally, even if it is generally recognized that the discovery of the Mettius *denarius* in the Königliches Munzkabinett at The Hague (unknown until 1952), and its description, was a brilliant stroke by Alföldi, it remains hazardous to draw very far-reaching inferences when only a single specimen is available for study. Alföldi's own analysis arouses serious doubt. Kraay is not convinced that the *denarius* shows Caesar's diadem hanging up in the temple, and takes it as unproven that a *lituus* is not here quite simply in question. Indeed, it is true that on the rest of the Mettius *denarii* with the legend CAES. DICT. QVART. a *lituus* inclined to the right instead of the left appears. But a *lituus* inclined to the left appears on Mettius *denarii* with the legend CAES. IMP., so it is not unusual.

The most important argument in opposition to Alföldi's views appeared in a long monograph by D. Felber.[114] Naturally, he follows the views of Kraay and Carson relating to the chronology of the coins. However, he returns to the conclusion that Caesar became dictator for life on February 15, and rejects Alföldi's interpretation derived from 'Sulla's Dream', that coins with different legends are to be put in chronological order and that all the issues with the *caput velatum* are posthumous.

We shall return to Felber in another connection; at this point it need only be remarked that his devastating criticism could lead to the conclusion that one should not attribute an exaggerated significance to coins. It would be worth while to ponder on Jones' sensible advice, 'If numismatists wish . . . to assist historians, I would suggest that they should pay less attention to the political interpretation of the coins . . . Latterly the value of numismatic evidence has tended to be over-strained and its interpretation has become over-subtle'.[115]

To sum up, it must be said that Alföldi's opponents have not actually proven any new theory, but have demolished his argument by their sceptical observations and thereby pointed in a new direction.

If one studies Alföldi's thorough criticism of Weinstock's book,[116] one might be surprised that the critic and the subject of his criticism belong to the same school, here termed the Revisionist. But in fact Alföldi's criticism was not fundamental. His attack on Weinstock's numismatic analysis was the more acute, mainly because the latter had taken scarcely any notice of the results of his own research. In numerous details, *inter alia* in matters of ancient Roman religion, he also stands apart from Weinstock.

By and large, however, there are no differences of opinion between the two scholars, as Alföldi dealt with the question of kingship, and Weinstock concerned himself with the deification. They agree that Caesar strove for both in his lifetime, even if Weinstock's precise wording was the more cautious and reserved. His enormous knowledge was steeped in German and Italian scholarship, but in the course of a long life in the atmosphere of an Oxford college he adapted to English style and English ways of thought. Using expressions like 'may' and 'might' he frequently softened the pointedness of an argument that would doubtless have aroused antagonism in another language.

Weinstock guarded against speaking of Caesar's far-reaching schemes, but likewise did not sketch him as a child of fortune or superman. Yet he, too, agreed with the view, as did Alföldi, that it was Caesar's first task to set up a monarchy (p. 281), and that at a certain point of time he was not satisfied with it, 'While fighting in Parthia, his rule was to be strengthened by religious means and his divinity was to be established gradually' (p. 286). Both Alföldi and Weinstock agreed that religious honours at this point became a constitutional necessity, since actual power was transferred from the annual magistrates to the one and only ruler.[117]

Weinstock's position on deification mirrored Alföldi's criticism of Meyer's idea of a Hellenistic monarchy and his substitution of the idea of a western monarchy, 'Caesar's new position in Rome was to be prepared in a Roman fashion: the influence of Greek Soteres, Gods, and kings can be felt, but what was made of it was due to the influence of an old Roman tradition' (p. 167), and, further, '[Caesar] did not want to appear as an innovator, nor to spread a new philosophy of life, but to be guided by tradition – yet one who at the end radically broke with it' (p. 411). This is the fundamental view that made Weinstock a representative of the Revisionist school. It is also the main theme of his book *Divus Julius*, which is not only a work on the deification of Caesar but a history of ideas, with the object of explaining how a particular atmosphere facilitated such deification. Since a mechanical incorporation of oriental rites into Rome appeared to him logically unacceptable, Weinstock described the development of the 'cults of personified values', *concordia, salus, pietas, victoria, honos, virtus, iustitia*, and finally, of course, *clementia*, in all their details, – one of the finest chapters in the book. The connection of these virtues with a statesman forms the core of the whole work.

In Weinstock's 450 closely-printed pages Caesar appears before us, not as the acute, tireless politician and army commander or the dictator driven by ambition, but 'as an imaginative and daring religious reformer who created and planned new cults, accepted extraordinary honours and died when he was about to become a divine ruler' (*ibid.*).

In contrast to this view Alföldi particularly stressed the enthusiasm with which the Senate compelled Caesar to accept all possible honours. But Weinstock forcefully maintained, 'Caesar was not a passive recipient. The decrees often fulfilled his expectations' (p. 412). 'He was involved in detailed planning of his cult and moved first towards an accumulation of priesthoods.' It was no accident that Caesar made every effort so that his adoptive son should inherit the office of Pontifex Maximus from him (p. 33). 'Varro dedicated to him his *Antiquitates Rerum divinarum* and Granius Flaccus *De indigitamentis* which was probably another antiquarian survey of prayer and ritual' (p. 32). Finally Caesar emerges as one who strove after a 'sacred kingship' (p. 323).

In Weinstock's favour it must be said that he warned his readers that some of his assertions were nothing more than learned conjectures, often emerging from evidence of doubtful reliability. His greatest service was to promote general public awareness of an elementary fact: that one ought not to judge Caesar without taking into account the religious background of the time (p. 260), and in this respect his work is preferable to that of B. E. Giovanetti published in 1937.

But even after a thorough study of his comprehensive work some questions remain, of which a single example may suffice. At one point Weinstock described in detail the religious tradition of the Julian family, a tradition that had its origins in Bovillae. He analysed a small incident related by Cassius Dio (XLI, 39, 2), of how Caesar set about sacrificing a bull to Fortuna, before putting to sea in pursuit of Pompey, and of how the bull eluded him. Weinstock arrived at a far-fetched interpretation – again taking assistance from the little word 'may', 'He may have intended to make the bull of Bovillae as popular as the she-wolf of Rome' (p. 7). The Julii had for years been responsible for local rites in Bovillae – and probably also in Alba. The ritual of the Feriae Latinae was celebrated on the Alban Mount by a *rex*, which explains why, in 45 BC, Caesar began to dress in the garb of the Alban kings.

But with the help of the word 'may' a different conjecture is also possible: the bull was also the ensign of the Italians, and if Vell. Pat. II, 27, 2 reports that Italian freedom was ravaged by the Roman wolves, so the Roman she-wolf's subjection by the Italian bull may be symbolically portrayed on the coinage (Hill, *Hist. Roman Coins* (1909), pl. XI, 49). Perhaps one should be permitted the conjecture that Caesar did not have his family emblem in mind at all, but was rather attempting to drop a hint to the Italians that their support in the war against Pompey could turn out to be profitable for them. And the question mark remains.

In addition, it is hard to be convinced that Caesar was a religious man, for Weinstock himself expressed astonishment that Caesar did not take the trouble in any of his writings to stress that he was a citizen who continually observed his religious duty (p. 26). It must also be added that Caesar – like every influential Roman – had a very good understanding indeed of how the masses could be manipulated with the aid of religion (Polyb. VI, 56), but he never allowed himself to be deterred from his purpose by religious scruples (Suet., *Div. Jul.* 59, 1; 81, 4).

Weinstock's assumption that Caesar treated Apollo as his ancestral god remains only a conjecture based on a passage of

Dio concerning the statement of Atia to the effect that Apollo begat her son. Likewise, no one allows himself to be convinced that Caesar became Jupiter Julius in his lifetime. None of the stories that appear in Dio (such as p. 264, n. 6, on Dio XLI, 15, 4; 16, 4), can be regarded as solid fact beyond all doubt.[118] All scholars from Mommsen to Adcock read these same sources, and the majority formed the conclusion that it was only after his death that Caesar legally became *divus*.[119] But the Revisionists stubbornly stick to their view, and eventually Balsdon desisted from further discussion: 'The truth is that in this sharp division of opinion scholars on either side preach to the converted.'[120]

In our view, Vogt's briefer and more penetrating article would have sufficed to present us with the insoluble problem. Some may have presumed that further discussion was futile. And yet it is not surprising that by way of reaction another group of scholars surfaced whom we term the Sceptics.

THE SCEPTICS

This section does not permit as simple a systematization as the earlier ones. There is no lack of common ground, yet most of the adherents of this school go their own ways. In general, it may be said that the Sceptics are usually prepared to accept the fact that even with the evidence that is available today it is impossible to penetrate to the full truth. At the outset they abandoned research into intentions and questions such as 'Did Caesar strive after honours, or was it the Senate that showered him with honours?', because satisfactory answers are not possible.

One has the impression that the consequences of World War II are readily discernible in the historical research of the last thirty years. Not only has Germany taken enormous strides towards the Anglo–Saxon democracies, but disapproving remarks about German historical research have disappeared from English works; on some issues an exchange of roles seems to have taken place. In fact, an extremely sceptical view on the divinity of humans might have been expected in the British Isles. Yet we read in Jocelyn Toynbee, a most distinguished archaeologist, that 'to the Greeks and Romans men and gods were not on two completely separated differential levels, and that a mortal could move godward by ascending degrees until he reached virtual identification with an immortal god'. She thinks that, with the aid of detailed research, 'the case of transition from man to god can be observed'.[121]

Precisely the opposite can be read in Carl Joachim Classen's article 'Gottmenschen in der römischen Republik'.[122] He comes to the conclusion that no individual Roman was honoured in a way that brought him nearer to the gods either in his lifetime or after his death. Contrary to the Greek conception, a deep gulf separated man and god. *Genii* are not divine, for there are as many *genii* as there are living men. Sacrifices are a way of offering honour and respect: they are also owed to gods, but not only to gods. They are a kind of thanksgiving for a particular achievement brought to fulfilment. Classen is prepared to admit that Caesar's measures were more audacious than those of all his predecessors, but no more than that.

Of course, everything cannot be blamed on World War II. E. J. Bickermann's warning, voiced in 1930, must not be forgotten, especially with regard to research into the emperor cult.[123] In his opinion it was not permissible 'to confuse ideology with the sacral law which alone determines worship, and nobody should confuse divinity and association with the divine'.[124]

A new view can be traced in the research of C. Habicht,[125] which was also mirrored in studies of Caesar and his desire for deification. R. Cohen remarked that the ruler cult is 'the most delicate question in the organization of monarchy',[126] and in L. Cerfaux and J. Tondriau we read, 'A cult is a matter of feeling, and the intentions that dictate it almost always escape us. Nothing is more dangerous than to try to reconstruct, above all in matters of religion, the mentality and reasoning of a man of the ancient world.'[127] These warnings were eventually heeded.

M. Liberanome, who was concerned with Caesar's aims for kingship, was much more cautious than Weinstock, although he admits the religious vitality of the people.[128] Elsewhere we noted Felber's decisive objections to Alföldi's chronology derived from the coinage, but he should again be mentioned in the present context, since he can serve as a prototype for the 'Sceptics'. Not content merely with a fresh examination of the numismatic material, Felber also reassessed the literary sources from which conclusions concerning Caesar's aim for kingship and deification may suitably be drawn, 'It is to be doubted that Caesar, in the attire in which he showed himself to the public at the Lupercalia, was unmistakably distinguished as the new Romulus and old Roman king.'[129] And, 'the assertion that Caesar had already introduced the title *imperator* as a personal name and mark of the ruler in the sense of the *praenomen imperatoris* of the empire, is untenable' (pp. 231 ff.).[130] And, 'the view that the dictator intended to acquire the title of king with the aid of a sibylline oracle does not hold water' (pp. 254 ff.). And finally (from the sources at our disposal), '. . . one can get no answer to the question whether Caesar, in fact, wanted to establish a kingdom' (p. 273).

Gustav Haber,[131] a pupil of Vogt, is also doubtful about Caesar's aims regarding kingship, and in 1968 Helga Gesche, a pupil of K. Kraft, published a brief, clear, and impressive book, which provides a fundamental analysis of all the literary, epigraphic and numismatic material connected with the deification of Caesar.[132] Her critics must be impressed by the meticulousness of her investigations, even if they do not agree with her conclusions.[133] Frau Gesche particularly stresses the difference between the concepts *Vergötterung* and *Vergottung*, and comes to the clear conclusion that on the coins struck before Caesar's death epithets such as *Deus* or *Divus Caesar* are missing, and that the dictator was never represented as a god (p. 16, especially n. 26).

Nevertheless, Helga Gesche, for all her caution, also believes that Caesar not only strove for deification, but also planned in advance for the time after his death. Of course, there is no evidence for such a view as yet, and, therefore, it is pointless to start the discussion afresh. As the source material at our disposal does not allow for a decision, it would be preferable to abandon the question for the time being, rather than hazard further guesses. As a sceptical English scholar put it, 'The foot of Hercules may be a sufficient clue to his stature, but we shall scarcely succeed in reconstructing him from the parings of his toe-nails.'[134]

The real protagonist of sober judgment in Caesar's case is Hermann Strasburger. As far back as 1937, in his review of H. Rudolph's *Stadt und Staat im römischen Italien* (Leipzig 1935), he warned against treating Caesar as a superman, and attempted to put him into measured perspective.[135] The proper perspective, however, was achieved in his brilliant essay 'Caesar im Urteil der Zeitgenossen', with which we introduced this historiographic section.

W. Schmitthenner, too, in a thorough analysis of all the events preceding the assassination of Caesar, had to take into account the doubts of numerous scholars, *viz.* that with regard to Caesar's final plans there can be only opinion, but no certainty, despite the pains and discoveries of the numismatists. Schmitthenner's sceptical view contained a warning, 'If we allow ourselves to be led by the search for truth, positions that are compulsorily established suddenly become open and inexact.'[136]

Strasburger's influence was felt as much in England as in Germany. Thus R. E. Smith, for instance, was not interested in whether Caesar really aimed at kingship, 'Whether Caesar ever had in mind to take the name of king we cannot know, nor does it greatly matter.'[137] Smith, like Strasburger, was mainly concerned with what Caesar's contemporaries thought about him, and assumed that they considered him a tyrant who put himself at the head of a Republic that stood for annual magistrates.

One finds similar conclusions, although based on a different theoretical foundation, in Christian Meier's brief remarks about Caesar.[138] In his opinion, the basic reason for Caesar's failure lay in the fundamental circumstances of the world in which he lived, not in this or that mistake or attribute of the dictator. Meier finds little value in posing the question of whether Caesar intended to found a monarchy. We simply do not know that. We know only that he reigned as a monarch and possessed the full powers of a monarch. 'He could command, dispose, forbid, establish institutions, do away with them, alter them, give laws, circumvent them, break them, elect and suspend magistrates as he willed.'

We know, too, that Caesar was given exaggerated honours, partly associated with royalty and partly with divinity, without being admittedly marked out as a king or god. Meier supposes that Caesar either had not given any thought to instituting a monarchy in Rome, or at least saw no viable way of approaching this aim. He was, above all, a pragmatist and improviser, and convinced himself that he could improve everything.

Meier stated that to Caesar and his followers the question of *regnum* and *respublica* was one and the same. His considerations were those of a typical Roman aristocrat who conceived no new constitutional ideas. 'Had the commonwealth been a piece of clay, politics a matter of manufacture, and not a vital process of manoeuvring, then Caesar would have been quite happy.' In truth, things appeared to be quite different. Meier pointed out that the omnipotent victor and dictator Caesar was actually powerless (*ohnmächtig*). That everything depended on him disturbed him no less than it vexed Cicero. Too many demands were made upon him; he felt oppressed, and as a result of *ennui* planned a Parthian war instead of restructuring the state and society. This was not due to Caesar's personality or character. Within Roman society there was no touchpoint which might have sparked off a direct conflict, in the course of which it might have been possible to work towards a new structure. To do this, there would have to have been some sort of articulated social group or class involved in a kind of emergency, surmountable only through a fundamental and comprehensive reform (or revolution). In the 50s and 40s of the first century BC the principle of the commonwealth was only extended, not supplanted, and Caesar's personality can be understood in the context of a crisis without an alternative.

Meier's view is contained in a popular work that until now has provoked only an insignificant response. Yet, a thorough investigation in the direction taken by this book would be desirable, although Meier himself doubted the interests of his professional colleagues in themes of this kind.

This survey would not be complete without a reference to J. H. Collins, a scholar who is not easily classified although he wrote many important works including an excellent article, 'Caesar and the Corruption of Power'.[139] An American who worked under Gelzer in Germany, he brought his critical examination of the sources to a high level, but did not hesitate to make use of the social sciences such as sociology and psychology in his research.[140] Collins believed that contemporary researchers shrink from generalizations, which are reserved for chatter in the corridors and the faculty common-rooms. He was convinced that there is one Caesar for the years between 60 and 48 BC and another for the years between 46 and 44 BC. The turning-point is thus the year 47 BC, the year that brought him into contact with the East and Cleopatra. She was more than a mistress. She was, as Horace put it, 'no ordinary woman'.

Collins maintained that Caesar's contemporaries also noticed changes in his nature and conduct. Initially they believed in him, but in the final analysis they were bitterly disappointed. Between 50 and 46 BC Sallust was still expecting Caesar to reform the Republic. Collins supported this view by reference to the *Letters of Sallust*, in which the writer addressed these words to Caesar,

But if you have in you the spirit which has from the very beginning dismayed the faction of the nobles, which restored the Roman commons to freedom after a grievous slavery, which in your praetorship routed your armed enemies without resort to arms, which has achieved so many and such glorious deeds at home and abroad that not even your enemies dare to make any complaint except of your greatness; if you have that spirit, pray give ear to what I shall say about our country's welfare.

(*Letter to Caesar* I, 2, 4)

Sallust suggested a series of ideas for reform, but later lost all hope. Caesar changed into a tyrant and was murdered. The serious doubts of H. Last, R. Syme and E. Fraenkel as to the authenticity of the letters did not prevent Collins from recognizing Sallust as the author. But Collins could have invoked the doubtless authentic work of Sallust, *The Jugurthine War* (3, 2), written after Caesar's death, 'For to rule one's country or subjects by force, although you both have the power to correct abuses, and do correct them, is nevertheless tyrannical . . .'

Cicero's relationship with Caesar (according to Collins) was similar. In the years between 55 and 53 BC they were intimate friends. Even after the civil wars Cicero continued to hope that Caesar would restore the Republic (his speech *Pro Marcello*). Later came disappointment, and then the irrevocable breach.[141] Cicero's mixed feelings towards Caesar were made abundantly clear in a letter of May 4, 44 (*ad Att.* XIV, 17). Cicero recalled that Caesar's behaviour towards him was moderate enough but otherwise unbending (*de div.* II, 23). Collins rightly emphasized that to Cicero Caesar was an enigma because he did not fit into any of the categories of his moral philosophy.

To sum up, in Collins' view there was sufficient evidence to suggest that Caesar's deepest political conviction was based on the old *respublica*. Only when he began to despair of it did he feel that despotism was the only other way open to him. But his arrogance, illusions of grandeur, aggressiveness towards the Senate and respect for *nobilitas* of great distinction was not purely arbitrary. The view that the Republic deserted Caesar and not Caesar the Republic is the truer of the two; and, if that is right, Balsdon also deserves credit for his statement (*Historia* VII (1958), 86, 94) that Caesar was not murdered because he had changed, but because he had not changed.

To add further notion or surmise to this medley of opinions would be a real presumption, but I would like to suggest some thoughts that might be worthy of further study.

Caesar is one of the phenomena that appear upon the stage of history in times of crisis and hope. His rule drew support from a heterogeneous social group, a fact impressively proved by Syme's research. Yet it does not clearly emerge from all the studies we have mentioned that each of these groups expected a different solution to the acute problems of the day from Caesar. Each group saw him in a distinct way: some saw him as a man of clemency, others as the harsh ruler. Some expected a land distribution, others the cancellation of debts. Some hoped he would restore the Republic to its former greatness, others wanted its abolition once and for all. Each individual was convinced that his picture of Caesar was the right one.

Collins drew a distinction between the Caesar of the years before 46 BC and the Caesar of later years, which does not solve the problem, however, since there were 'several Caesars' before 46 BC as well as after it. In 49 BC Caesar crossed the Rubicon, apparently to plead for the tribunes' rights, but in the same year he himself infringed on the rights of Metellus when he tried to make himself master of the treasury in the temple of Saturn.

In 49 BC a cancellation of debts was generally expected, but towards the end of that year the money-lenders, bankers and wholesale merchants were among Caesar's most loyal followers. After the crossing of the Rubicon, there was some expectation that Caesar would reach an understanding with all the members of the *nobilitas*; indeed, he made extraordinary efforts to reach such an understanding with them. Many were receptive to his canvassing, and the list of consuls for the years between 49 and 44 BC proves that the firmly entrenched *nobilitas* understood how necessary it was to preserve their influence in the state.

Who and what, then, was Caesar? Strasburger and Balsdon, Béranger and others proved that Caesar was a tyrant.[142] But that was only in the eyes of a limited group of senators in the latter days of Caesar's life. Did the people think so too? In another book[143] I have attempted to explore the masses' image of Caesar. It is not easy to free oneself of the picture of Caesar as portrayed, above all, in the writings of Cicero and Sallust because the common man wrote no literary works and it is difficult to say with certainty what the masses thought. But the attempt is worth while. From close consideration of his conduct, however, there is no doubt about how Caesar wanted to appear in the eyes of the people, and that he held himself up to the plebs as the popular father-figure freed from the shackles of the Senate.

There are historians who maintain that the similarities between Caesar and Pompey are greater than the differences. Even if that is true, and the difference is much less than we suppose, the Roman plebs were not of this opinion. When Julius Caesar organized games and festivals, on a generous scale, the people were jubilant. Yet, when Pompey permitted eighteen elephants and five hundred lions to be brought into the arena, sympathy was shown for the animals and he was met with angry abuse.[144] Why? How did the ideal figure of a leader appear in the eyes of the people? It is apparent that concern for the physical well-being of the masses was only one factor. All Roman rulers bribed the people with bread and circuses, and yet the one was popular and the other hated. Seneca provided us with the answer: the giving is not the decisive factor but the manner of the giving.[145] 'Idem est quod datur, sed interest quomodo detur'. The people were more easily swayed by how a ruler did than by what he did, and respected the one who at least took the trouble to appear popular.[146] When Caesar decided to live in the poor quarter (before the elections!), the people saw no false altruism in the action.[147] They preferred him to Pompey, who made not the slightest effort 'to climb down to the people'. Therefore, it is not surprising that after Ilerda all 'civil war games' played by Roman children ended with the victory of the 'Caesarians'.[148] The vast mass of the people loathed the members of the *nobilitas*, but were powerless against them. The most popular political leaders (all aristocrats in origin) were those who criticized and debased the existing 'establishment' of senators in public and *coram publico* made much of the fact that they – 'although senators themselves' – were not the slaves of their class.[149] The common people are not always as capricious as the sources make out. Perhaps Goethe was quite right when he wrote,

> Tell me, are we doing the right thing? We must
> deceive the rabble, See just how inept, how boorish, and how
> transparently stupid it is! It appears inept and stupid, just
> because you are deceiving it, Only be honest, and it, believe me,
> is human and shrewd.

> (*Venetian Epigrams*).

Caesar grasped every opportunity and spared no efforts to appear to be the people's friend, a man whose chief concern was the well-being of the common man.

Is that the true Caesar? I have never maintained so. I suppose there will be those who will say that my position is influenced by the conduct of those politicians in our age of mass media who are primarily interested in burnishing their personal image before the television cameras and the press.

Such criticism would be justified. Each generation writes history anew and adds its own ingredient to existing knowledge. I cannot quarrel with Friedrich Frhr. von Wieser's observation that the present is the teacher of the knowledge of the past. I have not discovered the quest for the 'image'. It does exist in the sources, but it seems to me that insufficient attention has been paid to it. In any case, this is not the last word on Caesar's place in history, and I am far from solving the enigma of Caesar the man.

If we tried to discover how the Gauls,[150] the Jews, the *municipales* in Italy or the merchants in Spain saw Caesar, it would become clear that there are still several 'Caesars'. But, even if we could not know which of them is the 'true' Caesar, we would better understand why he remains such an enigma to the present day. 'Maxima quaeque ambigua sunt' – it is precisely the most important state of affairs that remain ambiguous (Tac., *Ann*. III, 19, 2).[151]

However, nothing is achieved by extreme scepticism. A Cambridge modern historian explains, 'The historian who tries to reject everything that is unproven will be rejecting

much that is true. His talent lies neither in a corrosive and
tiresome scepticism about everything, nor in absolute
positivism, but in discernment and discrimination, best called
historical understanding'.[152]

If we knew exactly what Caesar's intentions were, our
subject would become wholly factual. But since we do not
know them, we must be content with the English maxim,
'People should be judged by facts, not by alleged intentions'.
What, then, are these facts? Thirty-eight laws and measures
are supposedly associated with Caesar's name. It ought to be
possible, by a thorough investigation of these laws and
measures, to understand how Caesar was assessed by different
sections of the public? It is worth making the attempt.
Moreover, can something be learned about Caesar's aims and
personality from his laws?

CHAPTER TWO

POLITICAL MEASURES

INTRODUCTORY NOTE

Three separate chapters will be devoted to a discussion of what Caesar's administration achieved in the areas of domestic, economic and social policies. For our purposes the general history of the years between 49 and 44 BC – the civil war – serves only as a background. The division is schematic, since every one of Caesar's measures operated in at least two areas. For example, laws regulating the collection of taxes in the provinces were based on political considerations, had an economic and social effect, and, finally, dovetailed into the administrative system. The decision to discuss a law such as, e.g., the *Lex Antonia de candidatis* in the chapter entitled *Administrative Measures of a Political Character* is quite arbitrary, but every classification entails a certain artificiality.

It would be better to establish a clear chronological order by fixing an exact date to each measure. This kind of chronological order might be preferable in so far as it could point to a logical development, but it involves the danger of the assumption *post hoc, ergo propter hoc*, and when chronology is as indeterminate as that of the legislation of Gaius Gracchus, such an arrangement can be confusing rather than useful. A schematic arrangement, at least, will not lead one astray, precisely because it is known to be artificial. But the classification is not a self-serving one. It should simply help one to find answers to the principal questions,

1 *Cui bono?* Who reaped advantages from this legislative activity with its many ramifications?
2 Is it really true that Caesar operated without a plan, or is a well-considered line of action detectable behind his activities?
3 Is it possible to pin down Caesar's image as reflected by

Roman public opinion, even if we cannot plumb the depths of his personality?
We should add two notes on the method used.

It is my intention first to present a straightforward description of Caesar's measures and then sum up these steps in an *Interim statement*. Caesar's legislative activity occupies a central position, although not all of his measures were brought about through legislation. The dictator was in no doubt that his proposals would be opposed in some quarters. Cassius Dio (XLIII, 27, 1) expressly reported that Caesar did not act unilaterally. In all matters, he made a habit of taking advice from leading members of the Senate, and frequently brought questions before the full body. In the tribal assembly (*comitia tributa*) Caesar had a decisive influence, and on no occasion were any of his proposals rejected. There is clear evidence on this point from Cicero (*ad Att.* XIII, 33a). Yet Caesar did not always operate through *leges rogatae*, but frequently preferred to use the method called *leges datae* by Mommsen (an expression for which there is no evidence in the sources), and governed by decree. Not only his instructions but also his ideas were preserved in writing as *acta Caesaris*, and after Caesar's death Antony attempted to put all of them into effect (Cic., *Phil.* I, 17; 18; 19; II, 109). Thus Caesar's legislation is to be considered as the most significant testimony of his activity.

It is also possible that Caesar, famous for his constant travelling, did not always allow himself enough time to follow the protracted procedures normally required for legislation. During his first dictatorship (in 49 BC), he spent only eleven days in Rome. During this short time he was so preoccupied with the problem of the debts that were oppressing so many that he could not take the traditional path of the legislator, and preferred magisterial enactment instead. Caesar himself admitted to this in *Bell. Civ.* III, 20 and coined the expression *constituere*, to signify that the decree was based on the dictator's authority. But we do not always have such reliable sources, and this causes considerable difficulties. G. Tibiletti took no notice at all of such transactions in his detailed article 'Lex'[1], while his compatriot G. Rotondi[2] always inserted a question mark in cases of doubt, an example that is followed here.

The credibility of various sources concerning Caesar is another crucial question. As mentioned in n. 76, Chapter 1, J.P.V.D. Balsdon divides the sources into three groups:

contemporary sources still extant (such as the writings of Cicero and Sallust); contemporary sources which are no longer extant, but whose content we know from other extant literature (such as Caesar's *Anticato*),[3] and later sources such as Cassius Dio and Plutarch.

The reader who, like Balsdon, concludes that later sources are worthless and, therefore, prefers to judge Caesar exclusively by the sources of his day, can do so easily on the basis of the material presented here. For this reason the sources for each individual statement are in parenthesis, with the result that another classification may be immediately established:

1 transactions described in contemporary sources
2 transactions described in later sources
3 transactions described in detail in later sources, but merely hinted at in contemporary sources

I accept Cassius Dio, Plutarch, Suetonius and Appian as more credible than do Balsdon and Strasburger. This statement requires further explanation.

Simply because a source is contemporary does not necessarily mean that it is credible. Cicero was a contemporary of Clodius, but no one takes seriously his estimate of Clodius in his speech on behalf of Milo. Caesar wrote a book about the civil war which attempted to prove that he had made superhuman efforts to avoid it. He was determined to have peace at any price (*Bell. Civ.* III, 90, 1), and it was, in fact, his enemies who drove him to war. We have every right to judge such an assertion with caution, although it comes from a contemporary source. Moreover, if we relied only on contemporary sources, we should be more or less dependent on Cicero's writings, and a greater part of the events reported in what follows would have to be rejected on the basis of *argumentum e silentio*, since later sources cannot be accepted or rejected just on the ground of their plausibility or implausibility – terms which mean nothing.

Some scholars believe that statements about Caesar's efforts to achieve divine honours are implausible, especially because they appear mainly in later sources. But they have difficulties in explaining facts found in Cicero that hint at such efforts (see pp. 32 ff.). Balsdon, who rejected every reference in Cassius Dio as a reference in a source of later date, undermined his position by the following argument: Caesar did not strive after divine honour – the fact is that he commanded the words 'to the demi-god' to be struck from an inscription dedicated to him. But the information relating to the deletion likewise comes from Cassius Dio (XLIII, 14, 6; 21, 2), and why should one accept one statement and not the other (see Balsdon, *ibid.* p. 84)? No one is in a position to establish on which sources Cassius Dio drew for his information. However, up to the present time no history has been written (of the era of Caesar and Augustus) which completely rejects pertinent accounts that appear in Cassius Dio and Appian.

Nevertheless, investigation of the sources requires caution. Just as portions should not be arbitrarily discarded, the whole should not be accepted without critical examination. An attempt should be made to trace the primary sources from which the later historian drew his material. Sometimes that is not very difficult. When, for example, Suetonius subsumed some detail about Caesar under a reference to Titus Ampius the Pompeian, it is not difficult to assess the quality of the source. But usually this is not so obvious, and unsupported assumptions should be avoided, and an attempt made to verify the account by means of epigraphic or numismatic material. That is the ideal situation, but, as far as the study of Caesar is concerned, very little has come to light in recent years.

Every account supplied by a later writer should, in principle, be assigned a question mark and certain problems should be left unresolved in preference to an unconsidered acceptance of such sources. An account which should be treated with suspicion is, for example, that of Cassius Dio XLIV, 7, 3, according to which certain persons dared to suggest that Caesar be allowed to associate with 'as many women as he wished'. The truth is that Caesar's promiscuity was proverbial, and Suetonius reported the most intimate details of such activity (*Div. Jul.* 50–52). Perhaps this 'advertisement' did not particularly impugn the image of the virile Caesar. On the other hand, it is doubtful whether other honourable senators were more chaste than he. It should not be forgotten that it was customary in ancient Rome to make personal attacks on political opponents by the publication of their intimate affairs. Caesar himself made use of this weapon in his abusive pamphlet, the *Anticato*. But a formal proposal in the *Senate* to permit him relations with 'as many women as he wished' is another matter.

Nevertheless, we can learn something even from this story. According to Suetonius, the tribune of the plebs Helvius Cinna publicly admitted that a written proposal for a law was before him to permit Caesar to take as many women as he chose, in order to provide for the succession (*Div. Jul.* 52), and that Caesar had arranged for it to be confirmed in his absence. Suetonius is thus speaking about a bill that was not passed, and that was perhaps never presented.

Again, Suetonius is not a contemporary source, and can hardly serve as proof or counter-proof for the assertions of Cassius Dio. Yet, Suetonius refers to a contemporary, Helvius Cinna. Helvius, however, was mistakenly killed in the disturbance that broke out after Caesar's murder, and could never confirm or deny the allegation made in his name. It is not impossible that the whole affair was part of the campaign of slander contrived by Caesar's murderers to justify their act. Their intention was to appear as executioners of a despot, and sensual pleasure (*libido*) is a notoriously distinguishing characteristic of the Greek tyrant. Naturally one can take the point of view that it was only malicious gossip, and no one can refute that. But in the following chapters we intend to consider no less than the 'true Caesar' – Caesar as he appeared in the eyes of the public – and we shall show that Cicero himself quoted the most hateful rumours circulating against Caesar in Rome, and that there is no reason to accept Cassius Dio's material as more credible than any pure rumour deserves. But propaganda, too, has its value, and much may be learned from it. That is the principal reason why data from later sources that are not contemporary should not be arbitrarily rejected. Admittedly, they contain statements at second and third hand, but rumours, too, should be cautiously classified into those current in Caesar's lifetime and those that began to circulate only after his death, for there are important differences between them. This will be discussed in Chapter 6.

I LEX ANTONIA DE PROSCRIPTORUM LIBERIS (49 BC)

This was a law passed by the popular assembly (*plebiscitum*) on Caesar's initiative and with the help of the tribune Antony. If we can believe Cassius Dio (XLI, 18, 2), Caesar stayed in Rome for only a short time at the beginning of 49 BC, and handed over to Antony the conduct of domestic administration. It is clear that Antony presented bills to the popular assembly only with Caesar's approval (XLI, 17, 3), and the *Lex Antonia de proscriptorum liberis* was most probably his first proposal.

If Cicero's speech 'De proscriptorum filiis', or 'liberis' (*ad Att.* II, 1, 3; *in Pis.* 4; Quint., *Inst.* XI, 1, 85) of 63 BC were extant, we would know more about this problem. The speech, however, has been lost so that we begin with Suetonius, who reported (*Div. Jul.* 41, 2) that the law made it possible for the sons of those proscribed (by Sulla), who until then had been excluded as candidates, to be elected to magistracies.

Caesar was consistent here. When he was aedile he attempted to demonstrate his rejection of Sulla's methods by restoring Marius' statues, despite the opposition of some of the *nobiles*. Velleius maintained that he simultaneously restored the right to hold office to the sons of those proscribed by Sulla (Vell. Pat. II, 43, 4, cf. 28, 4). That this actually happened as early as 65 BC is by no means certain, unless a proposal made in 65 BC had never come into force, and Caesar in 49 BC felt obliged to reintroduce it. The information was, in any case, confirmed by Cassius Dio (XLI, 18, 2) for the year 49 BC. Dio added by way of amplification that Caesar recalled those proscribed by Sulla from exile, and heaped honours and offices on the sons of those murdered by Sulla (XLIV, 47, 4). Plutarch (*Caes.* 37) wrote, 'He restored civic rights to the children of those who had suffered in the time of Sulla.' P. Castren in his research on Pompey also established this restoration as a fact.[4] We can thus confidently suppose that Caesar not only paved the way for their election to curule offices, but in due course also secured the return of their confiscated property.

The political motive behind this law is clear. Caesar was attempting to win the affection of all those who were damaged in any way by the old regime. It is important to emphasize that this law is not explicitly mentioned in any of the contemporary sources, but that Caesar frequently stood aloof from Sulla's methods, and on one such occasion even promised he would never imitate him (*ad Att.* IX, 7c, 1). The law is thus consonant with Caesar's wider policy, and can be accepted as fact without further discussion.

2 LEGES (?) DE RESTITUENDIS DAMNATIS (49 BC)

This series of measures was instituted in the second half of 49 BC, after Caesar's return from Spain and his election as dictator, and was continued, with interruptions, to 46 BC. There is no conclusive proof for a series of *Leges Juliae*, indeed not even for a single *Lex Julia*, but there are numerous references to the subject in contemporary and later sources. Plutarch (Plut., *Caes*. 37, 1) mentioned this act only in general terms, 'So, having been made dictator by the Senate, he called on the exiles to come back . . . '. Suetonius (*Div. Jul*. 41, 1) was more precise, 'He reinstated those who had been degraded by official action of the censors or found guilty of bribery by verdict of the jurors.' Reference is to the victims of the trials that took place during Pompey's consulship in 52 BC. At that time many of those accused of bribery at the elections were sentenced and banished from Rome. Caesar brought them all back again (App., *BC* II, 48; Dio XLI, 36, 2; XLII, 24, 2), and was even proud of it (Caes., *Bell. Civ*. III, 1, 4-5).

Caesar's own style is of particular importance in this context, for, willy-nilly, he also provided a key to his own political motivation. Above all he was trying to play down the importance of the bribes, for news of them had spread, while Pompey was guilty of a much more serious crime in keeping a section of his troops (*praesidia legionum*) as a bodyguard in Rome. In other words, how could anyone be charged with a crime while Rome lay under the sway of a despot? Caesar made it clear that every accused person offered him his services right away, but he (the exponent of law and justice) did not hurry to accept them, for (III, 5) he had decided the exiles must be recalled by a decision of the popular assembly (*iudicio populi*), and not just through his own dispensation (*suo beneficio*).

Caesar was primarily concerned with his image, and public reaction was much more important to him than the matter in hand. The verb *videri* indicates that 'it is his intention on the one hand not to be too ungrateful to repay a favour, nor on the other so presumptuous (*arrogans*) as to rob the popular assembly of its right to show a favour.' Obviously he was aware of the practical consequences, for who could object to a decision legally taken by the popular assembly?

Cicero was not very enthusiastic about the exiles' return (*ad Att*. IX 14, 2), because Caesar did not allow Milo's recall

(App., *ibid.*; Dio, *ibid.*). Why Caesar made an exception in Milo's case is hard to fathom. On the one hand, he appeared to have had no interest in undermining the dignity of the court, and Milo had been legally sentenced *de vi* (cf. p. 79). On the other hand, it is doubtful whether the rest of the accused had been illegally charged, and whether Caesar had carefully examined every other case. As a result, we must take into account the further assumption that he was not disposed to whitewash Milo, Clodius' murderer. The people of Rome remained loyal to the memory of the great tribune of the year 58 BC, and Caesar took care not to overthrow their idols. He allowed all the other exiles to return, without prejudice.

Caesar attempted to convert to his side anyone to whom Pompey had given favours at one time or another, and also publicly proclaimed this intention in his speeches, before crossing the Rubicon. Cicero heard of it as early as January 49 BC. In April, Curio promised in one of his speeches that after Caesar's victory all those sentenced under Pompey's law of 52 BC would be rehabilitated (*ad Att.* X, 4, 8). On May 2, Cicero wrote in a state of panic, '. . . I foresee a bloodbath . . . an onslaught on private property, the return of exiles and cancellation of debts' (X, 8, 2).

Ultimately many of Cicero's fears turned out to be unfounded, but in relation to the exiles Caesar kept his promise. Moreover, in 46 BC he took further steps in this direction, '. . . he instructed some of the tribunes to restore many of those who had been exiled after due trial and who had been convicted of bribery in canvassing for office, and gave them permission to live in Italy' (Dio XLIII, 27, 2).

In September 46 BC Cicero complained of the affair to Aulus Caecina, and wrote that it was no great privilege to live in a country to which so many criminals were brought back (*ad fam.* VI, 6, 11). Cassius was much more sarcastic. Publius Sulla, the scoundrel, served as *legatus* in Caesar's army; in the battle of Pharsalus he commanded the right wing, but made use of his high position to obtain personal advantages for himself, and thus incurred the hatred of the public. At auctions of confiscated property he acquired valuable books at a low price. When Cassius learned of his death, he did not grieve for him, but wrote to Cicero, 'Caesar, however, will not let us feel his loss too long; for he has a lot of criminals to restore to us in his stead . . .' (*ad fam.* XV, 19, 3, cf. IX, 10, 3).

But Caesar was not disturbed by criticism, which he hoped would gradually die away by itself. Pompey's enemies were his potential supporters, and he took every opportunity to make new friends for himself. Moreover, he attempted to concentrate the public's attention on the fact that Rome could now look forward to a lawful and moderate regime, in contrast to the widespread despotism under Pompey's consulship. There is no certainty at all that the restoration of the exiles was carried out by only one law. We referred at the beginning of the chapter to the possibility that a whole set of ordinances was issued for this purpose between 49 and 46 BC.

3 LEX ROSCIA DE GALLIA CISALPINA (49 BC)[5]

It is assumed that this law, too, was a plebiscite, although there is no conclusive evidence. The proposer seems to have been the Lucius Roscius, designated in Caesar's writings as praetor of the year 49 BC (*Bell. Civ.* I, 3, 6; 8, 4; 10, 1), and also mentioned by Cassius Dio (XLI, 5, 2). Many scholars assume that his full name was L. Roscius Fabatus (Cic., *ad Att.* VIII, 12, 2); others identify him with the Roscius known to us through the *Lex Mamilia-Roscia-Peducaea-Alliena-Fabia*. Nothing else is certain (see pp. 119 ff. and pp. 138 ff.).

The date for the proposal of the law is derived from information that comes from a fragment of the inscription known as the *Fragmentum Atestinum*. It runs, '. . . as before the law or plebiscite that L. Roscius put to the people or the plebs five days before the Ides of March' (Riccobono, *FIRA* I, 20, 14).

Cassius Dio explained (XLI, 36, 3) that Caesar had granted citizenship to the Gauls settled south of the Alps and beyond the Po in recognition of their loyal services to him. Doubtless this means the Transpadanes, and the services rendered go back to the time when Caesar administered the area. Tacitus also mentioned the extension of citizenship in a speech put into the mouth of the Emperor Claudius, '. . . finally Italy itself was extended to the Alps, so that not only individuals (*singuli viritim*) but countries and nationalities should be united under the name of Rome' (*Ann.* XI, 24).

It is not easy to work out Caesar's intentions from these scanty pieces of information. One first needs to survey briefly the situation in Gallia Cisalpina down to the time of Caesar, and then to consider the connection – if indeed there is one –

between the *Lex Roscia*, the *Lex Rubria* and the *Fragmentum Atestinum*.

There were Roman settlements of various types in Gallia Cisalpina from the third century BC, before it became a province. Placentia and Cremona (218 BC), Bononia (189 BC) and Aquileia (181 BC) were *coloniae Latinae*, and thus possessed only *ius Latii*, and not full citizenship. On the other hand, Parma and Mutina existed from 183 BC as *coloniae civium Romanorum*. Further, there were market centres (*fora*) such as Forum Popilii, Livii, Cornelii and Lepidi, as well as two Roman outposts from the second century, Dertona and Eporedia.

Modern research has made one point clear: the *Leges Juliae* and *Papiria Plautia* (which, after the war with the Socii, granted citizenship to all those who had remained loyal to Rome throughout the war, or who were prepared to lay down their arms) were subsequently put into operation in Gallia Cisalpina in a manner apparently different from the way in which they were applied to the rest of Italy. The reason can be traced to the lesser degree of romanization and urbanization, and the backward status of the Transpadana, which obtained only the *ius Latii* from Pompeius Strabo in 89 BC (Asc. 3 Clark, 'Cn. Pompeius Strabo, pater Cn. Pompei Magni . . . non novis colonis eas constituit, sed veteribus incolis manentibus ius dedit Latii, ut possent habere ius quod ceterae Latinae coloniae . . .'). The problem of whether Gallia Cisalpina was transformed into a province as early as 89 BC or not until the time of Sulla is not a matter for discussion here. But the mere fact that Roman generals levied troops among the Transpadanes is still no proof that the latter had full Roman citizenship. P. A. Brunt (*Italian Manpower*, p. 240) rightly draws attention to the fact that the recruits hoped to obtain citizenship on discharge (*virtutis causa*). This state of affairs also explains some sporadic references that point to a certain unrest in the area in the 70s.

In 69 BC Hispania Ulterior fell to Caesar as *quaestor*. He left it hurriedly, and travelled through the Latin colonies of Gaul beyond the Po. Suetonius (*Div. Jul.* 8) reports on the tense situation throughout the area as a result of the Latin colonies' urgent demands for grants of citizenship. Some years later (65 BC) M. Licinius Crassus attempted (as censor) to obtain full citizenship for the Transpadanes, but failed because he was opposed by the conservative Q. Lutatius Catulus (Dio XXXVII, 9, 3; cf. Cic., *Pro Balb.* 50). Therefore, it is not

surprising that Julius Caesar took pains to offer to the Transpadanes in 49 BC what he might have attempted to procure for
them at an earlier stage as a young pro-magistrate. If the date
that appears in the *Fragmentum Atestinum* tallies, the law was
already promulgated by March 5, 49 BC. But a problem arises
here, for C. Niccolini had already established that Cassius Dio
was talking about the autumn, and not the spring, of 49 BC, as
in the *Fragment*.[6]

Numerous scholars have attempted to extricate themselves
from this problem by trying to establish some connection
between the *Lex Roscia* on the one hand and the *Lex Rubria*
and the *Fragmentum Atestinum* on the other. But this solution,
too, presents considerable difficulties. We have, in fact, no
single source that cites the Rubrian law, but it is concerned, as
is clear from the large extant fragment from Veleia (*FIRA*, I,
19), with the regulation of judicial competence of municipal
magistrates in Gallia Cisalpina, and with directions for civil
proceedings (such as charges concerning *pecunia certa credita*
(XXI), or the complaints of a landowner against building
works carried out on a neighbouring plot, *operis novi nuntiatio*,
etc.). The inhabitants of the plain of the Po were subject to the
jurisdiction of the praetor in Rome, and thus were also made
equal with the other citizens of Italy when it came to legal
matters.

Because we lack precise information about Rubrius, there
are different views regarding the date of the law. Some
historians maintain that the *Lex Rubria* was not an independent
law, but rather an outcome of the *Lex Julia Municipalis*, and, as
such, formed the basis of the organization of Gallia Cisalpina
(see Rudolph, pp. 119–21). However, it is difficult to explain a
doubtful event with the aid of a no less doubtful document.

According to other views, the *Lex Rubria* belongs to the
year 42 BC, when Gallia Cisalpina's provincial status was
elevated, and Bruna recently put forward the attractive theory
of a connection between the *Lex Roscia* and the *Fragmentum
Atestinum* discovered in Este in 1880. It is no accident that
Roscius' name appears in the law: the latter, in turn, hangs
together with the *Lex Rubria*, which had its origin in 49 BC or,
at latest, 48 BC.

The *Fragmentum Atestinum*, intended to initiate certain
changes in the duties of local magistrates in Gallia Cisalpina,
was simply a transitional provision relating to a district whose

inhabitants had until then possessed highly varied legal positions. Since it was impossible, in such a distant district, to implement a commonly applicable legal assimilation in one fell swoop with any degree of efficiency, it was decided to proceed gradually.

The first step, as stated, consisted of the *Fragmentum Atestinum*, whereby those local magistrates who were in office at the time of the passing of the *Lex Roscia* could continue, for the time being, to settle judicial business according to their own, previously valid, ordinances, if they were not otherwise expressly provided for by the legislator (Bruna, p. 321). Detailed reorganization for all the inhabitants of Cisalpine Gaul in towns (*oppida*), municipalities (*municipia*), colonies (*coloniae*), prefectures (*praefacturae*), market centres (*fora*), villages (*vici*), places of assembly (*conciliabula*), forts (*castella*) or territories (*territoria*) were established for the first time by the *Lex Rubria*.

There is no basic difference between the views of Bruna and Mommsen. Even if we accept that Bruna's compromise solved the problem of the different dates in Cassius Dio and the *Fragmentum Atestinum*, the question of Caesar's political views, as incorporated in the *Lex de Gallia Cisalpina*, still remains, since we probably cannot assume that Roscius was acting on his own initiative.

The Minimalists, Maximalists, and Sceptics will continue to argue the question, just as they will argue about Caesar's intentions on deification or kingship – or will argue about both simultaneously. An example may suffice: Vittinghoff sees in the *Lex Roscia* not merely an increase in Caesar's personal political power, but also an imperial policy that would affect the future: 'The Caesarian notion of empire, too, which included the Rhine as boundary, and embraced greater Italy beyond the Po as a territory with Roman citizenship, was closely connected with it' (Vittinghoff, p. 51). Minimalists will summarily dismiss this statement, since there is no evidence of any kind for so far-reaching a conclusion. Sceptics will not be prepared to admit that Caesar was the first to understand that Rome must initiate a purposeful policy for the Empire, and enlarge the number of Roman citizens. In fact, it is indisputable that Caesar's policy of granting citizenship was more liberal than that of the traditionalists. This would hardly be challenged by experts on Roman citizenship but in the last resort this was a typical line of Roman policy that had had its origin many years before.

Cassius Dio positively stated (XLIII, 39, 5) that Caesar had never granted privileges without compensatory expectations, yet Pompeius Strabo was acting from motives no more altruistic in 89 BC, when he granted certain Transpadanes the *ius Latii*. There is no need to ascribe to Caesar any farsighted considerations of imperial policy because practical explanations on an *ad hoc* basis suffice. On the eve of his decisive war with Pompey, he knew he had to trump his opponent in every area. He wanted to offer the Transpadanes more than Pompeius Strabo had, and thereby make sure of the support of all the inhabitants of northern Italy, particularly since many of his troops had been recruited in the plain of the Po (*BG* III, 20, 2).

Cassius Dio (XLV, 9, 3) also explicitly stated that Gallia Cisalpina was important on account of its troops and financial resources. It was no coincidence that Antony took the trouble, in 44 BC, to keep Gallia Cisalpina as a province, nor does his reproach, levelled against Octavian, that he had revoked the provincial status of Gallia Cisalpina only to damage Antony by this deception, come as a surprise (App., *BC* V, 3, 22). But we shall never discover whether this step agreed with the intention of the elder Caesar. After Caesar's death his heirs frequently attempted to win the affection of the public by maintaining that they based their measures on Caesar's ideas and plans, and discussion will continue for a long time about whether a plan of Caesar's actually did lie behind such measures.

Caesar's intentions cannot be discerned on the basis of the *Lex de Gallia Cisalpina* alone. Further measures and laws require additional study, so that a fuller context may perhaps yield conclusions. Yet all the arguments and facts cited here confirm Cassius Dio's report (XLI, 36, 3) that Caesar granted citizenship as a personal *beneficium*, and thus enlarged the scope of his *clientela*.

4 LEX JULIA DE CIVITATE GADITANORUM (49 BC)[7]

In 49 BC Caesar went to Spain to take the field against the Pompeians, or, as he put it, 'the army without a general' because Pompey had moved on to Greece while his army remained behind under Afranius and Petreius. Caesar defeated the enemy at the battle of Ilerda. Cassius Dio recorded the event: '(Caesar) advanced as far as Gades, injuring no one at all except in so far as the exacting of money was concerned' (in fact, he extorted considerable sums). Many of those domiciled in the district obtained all kinds of gifts from him, and he granted citizenship to all the inhabitants of Gades. These measures were later confirmed by the popular assembly in Rome (XLI, 24, 1; see also Livy, *Per.* 110; Flor. II, 13, 29). If these were the only sources at our disposal, the following line of argument could explain the above mentioned facts.

Caesar had an easy task in Gades. Since the Punic Wars the inhabitants had remained loyal to Rome, and the town was associated with Rome by a *foedus* (206 BC), renewed by the Senate in 78 BC. The romanization of Spain proceeded rapidly, and the inhabitants revealed a marked opportunism: whenever possible they attempted to steer clear of political intrigues in Rome. They were initially loyal servants of Sertorius and later of Pompey. They had no reason to come into conflict with Caesar. Subject peoples usually develop a defence mechanism of this sort, and when a split occurs at the centre of power, sometimes they support one and sometimes the other dynast. Antipater and Herod in Judaea behaved in a similar fashion.

Pompey won the trust of the elder Balbus of Gades, and even granted him citizenship in 72 BC. Balbus went to Rome, and his association with Caesar in the years between 62 and 59 BC was not any cause for Pompey's suspicion. He was *dominus*, while Caesar was considered as one of the *advocati*.

Caesar himself maintained substantial connections with Spain. In 68 BC he served as quaestor in Hispania Ulterior (Suet., *Div. Jul.* 7), and seven years later returned there as propraetor (Cic., *Pro Balb.* 43), possibly with the title of proconsul (Suet., *Div. Jul.* 54, 1). Balbus rendered Caesar sterling service, distinguished himself as *praefectus fabrum* (Cic., *Pro Balb.* 63) and after Pharsalus became a trusted member of Caesar's circle.

But Caesar did not use Balbus as an intermediary for his Spanish connections. He was himself very active in Gades, and showered the city with *beneficia*. Cicero recounted that he smoothed out disputes and, with the agreement of the population, issued laws 'iura ipsorum permissu statuerit' (*Pro Balb.* 43). In addition, Caesar was concerned with the cancellation of debts, and decreed that a creditor had an annual claim to two thirds of his debtor's income until the debt was settled (Plut., *Caes.* 12, 2). Plutarch stressed that Caesar was a highly respected man when he left the province; had Plutarch written Latin, he would surely have said Caesar's *existimatio* had reached a peak.

Yet, there are scholars who maintain that Cassius Dio, in writing that Caesar granted Gades *politeia* did not mean *civitas romana optimo iure*, but only *ius Latii*. Therefore, we have no choice but to turn to Caesar's own account (*Bell. Civ.* II, 17-21). Initially Pompey's legate in Hispania Ulterior, M. Varro, promised allegiance to Caesar; however, he changed his attitude for reasons unknown to us (for we must surely not accept Caesar's accusations at face value).

Eventually Caesar reported that Varro had ten warships built by the Gaditani, brought all money and *ornamenta* from the outlying temple into the city, laid in provisions and appointed C. Gallonius prefect with six cohorts. Varro believed that, entrenched in Gades with two legions, he could hold out until Caesar was compelled to return to Italy and the East, since the threat was much more serious there. But the citizens of Gades refused to cooperate and threw Varro's calculations out of balance. With the aid of some *tribuni cohortium*, they drove Gallonius out, and then delivered the city and island to Caesar. One of the legions, the *Vernacula*, recruited from among the natives of the province, betrayed Varro, and went to Hispalis, so that eventually Varro, together with his remaining legion, had to surrender to Caesar and even had to hand over his money and warships.

Caesar convened a public assembly (*contio*) in Corduba, and expressed his thanks to all sectors of the population ('generatim gratias agit', *Bell. Civ.* II, 21). He particularly praised the Gaditani for frustrating the attempts of his enemies, and for defending their own freedom. Even though he stayed only two days in Corduba, he took the time to go personally to Gades, where he made arrangements for the restoration of the treasures confiscated by Varro to the temple of Hercules. But he was extremely cautious concerning a grant of civil rights and said only that he had guaranteed certain groups public and private rewards ('tributis quibusdam populis publicis privatisque praemiis'). Doubtless *populis* could mean the same as *civitatibus*, and the expression *publicis praemiis* may mean not only cash rewards but also, as is the case in certain associated passages, *honores* (as in II, 21, 5, 'Eadem ratione privatim ac publice quibusdam civitatibus habitis honoribus' etc.). In no sense is it explicit here that Caesar granted citizen rights *optimo iure* to all the inhabitants of Gades. Minimalists and sceptics will have their doubts. Others might justifiably make the following surmise.

Apparently Caesar's method was first to grant citizenship to the local residents on his own responsibility, and later, after his return to Rome, to have this personal initiative legalized, as other magistrates had done before him. Also, in the case of the restoration of the exiles, he preferred that it be granted *iudicio populi* (*Bell. Civ*, III, 1, 5). There is no cogent reason to doubt Dio's statement that these measures were later confirmed by the people of Rome (XLI, 24, 1). Dio also made the point that citizenship was granted to all (and not just some) inhabitants of Gades, and in Livy it is expressly stated, 'Gaditanis civitatem dedit'. In any case, the date of ratification by the popular assembly remains obscure.[8] That Caesar did not hesitate to take any step that would establish his popularity with both old and new citizens in Spain, and that during his lightning campaign of 49 BC he could not remove Pompey's *clientela*, is not in any doubt. It is no coincidence that there were still considerable pockets of opposition in Spain in 45 BC, although Gades itself apparently maintained its allegiance to Caesar (*Bell. Hisp*. 37; 39; 40; 42).

5 DE AGRIS MASSILIENSIUM (49 BC)

The Massiliots broke the truce with Caesar and went over to Pompey's side. They even made it possible for Domitius Ahenobarbus, whom Caesar had pardoned in Corfinium, to take over the Massilia garrison, and thus disrupt or halt Caesar's advance on Spain. Caesar, however, was not particularly alarmed by the Massiliots' opposition, but marched around the city and left his deputies, Decimus Junius Brutus and C. Trebonius, to besiege it. He then advanced by forced marches against the troops under Afranius and Petreius in Spain. After victory, on his way back to Italy he besieged and overcame the rebellious city, '. . . he deprived them of their arms, ships and money, and later of everything else except the name of freedom' (Dio XLI, 25, 3). It was only after Caesar's

death that Antony took the trouble to restore to Massilia everything taken from it under martial law. (Cic., *Phil.* XIII, 32).

There remains only one point beyond doubt – that Massilia
had to endure hardship under Caesar. Yet there is no conclusive proof that a *Lex Julia de agris Massiliensium* might have
been the instrument for punishing Massilia. For this reason we
have not used the word *Lex* in the heading for this section.
Admittedly, if Cassius Dio's account is subjected to minute
scrutiny, the word 'later' (*hysteron*) might suggest that Caesar
took the Massiliots' weapons, ships and money on the spot,
whereas these punitive measures were implemented only
later, after Caesar's return to Rome, and legalized *post factum*
by a special law passed by the popular assembly. But such an
assumption would be exaggerated. Neither Cicero nor
Cassius Dio spoke of a law, and it is difficult to believe that the
word 'later' is so significant. It is true that the word also
occurred in Cassius Dio's description of the events at Gades
(see pp. 70–73) but there he explicitly stated, 'the people of
Rome later confirmed this measure'. No similar sequel
attaches to the word 'later' in connection with Massilia. Had
there been any question of similar proceedings in this context,
Dio would certainly have found the appropriate words to
describe them. It is thus preferable to suppose that the punitive
measures against Massilia were carried out by a decree, issued
by Caesar on the spot. That was Caesar's way: generous
rewards to those who served him faithfully, and implacable
anger against all who stood in his way (Dio XLIII, 39, 5; cf.
Cic., *Phil.* VIII, 19).

Megara, too, was punished in the same way in 48 BC, when
it opposed Caesar's legate Q. Fufius Calenus (Dio XLII, 14,
3-4). Servius Sulpicius provided proof of this in a letter to
Cicero, in which he described Megara as 'broken and destroyed' (Cic., *ad fam.* IV, 5, 4). In 45 BC Caesar severely
punished the Spanish supporters of the younger Pompey (Dio
XLIII, 39, 4; *Bell. Hisp.* 42), also without passing a special
punitive law. Apparently there was no necessity in this
instance to take special care to invest all his measures with the
dignity of law, so that they appeared to be legal and un-
impeachable. In cases of punishing rebels, Caesar operated
within the framework of *mos maiorum*, and according to the
well-established principle, 'parcere subiectis et debellare
superbos'.

6 LEX HIRTIA DE POMPEIANIS (48 BC?)

This law was passed after Pharsalus in Caesar's absence but we have no incontrovertible knowledge of its detailed provisions. Cassius Dio (XLII, 20, 1) said, quite generally, that Caesar was given the right to treat the Pompeians entirely at his discretion. This statement needs further discussion. In *Verr.* II, 3, 82, Cicero maintained that the Roman people had decided to recognize Sulla's *voluntas* as legally binding ('pro lege esse'). Might this have been the case with Caesar too? Dio stated that Caesar had considered such a law a necessity to give his actions at least the appearance of legal authority.

Hirtius was tribune in 48 BC (the corresponding passage in Cassius Dio fits the year 48 BC), and it is, therefore, assumed that he introduced this law. As we have stated, the matter is not at all clear. Cicero mentioned Hirtius' law in his argument with Antony (*Phil.* XIII, 32), and explained that this measure should not be called a law. His venomous, demagogic remarks actually do not throw any light on the content of the law, but only prove that Cicero knew of its existence. He expressly mentioned a *Lex Hirtia* and not a *Rogatio Hirtia*, as can be read in a poorly preserved inscription (*CIL I* 2, 604-5).

It is worthwhile citing the corresponding passage of Cicero in full,

You repeat that no surviving adherent of Pompeius is bound by the Hirtian law. Who, I ask, now mentions the Hirtian law? a law, I think, the proposer himself regrets no less than those indeed against whom it was passed. In my opinion, indeed, it is not right to call it a law at all; and, even if it be a law, we ought not to regard it as a law of Hirtius.

Cicero was referring here to a law proposed by Hirtius at Caesar's instigation (which was repealed after Caesar's death), and complained that it is termed the *Lex Hirtia*, whereas it should be called the *Lex Julia*. We can confidently connect this passage with Cicero's letter to Atticus of December 48 BC (*ad Att.* XI, 7, 2), in which he said that he came close to being banished from Italy himself,

Antony has sent me a copy of a letter from Caesar to himself, in which Caesar says that he has heard that Cato and L. Metellus have returned to Italy intending to live openly in Rome, and he does not approve of this in view of the risk of disturbances resulting, and that all persons are barred from Italy except those whose cases he has personally reviewed.

It is further reported that Antony apologized to Cicero but emphasized that he could not contradict Caesar. Cicero permitted Antony to let it be known through Lucius Lamia that he had really returned to Italy at Caesar's request. Thereupon Antony hastened to publish an edict excepting Cicero and Laelius from the decree. But Cicero expressed his anger on this point too, 'he could have solved the problem without mentioning my name' (*loc. cit.*).

Everything depends, of course, on the way we read the passage cited from *Phil.* XIII. The generally accepted reading is suggested by Orelli (and by the majority of scholars who agree with him), 'Neminem Pompeianum, qui vivat, teneri lege Hirtia dictitatis'. But this interpretation is disputed, and it is no coincidence that Lange (*Röm.Alt.* III, p. 455) came to the conclusion that the *Lex Hirtia de Pompeianis*, rather like the *Lex Sempronia de abactis* of 123, regulated the *ius honorum* for a certain category of Pompeians. He probably read, 'Neminem . . . tenere lege Hirtia dignitates'. R. A. Baumann, on the other hand, maintained[9] that we have here a *Lex Hirtia maiestatis* directed against those who carried arms against the Roman people ('qui arma contra populum Romanum tulerunt').

The question mark in the heading of this section is, therefore, appropriate, and even after the textual difficulties in *Phil.* XIII are resolved, the question remains whether the law was actually necessary from Caesar's point of view. For was not *clementia* inherent in the nature of his regime? Was not *clementia* especially popular with a wide section of the Roman public? Was it merely chance that a temple to *Clementia* was erected in Caesar's honour?

Caesar wrote in a letter to Cicero, 'You rightly surmise of me (you know me well) that of all things I abhor cruelty. The incident gives me great pleasure in itself and your approval of my action elates me beyond words' (*ad Att.* IX, 16, 2). The fact is that Caesar never made use of the full authority of the *Lex Hirtia*, and his forbearance towards his former enemies was proverbial.

7 LEX JULIA DE LEGATIONIBUS LIBERIS (46 BC)

'He made a law . . . that no senator's son should go abroad except as the companion of a magistrate or on his staff' (Suet.,

Div. Jul. 42, 1). Some scholars are convinced that Caesar provided for a special law on this occasion, others believe that the provision was contained in a comprehensive law, the *Lex Julia de repetundis*.

According to yet another view, there is a connection between this law and a certain *Lex Julia militaris* (Lange, *Röm. Alt.* III, 449), and the passage concerned with *legatio libera*, too, is associated with precisely this passage of Suetonius (*Div. Jul.*, 42). It runs as follows, 'He made a law that no citizen older than twenty or younger than forty, who was not detained by service in the army, should be absent from Italy for more than three successive years.' This view is without foundation. Nothing is known of a *Lex Julia militaris*, and G. Rotondi's idea (p. 423) that a *Lex Julia de absentibus* is intended here is equally baseless. On the other hand, contemporary texts also mention a law concerned with missions abroad, and this suggests that part of the *Lex Julia de repetundis* is concerned here; the *Lex de legationibus* remained in force even after Caesar's death, and on June 8, 44 BC, Cicero wrote, '. . . free commissions have a time limit under the *Lex Julia* . . . and it is not easy to add to that type of commission a licence to come and go as one pleases' (*ad Att.* XV, 11, 4). On the pretext of '*liberae legationes*' senators travelled with their sons to the provinces at state expense, but went chiefly on private business to bolster their personal standing. It was precisely this that Caesar wished to prevent at all costs and this law was meant to serve that purpose.

8 LEX JULIA DE VI (?) (47 OR 46 BC?)[10]

The question marks in the heading are there for two reasons: first, it is impossible to determine the exact date of the law's origin, and second, it is not at all certain that Julius Caesar promoted such a law. The only relevant text, on which widely varied theories are based, does come from a contemporary source, but it yields extremely sparse information.

This law established that '. . . he who is convicted of riot . . . shall be refused water and fire', as Cicero wrote in *Phil.* I, 23, but nothing more is known about it. According to an attractive conjecture by A. W. Lintott (p. 107), Caesar's law was chiefly concerned with *vis publica*, while a *Lex Julia* from the time of Augustus dealt with the distinction between *vis publica* and *vis privata*. From later legislation we discover that

the Romans understood the concept of *vis publica* to be concerned with the carrying of weapons in public, the formation
of violent gangs, the building of arsenals, the breach of the
peace in court or in the elective assemblies, and similar
offences. The usual penalty was 'interdiction from fire and
water', that is, banishment (*Dig.* XLVIII, 6, 1-3). It is possible
that such a distinction already existed under the Roman
Republic as early as the first century BC, but we must be
extremely wary of taking a passage from the *Digest* as a reliable
source of information on the republican period. It makes sense
to assume that the bearing of weapons was also permitted
under the republic for the purposes of hunting, or for self-
defence while travelling by land and sea; this statement, in fact,
occurs only in the *Digest*, but there are hints of the occasional
necessity for self-defence in the works of Varro (*RR* I, 69) and
Cicero (*Pro Mil.* passim).

But the *quaestio de vi* was initially established in the first
century BC. Apparently the *Lex Lutatia* of 78 BC was principally directed against the revolt of Lepidus, and was chiefly
concerned with *vis contra rem publicam* (*Pro Cael.* 1). Shortly
afterwards the *Lex Plautia de vi* was passed, which was
probably particularly concerned with *vis contra privatos*. But
Cicero's *Pro Caelio* (70-71) does not reveal all these details.
Instead of clear definitions we find confused hints in a blast of
rhetoric. An extract should suffice by way of example. Cicero
addressed the *iudices* (70),

> You are enquiring into a question of violence. The law which has to
> do with the rule, high estate and existence of our country, and the
> welfare of all; the law which Quintus Catulus carried through at a
> time of armed civil strife, when the State was at almost its last
> extremity.

It would thus be legitimate to assume that the *Lex Lutatia* set
up a *quaestio* (*extraordinaria*) to try the rebels who had sided
with Lepidus. The *Lex Plautia* provided for a *quaestio perpetua*,
which later carried out the investigation of the Catilinarians.
Mommsen, on the other hand, thought it possible that the *Lex
Lutatia* and the *Lex Plautia* are identical (*Strafrecht* 654).
Bauman (pp. 87-88) explained that the legislation *de vi* became
necessary (in spite of the *Lex Cornelia de maiestate*), because the
leges de maiestate applied only to magistrates and members of
the Senate. Mommsen believed that it was more in keeping
with the character of the dictator Caesar than for Augustus to

initiate a double law dealing with criminal and civil procedure. These procedural regulations appeared partly in the guise of a *Lex (iudiciorum) privatorum* and partly grouped together as *Leges iudiciariae Caesaris* (*Phil.* I, 19; *Strafrecht* 128-29, *cf.* 655).

If Mommsen's view is accepted (even though there is no conclusive proof for his assumption), it is easy to work out Caesar's intentions. At the end of 47 BC or at the beginning of 46 BC, he wanted to punish all the more or less active participants in the unrest organized by Caelius, Milo, and Dolabella (p. 83), and it may be assumed that, when Suetonius (*Div. Jul.* 42, 3) said that Caesar increased the penalties for crime, he meant that the transgressions were considered within the framework of *vis privata*.

9 LEX JULIA DE MAIESTATE (47 OR 46 BC?)[11]

This law is even more problematic than the *Lex Julia de vi*, for here, too, the notorious passage from the first *Philippic* serves as our principal evidence (*Phil.* I, 23): 'He who is convicted of treason shall be refused fire and water.' We do not know the text of the law, and Cicero complained that even for him it was not clear enough (*ad fam.* III, 11, 2). 'Definitions of high treason are seldom precise', Jolowicz wrote, 'but the Romans do not seem to have attained even a moderate degree of precision in the matter, and trials for *maiestas* were decided . . . mainly on political considerations.' An entire book could be written on the different views of legal historians because, owing to the lack of reliable sources, modern theories are no more than conjectures based on few historical facts.

Even at the time of the Twelve Tables in the fifth century BC the Romans used to punish any crime against the Roman state with the death penalty. The offence was called *perduellio* and was dealt with by *duoviri perduellionis*. In the later Republic *perduellio* was absorbed into the more comprehensive crime of *maiestas*. The most explicit definition is found in Cicero (*de inv.* II, 53): 'Lèse-majesté is a lessening of the dignity, the greatness or authority of the people or of those to whom the people have given authority' (Maiestatem diminuere est de dignitate aut amplitudine aut potestate populi aut eorum quibus populus potestatem dedit aliquid derogare). From this definition legal scholars logically concluded that true *maiestas* was that of the Roman people, whereas that of the magistrates was a derivative form. The earliest known text of a *lex de maiestate* is the *Lex Appuleia*, probably of the year 103 BC (according to another view, 100 BC). It is generally supposed that Saturninus felt it necessary to bring in such a law, because he wanted to impeach Roman generals who had not fulfilled their duty in times of war (Rotondi, p. 329), whereas Mommsen connected the law with events that took place in Tolosa in Gaul.

In 90 BC the scope of *maiestas* was enlarged through the *Lex Varia de maiestate* (Rotondi, p. 339) in order to make the law also applicable to those who instigated the *socii* to take up arms against Rome.

The *Lex Cornelia* of 81 BC (Rotondi, p. 360) extended *maiestas minuta* to deal with the case of a Roman proconsul who might desert his province without a *Senatus Consultum*, or lead his troops into neighbouring territory without the approval of the Senate. Thus Julius Caesar could have been impeached in 49 BC under the existing laws, and when he crossed the Rubicon, he was afraid that he would be accused of *maiestas minuta* because of his activity in Gaul – if he should actually return to Rome as *privatus*.

If the passage cited from Cicero's *Philippics* is correct, the question arises why Caesar considered another law *de maiestate* necessary in 46 BC. Was it because he wanted, by means of an unambiguous edict, to prevent someone else from using his own manoeuvre, and then basing his claim on the fact that he should also be allowed what had been permitted to Caesar? Or did Caesar wish to extend the existing law so that an attack on his person also signified *laesa maiestas* or *maiestas minuta*? If these hypotheses could be proven, the adherents of the 'king and god' theory would be justified in offering them as conclusive evidence that Caesar was not merely the last patrician but the first monarch. H. Drexler, for instance, believed that Caesar's personal *dignitas* became *maiestas*, replacing the *maiestas populi Romani* as an immediate result of his victory.

Minimalists again consider guesses unnecessary and irrelevant. They do not believe that there is any basis for asserting that the *Lex Julia de maiestate* known to us from *Dig.* XLVIII, 4 derives from Caesar and not from Augustus. They do not categorically deny the fact that Caesar passed such a law, but they prefer to leave the question open.

Mommsen believed on the evidence of the Cicero passage (*Phil.* I, 23) that Julius Caesar certainly regulated the penalties for the crime of *maiestas*, not, however, by means of a special law, but within the frame of his *Lex iudiciorum publicorum* (*Strafrecht*, p. 541); on the other hand, the *Lex Julia de maiestate* which remained in force for the following period, and is related to *iniuriae* against a *princeps* and his father (Tac., *Ann.* IV, 34), is to be traced back to Augustus.

J. E. Allison and J. D. Cloud, on the other hand, vigorously insist (p. 713) on a *Lex Julia Caesaris de maiestate*, but do not firmly establish whether this is a completely new law or perhaps a *lex tralaticia*, taking certain elements from the *Lex Cornelia de maiestate*, which is from the time of Sulla. Yet they have no doubt that Julius Caesar introduced at least one innovation: he abolished the death penalty for this crime, made clear in defining the penalty as *aqua et igni interdictio*.

A book on *maiestas* by R. A. Bauman is invigorating and captivating, clearsighted and lucid. It seems to me that even those who remain unconvinced by its arguments can no longer disregard them. The book is preponderantly based on the views of German legal scholars of the nineteenth and early twentieth centuries, and appeals primarily to readers who are not familiar with the older German literature. Yet, at the same time, it offers many original and bright ideas.

We must deal in greater detail with his hypothesis that Roman laws *de maiestate* were not laws of consolidation but of amplification. None of the *leges de maiestate* consolidated earlier legislation, or covered the whole subject in comprehensive form. Bauman is not disturbed by the fact that the concept of *maiestas* is not clearly defined. This problem is the principal concern of the legal historians of our time. The Romans had no need to define clearly their *maiestas*, which was an integral component of their view of themselves and their role in the world.

Bauman's argument is that Roman politicians tried to pin down their opponents by precisely defining specific crimes, and bothered little about affairs that were of no consequence to their immediate aims. Whether the accused had committed a crime that, in its wider sense, constituted an offence against the *maiestas populi Romani* was left to the consideration of the court. Therefore, the attempt to formulate a comprehensive definition of the concept of *maiestas* is scarcely worth the trouble. The Romans in any case took another path: in a series of laws promulgated from time to time they dealt with certain

aspects of high treason, selected according to the then prevailing political situation.

If such were the situation, one would have had to suppose
that a general law *de maiestate* existed before the time of
Augustus. However, the opposite is the case, as shown by a
series of 'small' specific laws:

1 the *Lex Appuleia* which concerned the protection of tribunes
from violent riot (thus Bauman as opposed to the view that
the law was directed against negligent proconsuls);
2 the *Lex Varia* which was directed against the allies of the
Italian rebels and,
3 the *Lex Cornelia* which was directed against irregular
conduct of proconsuls. Since Sulla wished also to reduce the
competence of tribunes, whereas the *Lex Appuleia*, in fact,
protected them, he needed an additional law.

Thus the question arises again; to what end did Caesar
require new legislation if at all, and why did the law *de vi* not
satisfy all his demands?

The existence of a *Lex Caesaris de maiestate* at the end of 47 BC
or at the beginning of 46 BC is not immediately provable,
especially as the passage in Cic., *Phil.* I, 23 gives no detailed
information. In his first *Philippic* Cicero attacked Antony, who
pressed for ratification of a long series of *acta Caesaris*, disordered memoranda taken from Caesar's papers. Cicero
chided Antony for endangering the *leges Caesaris* that had been
legally confirmed: these laws should be protected by all the
means at one's disposal, since they guaranteed *quietas* and *otium*
for Rome (*Phil.* I, 16; 25). By this demagogic trick Cicero
made himself the defender of Caesar's genuine laws, and
accused Antony of attempting to destroy them by amendments contrary to the intentions of the real law-giver, Julius
Caesar. Bauman suggests that we refer to Cic., *Phil.* I, 21-22,

A second law has been advertised, that persons convicted of riot and
treason should appeal to the people if they will. I ask you, is this a law
or a recision of all laws? For who is there today concerned that that
law should remain? There is no one now accused under those laws,
no one we think is likely to be; for things done by men in arms will
doubtless never be brought into court. 'But the proposal is a popular
one.' Would to heaven you contemplated something that is popular!
For all citizens are now agreed in mind and voice about the safety of
the State. What means then that eagerness of yours to propose a law
which involves the greatest disgrace and no gratitude? For what can

be more disgraceful than that a man who has by violence committed treason against the Roman people, and been convicted, should then resort to that very violence for which he was by law convicted? But why do I argue any more about the law? As if forsooth its object were appeal! Its object, and your proposal, is that no one at all should ever be accused under those laws. For who – if he be prosecutor – will be found so mad as to be willing by the conviction of an accused to expose himself to a hired crowd? – or – if he be juryman – as to dare to convict an accused man at the price of being himself at once hailed before a gang of suborned labourers? No! It is not an appeal that is granted by that law: rather are two very salutary laws and courts abolished. What else is this than to urge young men to be turbulent, seditious, pernicious citizens? And to what ruinous lengths may not the frenzy of tribunes be impelled when these two courts on riot and treason have been abolished? And what of this, that those laws of Caesar's are in part altered which declare that he who is convicted of riot, and also he who is convicted of treason, shall be refused water and fire? When an appeal is given to such men, are not the acts of Caesar annulled? Those acts indeed, Conscript Fathers, though I never approved them, I have thought should be so carefully maintained for the sake of peace that I disagreed with the annulment of his laws, not only of those he had proposed in his lieftime, but even of those which you see brought forward and posted after Caesar's death.

The argument is clear. Antony is accused of *abrogatio* of Caesar's own law expressly mentioned in *Phil.* I, 23, in which there is no question of *provocatio* to the people, but established as the penalty for an offence against *maiestas* 'interdiction from water and fire' (banishment). Cicero charged Antony with trying to nullify the judgment of the *quaestio de maiestate*, which was final, and put the decision instead to the popular assembly. Such a law would not only have failed to guarantee *otium* and *quietas* in Caesar's sense, but would have provoked even more dangerous unrest, because rebels would be actually encouraged to incite further disturbances. Then the rebels, when brought before the court, could terrorize that same popular assembly with the aid of armed gangs, before which an appeal against the judgment of the *quaestio* could be lodged. This was the best way to abolish Caesar's *salutatores leges* and sacrifice everybody to the *furor tribunicius*. Naturally one can take the view that after the uprising initiated by Caelius, Milo and Dolabella, Caesar needed a law which would bring *adulescentes* and *perniciosi cives* before the court. Cicero, in fact, also spoke of an accusation against him 'qui maiestatem populi Romani minuerit per vim' in I, 21.

Thus far one can agree with Bauman, but numerous queries still remain. It is still not quite clear whether the different *leges de maiestate* were really each restricted to just one count of an accusation. The fragmentary material available does not permit clear conclusions about any of the various laws. If it is correctly assumed that only magistrates in high positions and senators could be accused under the *Lex Appuleia de maiestate*, and that Caesar wished to bring in a law to facilitate the accusation of persons of all classes and conditions for *maiestas minuta per vim*, it is difficult for us to understand the purpose of the *Lex Julia de vi* discussed in the previous section, for no one doubts that *leges de vi* were applicable to magistrates as well as to *humiles*.

In conclusion, it may cautiously be stated that the sceptics could have grounds for maintaining that a complete law cannot be reconstructed from the words 'qui maiestatem populi Romani minuerit per vim'. The existence of a *Lex Julia de vi* is likewise not open to question, for it is expressly mentioned by Cicero. However, that should not indicate that Caesar's *maiestas* was synonymous with the *maiestas populi Romani* in his lifetime.

From Tacitus, *Ann.* I, 72, we discover more about the nature of such laws under the Republic in contrast to the situation in the time of Tiberius,

For he had resuscitated the *Lex Maiestatis*, a statute which in the old jurisprudence had carried the same name but covered a different type of offence – betrayal of an army; seditious incitement of the populace; any act, in short, of official maladministration diminishing the 'majesty of the Roman nation'. Deeds were challenged, words went immune. The first to take cognizance of written libel was Augustus; who was provoked to this step by the effrontery with which Cassius Severus had blackened the characters of men and women of repute in his scandalous effusions: then Tiberius, to an enquiry put by the praetor, Pomponius Macer, whether process should still be granted on this statute, replied that 'the law ought to take its course'. He, too, had been ruffled by verses of unknown authorship satirizing his cruelty, his arrogance, and his estrangement from his mother.

Augustus was therefore the first to impeach those who published libels under this law. This fact may also be deduced from Suetonius, *Div. Jul.* 75, 4-5,

. . . In his later years . . . if any . . . slanders (were) uttered (against him), he preferred to quash rather than to punish them. Accordingly he took no further notice of the conspiracies which were detected, and of the meetings by night, than to make known by proclamation that he was aware of them; and he thought it enough to give public warning to those who spoke ill of him, not to persist in their conduct, bearing with good nature the attacks on his reputation made by the scurrilous volume of Aulus Caecina and the abusive lampoons of Pitholaus.

This, therefore, indicates that Caesar, true to the principles of the Republic, impeached individuals only for acts, and not for words.

10 DE COLLEGIIS? (46 BC?)[12]

The question marks in the heading indicate the difficulty of establishing conclusively whether Caesar passed a law entitled the *Lex Julia de collegiis* or merely issued a decree, and whether the law, or decree, belongs to the year 46 BC. We have one terse piece of information for this investigation: (Suet., *Div. Jul.* 42, 3): 'He dissolved all guilds (*collegia*) except those of ancient foundation.' No indication whatsoever is to be found in contemporary sources, and pedants have good reason to assume that Suetonius, confused by the *Lex Julia* of Augustus, referred certain vague remarks to a *Lex Julia Caesaris de collegiis*. The corresponding passage from Suetonius' life of Augustus (*Div. Aug.* 32, 1) runs,

Many pernicious practices militating against public security had survived as a result of the lawless habits of the civil wars, or had even arisen in the time of peace. Gangs of footpads openly went about with swords by their sides, ostensibly to protect themselves, and travellers in the country, freemen and slaves alike, were seized and kept in confinement in the workhouses of the landowners; numerous leagues, too, were formed for the commission of crimes of every kind, assuming the title of some new guild ('plurimae factiones titulo collegii novi ad nullius non facinoris societatem coibant'). Therefore to put a stop to brigandage, he stationed guards of soldiers wherever it seemed advisable, inspected the workhouses (*ergastula*), and disbanded all guilds, except such as were of long standing and formed for legitimate purposes ('collegia praeter antiqua et legitima dissolvit').

No wonder that Mommsen wrote in his *History of Rome*:

'There is no aspect of the life of the Roman people respecting which our information is so scanty as that of the Roman trades'.[13] And yet it was the youthful Mommsen who, in 1843, wrote the epoch-making work *De collegiis et sodaliciis Romanorum* (Kiel), and at that time came to the conclusion that the nature of the Roman *collegia* was such that it 'perpetuam interpretationem vix recipiat'.

There are very few differences of opinion about Augustan legislation regarding *collegia*. The passage of Suetonius cited above (*Div. Aug.* 32, 1) is additionally confirmed by *CIL* VI, 2193, and some scholars believe that an indication of Augustus' motives was revealed by a sentence of Cassius Dio (52, 36, 1-2) in which Maecenas advised Augustus not to tolerate foreign cults, not merely because native gods lose their influence, but because foreign deities also bring foreign customs in their train. This ends in conspiracies, unrest and secret assemblies, all dangerous occurrences for a monarchy.

The situation is far more complex with regard to Caesarian legislation on *collegia*, on which there are numerous views. The most important trends of research merit a brief reference here. There are historians who dispute the fact that so brief a notice in Suetonius (*Div. Jul., loc. cit.*) justifies the assumption of the actual existence of a special Caesarian law. It is much more likely that what we have here is merely a decree.

In what capacity did Caesar publish this decree? Cohn (p. 71) believed he introduced it as *praefectus morum*, Liebenam (p. 27) as *pontifex maximus*, and Karlowa (II, 67) as *dictator rei publicae constituendae*. Many years later de Robertis returned to the idea of legislation assuming that Caesar passed a law concerning *collegia*, whereas Augustus was satisfied with an ordinance renewing Caesar's law. In his view Caesar established a system of strong state control over the *collegia*, which lasted for five hundred years. Caesar's law was chiefly amplified by *senatus consulta* and *constitutiones*, but the principles of the law remained intact (see especially ILS 4966).

While Suetonius, in the passage relating to Caesar, mentioned only *collegia antiqua* (or *antiquitus constituta*) he dealt with *collegia legitima* as well as *antiqua* when speaking of Augustus. If *legitimus* is translated 'in accordance with a particular law', and not, as ordinarily, 'in accordance with the general legal system', there is no difficulty in construing Suetonius, *Div. Aug.* 32, 1, as follows: The Augustan ordinance was made with explicit reference to the *Lex Julia de collegiis*, and *collegia legitima* are those which were lawful under Caesar's legislation. Obviously the *antiqua* too remained lawful, as they had been earlier.

When J. P. Waltzing stated vaguely, 'It is generally admitted that a law is in question' (I, 113), the remark is merely a throwback to the young Mommsen, who believed in a Caesarian law (*De coll.* p. 73, n. 3).

A series of impressive studies by J. Linderski deserves special attention. While in his view too it is possible to speak confidently of a *Lex Julia* of the time of Augustus, there are no compelling reasons to reject a *Lex Julia* of the time of Caesar. Linderski's healthy scepticism teaches us how to gain maximum results from the material at our disposal without reading into the texts what is not there. Before turning to him here are some general remarks: Gerhard Schrot was wrong in blaming 'bourgeois' historical writing for 'suppressing the real impetus of the history of the masses and stressing the role of important personalities' (p. 245). The fact is that 'bourgeois' historians, too, would like to know much more about artisans and traders than they can discover from the material at their disposal. The truth is that our knowledge about the formation of *collegia* is very scanty. We do not know whether *collegia* (with the exception of the priestly colleges) were founded and established from above and from the outside, rather than through the initiative of their members. It would be logical to suppose that *collegia* of artisans could come into being only after various crafts had ceased to operate within the household but no one can establish a date for this process in Rome. There is no doubt that all *collegia* were under the protection of a deity, which is why there may have been a religious tone to their activities.

We also know that many city neighbourhoods took their names from particular crafts, but why did the workers in a craft settle in a certain neighbourhood? One might, of course, be satisfied with calling it a natural urge to encourage social intercourse, which was especially marked in a class-conscious society such as that in Rome. Honourable positions in the *collegium* carried lofty titles such as *magister*, *curator*, and *quaestor*, not only to satisfy the members' desire for esteem, but also for the reason so neatly formulated by W. Liebenam (p. 260): 'Through acceptance into a *collegium* even the common man could achieve an influence denied to him as an individual' (*ILS*, 7237).

Even if one is satisfied with the superficial statement that there were several reasons for the foundation of professional associations, numerous questions remain. For instance, we have no notion of what was discussed at the meetings of the *collegia*. Was there ever a lobby for the advancement of professional interests? Did it ever occur to the members to discuss the professional competition caused by slaves, or at times of inflation to demand higher wages for members of *collegia*? Did they have any conception of the power available to them through threat of strikes and other co-operative actions?

The source material from the Caesarian period tells us that it was not especially difficult to be admitted to a *collegium*; that *collegia* were interested in acquiring the greatest possible number of members; that a new member was accepted by vote of the whole assembly and had to pay an entrance fee and then a monthly subscription (*stips menstrua*) but we know nothing about the size of these contributions.

A passage from the *Digests* cannot be used as a primary source to illuminate this period of the Republic, and, where contemporary sources are lacking, we have no recourse but to make conjectural reconstructions or admit ignorance.

Turning again to Suetonius' passage about Caesar, we must first attempt to discover what he could have meant by *vetera collegia* or *antiquitus constituta*. His main intentions were apparently as follows:

1 The old priestly colleges, mentioned as the *summa quattuor collegia* (*pontifices, VII viri epulones, XV viri sacris faciundis* and augurs). To be added to these are the smaller colleges of the *Fetiales, Arvales, Titii,* and *Salii*.

2 The *sodalitates sacrae*, which, at least to some extent, originated from the period when the state allowed the *gentes* a share in the public rites ('From earliest antiquity certain public cults were entrusted by the state to families (*gentes*)', Waltzing, p. 34). Thus the *Luperci*, for instance, were split into the *Fabiani, Quinctiales* and *Juliani*. Under this category the *montani* and *pagani*, and likewise the *collegia compitalicia*, must be subsumed. The latter came into being because the inhabitants of districts surrounding a crossroads joined together to celebrate the *compitalia* in the neighbourhood of

aediculae (small sanctuaries). It is possible that it was those very *collegia* of which slaves were already members in antiquity (with the agreement of their masters – *volentibus dominis*) that in the course of time developed into the most politically dangerous, whereas in early days they were totally harmless.

3 Within this framework of innocuous associations can be included those *collegia* whose members met for purely cultural purposes, and which were somewhat similar to dining clubs. (Obviously the waggish inscriptions from Pompeii, which mention associations of *seribibi* (late-drinkers), *furunculi* (pick-pockets) and *dormientes* (sleepers) are not to be taken seriously. On the other hand, colleges of ball players (*pilicrepi*) are conceivable.) Perhaps Varro was thinking of such associations when he spoke of the *cenae collegiorum*, whose extravagant feasts raised food prices (Varro, *RR* III, 2, 16). But these were clubs of bon viveurs, and it is improbable that Varro was referring to conventions of poor artisans.

4 The *collegia* most important to our enquiry had existed since antiquity; these were the associations of *opifices*, *artifices* and *mercatores*, which, according to tradition, had been founded in the time of Numa Pompilius. Plutarch even maintained that the most admirable of Numa Pompilius' measures was the division of the people into groups according to their occupations (Plut., *Numa* 17). Plutarch referred in this passage to musicians (*tibicines*), who played during sacrifices, goldsmiths (*aurifices*), carpenters (*fabri tignarii*), dyers (*tinctores*), saddlers (*sutores*), tanners (*coriarii*), coppersmiths (*fabri aerarii*) and potters (*figuli*).

A quick glance at A. Degrassi's index extends Plutarch's list to include many other *collegia*. Some of the more important were the *anularii* (769), *violarii*, *rosarii* and *coronarii* (99), *lanii* (98), *serrarii* (774), *cisiarii* (103a), *fullones* (240), *nummularii* (106), *olearii* (344) and *retiarii* (231). Naturally, the statement in Dionysius of Halicarnassus (II, 28; IX, 25) that free men were forbidden all manual labour except of an agricultural kind is without foundation.

It is hardly likely that Caesar wanted to attack any of these *collegia* so long as they remained guilds of artisans *sensu stricto* (as explained below); therefore they may also be numbered among the *collegia vetera*.

5 Finally, there were the various *collegia* of *apparitores*, such as those of the *scribae, viatores, praecones, lictores*, etc.

No mention is made of *collegia funeraticia*, in the days of the Republic; they apparently came into being for the first time under the Empire. There were three main aspects of *collegia*: those of trade guild, religious brotherhood and local association. These were not mutually exclusive but often interdependent.[14]

In conclusion, it may be observed that during the first four hundred years of the Republic nothing is known of any interference by the state in the internal transactions of existing *collegia*. But the situation took a decisive turn when the *collegia* became increasingly significant at election time. Bursting with pride, Cicero boasted of the influence of the *scribae* and of other *collegia* in the popular assembly (*de Dom.* 74), and, in the light of his remarks, the advice given in *Comm. Pet.* VIII, 29–30, is of special significance,

There are many hard-working citizens, many freedmen who find favour in the forum and are active there. Through your own efforts and those of mutual friends, with great care you will be able to achieve their support for you. Stir yourself, seek them out, tell them how greatly obligated you are to them. Then consider the whole city, all the colleges, districts, neighbourhoods. If you win over the leaders (*principes*) to your circle, you will quickly get a hold on the remainder through them ('per eos reliquam multitudinem facile tenebis').

Indeed, towards the end of the Republic, the *collegia* were already organized and well drilled for election campaigns. There were the *sequestres*, with whom the candidate deposited funds, and the *divisores*, who distributed money to the voters.

The more active the *collegia* became in politics, the more comprehensive were the legal measures directed against them. Unfortunately, we have only scattered information on the subject, but the fact that we have no more than a single sentence about particular problems is often the reason why so much has been written about the subject.

In order to understand the *Lex Julia de collegiis* properly, earlier legislation must be considered, and the following remarks draw heavily on Linderski. In 64 BC, the year Catiline became a candidate for the consulship, the *collegia* were especially active, and, therefore, those that appeared to be particularly dangerous to the Senate were disbanded ('collegia quae adversus rem publicam videbantur constituta', Cic., *In Pis.* 8; Asc. 7 [Clark]). In his article on the Senate and the *collegia*, Linderski convincingly remarked 'that this decree made no change in the existing legislation affecting *collegia*, and created no new rules of state policy with regard to them' (p. 97).

It is not known exactly which *collegia* were dissolved, whether perhaps the reference is only to the *collegia compitalicia* (which also accepted slaves), as Mommsen believed, or whether professional associations were also disbanded, as M. Cohn and J. P. Waltzing maintained. It is quite possible that both were affected, irrespective of the degree of danger they posed to the state. But, if we consider the moderate conduct of the *tabernarii* (who were nothing more than working shopkeepers) towards the end of the Catilinarian conspiracy, it must be concluded that they constituted a more conservative element, and were therefore less affected. But that, too, is uncertain.[15]

It is clear that a latent unrest prevailed in Roman society. As early as 61 BC Cicero (*ad Att.* I, 13, 3; 14, 5) wrote about the *operae*, which in the course of time, especially in the years between 58 and 56 BC, became a significant factor, quite contrary to the *senatus consultum* of 64 BC (*Pro. Sest.* 55). Clodius collected his supporters *vicatim*, divided them into groups of ten (*decuriae*) (*ibid.* 34), and permitted the recruitment of slaves and freedmen (*de Dom.* 54; *pro Mil.* 25).

It is still uncertain how Clodius recruited his followers, and whether F. M. de Robertis was right in saying that he made use of the *compitalia* to win the favour of his slaves who participated in them. Clodius' gangs were superbly organized, with subordinate squads under *duces*, some of whose names we know: Sex. Clodius, Gellius, Titius, Fidulius, Lollius, Sergius, Lentidius and Plaguleius (*de Dom.* 25; 89), and no power, except for the army or well-trained units of gladiators, was a match for them (*pro Sest.* 78; 85). These gangs terrorized the whole city. The authorities constantly tried to drive a wedge between Clodius and the masses by saying that his gangs were made up exclusively of slaves and criminals. In the course of the Catilinarian conspiracy this propaganda was successful with the *tabernarii* (*In Cat.* IV, 17), and in the days of Clodius too.

Although Clodius had considerable backing at the beginning of 58 BC, the man in the street did not support him
wholeheartedly, and he was never the leader of the entire
plebs. With the increase of violence, uproar, disturbance and
anarchy, the conservative elements increasingly deserted him
(*ad Att.* IV, 3, 2), and it was perhaps precisely for this reason
that some, maybe even the majority, of *societates* and *collegia*
voted for Cicero's recall from exile (*In Pis.* 41; *Pro Sest.* 32).
Obviously this does not imply that Clodius had at the time
been deserted by all of the people: some remained loyal to him
throughout his whole career, and probably an even greater
number mourned him after his death (Asc. 32-33 [Clark]; Dio
XL, 49, 2-3), just as Catiline's grave was adorned with flowers
after his crushing defeat (Cic., *Pro. Flacc.* 95).

In this struggle between Senate and *collegia*, a *Senatus
Consultum* of February 56 BC played an important role. The
information comes from *ad Q.fr.* II, 3, 5, where it is related,
'On the same day a decree of the Senate was passed that
political clubs and caucuses should be broken up, and that a
law concerning them should be proposed, whereby all who
refused to disband should be liable to the penalty fixed for
breaking the peace.' In fact, this law was passed in 55 BC in the
consulship of Pompey and Crassus, under the name of the *Lex
Licinia de sodaliciis*. It immediately presents scholars with the
problem that neither in 56 BC nor in 55 BC do we hear about
collegia, only about *sodalitates*.

A *sodalitas* was originally an innocuous dining club (Festus
298, 24; Isidore X, 245), and later a technical term for a sacred
brotherhood; *sodalis* is still a synonym for a relative in the *Lex
Acilia Repetundarum* (Riccobono *FIRA* III, 7, p. 87) and *sodalis*
was not necessarily used in Cicero as a term of abuse (*Pro Planc.*
29). Under the Empire the word *sodalitas* disappeared, and
sodalicium was used as a synonym for *collegium*. Only in the 60s
of the Late Republic (the exact date cannot be established) did
sodalitas take on the meaning of an association that pursued the
sole objective of influencing elections by bribery and, if
necessary, by force and was therefore a danger to the state. This
has been convincingly argued by Linderski.

Laterensis abused Plancius' followers as *sodales*. Cicero, on
the other hand, spoke of a polite friendship ('officiosa
amicitia') between Plancius and his partisans: 'Quos tu si
sodales vocas . . . nomine inquinas criminoso' ('if you call

these persons *sodales*, you sully them with a criminal connotation', *op. cit.* 46).

This is not the place to describe the process of trans-
formation of *sodalitates* (Waltzing I, 48-51); suffice it to say that
for many years scholars have made a distinction between
sodalitas and *collegium*. De Robertis remarked that aristocratic
conservatives founded *pseudo-collegia* for the purpose of
ambitus, whereas revolutionary democrats formed them for
vis. The *Senatus Consultum* of 56 BC was directed against the
latter, the *Lex Licinia* against the former. Linderski essentially
agreed with this view but his amendments to it are extremely
illuminating. He also stated that the *sodalitates* consisted mainly
of members from the middle and upper classes of society, and
stressed that the members were very faithful to their principal.
While we never encounter a *collegium Cornelii*, a *sodalitas Cornelii*
is quite possible (p. 110). In *Comm. Pet.* 19 it is clearly stated, 'for
in the last two years you have bound to yourself four *sodalitates*
most favourable for furthering your ambition, those of C.
Fundanius, Q. Gallus, C. Cornelius, C. Orcivius'.

When Cicero abused the Roman *jeunesse dorée* as *barbatuli
iuvenes*, and spoke of it as the *grex Catilinae* (*ad Att.* I, 14, 5), he
was not talking about slaves, artisans and shopkeepers, but of
political associations of the eminent, 'whose effect made itself
felt in all areas of social life, especially those who bribed the
electorate and participated in armed street fighting'.

At the time of the Senate's efforts to create a breach between
the *collegia* of artisans and Clodius, the reputation of the
collegia, their early origin, and association with the state had to
be increasingly praised, while other associations, which were
actually *sodalitates*, but posed as *collegia*, had to be vilified.
Hence the expression *nomine, simulatione* or *titulo collegiorum*
(*Post red. in sen.* 33; *pro Sest.* 34). Those that bore the name
collegium without justification (and it is no accident that the
presence of slaves is stressed, whose attitude represented
destruction, ravage and ruin) must be dissolved, and failure to
submit to the ruling should be punished 'ea poena quae est de vi'
(*ad Q.fr.* II, 3, 5).

Thus the senatorial decree established the link between *vis*
and *ambitus* (*Pro Cael.* 16). The *Lex Licinia de sodaliciis* of 55 BC
(*Pro Planc.* 44-48; *Schol. Bob.* 152 [Stangl]) officially made the
employment of organized bodies for the bribery or constraint
of electors an offence.

If this analysis is correct, there is still the question of the purpose of the *Lex Julia Caesaris de collegiis*. In the nineteenth century scholars clung to the concept of Caesarism, and in 1866 Rodbertus wrote that Caesarism took away the right of association from the upper classes, but left it freely available to others.[16] Using this theory, Caesar would have had to proceed against *sodalitates* but not against *collegia*, for as a tyrant he had more to fear from associations of frustrated aristocrats than from those of the lower classes.

The *collegia* had no life presidents; their *magistri*, *quaestores* and *decuriones* were elected by the full membership. Thus they were not a threat, and such organizations must have been of little consequence to a democratic ruler like Caesar. But what can one do when it is expressly stated that Caesar's action was directed against *collegia* and not against *sodalitates*? Rodbertus' thesis leads us nowhere.

Meanwhile, enthusiasm for the 'democratic tendencies of Caesar's government' had somewhat ebbed. And, as we shall see later, anything might be said of this regime other than that it was associated with, or based on, a single class of society. De Robertis,[17] it is true, continued to speak of Caesar as 'head of the democratic party' (*Cappo della parte democratica*), although before he died the dictator broke with the democrats who had helped him. We do not know how Caesar built up his connections with the masses and with the different *tribus*, but we do know that he chose his candidates carefully, to be certain that the election results would turn out as he expected (Suet., *Div. Jul.* 41, 2). It may be supposed that Caesar had at his disposal a number of *duces multitudinum* (Sall., *Cat.* 50, 1), or *auctores turbarum* (Asc., *Corn.* 66 [Clark]), and, provided only that they operated in his favour, the democratic or undemocratic structure of any of the associations was of precious little interest.

Caesar could make immediate use of the *Lex Licinia* of 56–55 BC against *sodalitates*. But should he wish to prevent some more popular tribunes (after the fashion of Clodius) from forming new *collegia*, and then from using them for their own purposes, he required a new *lex de collegiis*. The law of 47 BC or 46 BC must therefore be interpreted in this sense. *Collegia* established in antiquity were not affected. They included not only Numa's eight *collegia*, but also, as Accame has already shown, all the others that were established before political agitation became one of their central activities. Caesar wanted to be certain that they would not persuade their members to take part in intrigues against the state.

Caesar's attitude towards the Jews may serve as an example to prove that in this instance he was prosecuting political aims in the sense, say, of ensuring the security of the state and of entrenching his own position. He did not disturb their synagogues, for he was apparently convinced that they were not a cloak for dangerous political organizations. On this, see a pertinent passage of Flavius Josephus (*Ant.* XIV, 213-5), where it is reported that Servilius Vatia Isauricus, proconsul of Asia, relied on a provision of Caesar's pertaining to Rome to allow the Jews of Paros to live by the laws of their fathers,

The Jews in Delos and some of the neighbouring Jews, some of your envoys also being present, have appealed to me and declared that you are preventing them by statute from observing their national customs and sacred rites. Now it displeases me that such statutes should be made against our own friends and allies . . . for this they are not forbidden to do even in Rome. For example, Gaius Caesar, our consular praetor (*strategos hypatos*), by edict (*diatagma*) forbade religious societies to assemble in the city, but these people alone he did not forbid to do so or to collect contributions of money or to hold common meals.

The text is not clear, and Josephus' practical knowledge of Roman law is not especially impressive. No one knows the significance of the remarkable expression *strategos hypatos*,[18] and it is doubtful whether one may translate *diatagma* by *Lex Julia de collegiis*. But the content is beyond doubt,[19] and fits in with the general picture sketched here.

Caesar abolished all associations *adversus rem publicam constituta*, and activity dangerous to the state could be found in the sacral *collegia* as well as in those of the artisans. Thus he was compelled to dissolve all of them because Caelius and Dolabella, when instigating the unrest of 48 BC and 47 BC, had a large following. It is true that the *tabernarii* in general constituted a conservative element (Cic., *In Cat.* IV, 17); however, in times of economic or political confusion it was not difficult to incite them too, as we read in the works of Cicero and Sallust (Cic. *de Dom.* 18; *Pro Flacc.* 17-18; Sall., *Cat.* 50; *Jug.* 73).

We shall never know whether a specific event drove Caesar to this type of legislation, or whether it was part of his general policy for the establishment of law and order in a state torn to shreds by civil wars and demagogy. The *Senatus Consultum* of 64 BC did not forbid the right of association, but allowed the state to initiate ordinances and senatorial decrees from time to time against associations that appeared to be dangerous. Asconius' testimony is explicit (Asc. 75 [Clark]), and Caesar's legislation in this area is no exception.

I I RE-ERECTION OF THE STATUES OF SULLA AND POMPEY (44 BC)

This measure was carried out by means of a decree and not through special legislation. In his fifth consulship Caesar removed the *rostra* from the centre of the forum to another place; at the same time he permitted the statues of Sulla and Pompey to be re-erected there (Dio XLIII, 49, 1). Suetonius also reported that he 'actually set up the statues of Lucius Sulla and Pompey, which had been broken to pieces by the populace' (Suet., *Div. Jul.* 75, 4). Although this statement is not confirmed in contemporary sources, it is, however, undoubtedly reliable. Plutarch (*Caes.* 57, 4) on this occasion cited Cicero, who, glancing at the full-length statue of Pompey re-erected by Caesar, said 'that in setting up Pompey's statue Caesar firmly fixed his own'. The statues of the dead Sulla and Pompey could not damage his position. On the other hand, however, the gesture raised his standing even among his opponents.

12 GENERAL AMNESTY FOR POLITICAL OPPONENTS (44 BC)?

Caesar's policy of reconciliation was guided by *clementia*, and its terms of reference extended beyond the monuments of his enemies. After Pharsalus 'he allowed each of his men to save any one man he pleased of the opposite party' (Suet., *Div. Jul.* 75, 2). In his later days he remembered all those whom he had not yet pardoned, allowed them to return to Italy, and even permitted them to take up civil and military posts (*op. cit.* 4). This sentence indicates that he guaranteed a general amnesty in the evening of his life, which is why we have not introduced these measures under sections 1 and 2 of this chapter, which are only concerned with those of the year 49 BC. In his book on the events of 44 BC, Cassius Dio reported (XLIII, 50, 1-2),

Caesar, however, removed the ban from the survivors of those who had warred against him, granting them immunity on fair and uniform terms; he promoted them to office; to the wives of the slain he restored their dowries, and to their children he granted a share of the property, thus putting Sulla's cruelty mightily to shame and gaining for himself a great reputation not alone for bravery but also for goodness.

It must be supposed that Caesar carried out this measure without a special law, even if Antony maintained after Caesar's death that Caesar had prepared the relevant proposals, but had not reached the stage of presenting them properly, among them a *Lex Julia de exilibus revocandis*. We shall never discover the truth, for Cicero accused Antony of forging documents purported to come from the hand of Caesar (*Phil.* V, 11), and even doubted that Caesar ever proposed such a law (*Phil.* II, 98).

Antony probably proposed a selective pardon within the framework of a *lex de actis Caesaris confirmandis* for those exiles he knew personally (Dio; XLV, 25, 2; XLVI, 15, 2). Caesar's intention was probably wider in scope, and, therefore, the heading *General amnesty* for this section is justified.

13 LEX JULIA DE CIVITATE SICULIS DANDA (44 BC)?[20]

This law was also presented by Antony in the guise of his 'law to ratify Caesar's measures', indeed, with the statement that the draft had been found among Caesar's papers. Numerous persons with full Roman citizenship lived for a long time before Julius Caesar in Sicily, yet every one of them had been granted his citizenship personally (Cic., *Pro Balb.* 24). Cicero, who was always proud of his good connections with the Sicilians, said that he loved them, defended them against Verres' rapaciousness, and wholeheartedly supported the many privileges Caesar had granted them, yet considered the grant of *ius Latii* to the Sicilians intolerable. That was too much of a good thing, even for a friend of the Sicilians such as he.

The fact that Caesar granted the Sicilians *ius Latii* is not questioned, yet many historians doubt his plans to make them full citizens a short time later. Hence the question mark in the heading, since Antony's assertion does not provide proof.

In one of his letters Cicero vented his anger against Antony,

Well, here is Antony posting up (in return for a massive bribe) a law allegedly carried by the Dictator in the Assembly under which the

Sicilians become Roman citizens, a thing never mentioned in his lifetime! (*ad Att.* XIV, 12, 1)

Here too we are unable to discover the truth. Antony was trying to acquire a new *clientela* for himself, on which to build up his political future. To appear as heir of the popular Caesar and executor of his will was to his advantage, whereas Cicero could not imagine that Caesar would have agreed to liberate whole provinces of the Roman Empire (cf. *Phil.* I, 24; II, 92; III, 30).

If such had also been Antony's intention, it would never have come to pass. Towards the end of 43 BC Sicily was already under Sextus Pompeius control, and when it fell again to Octavian, he was in no hurry to grant all Sicilians Roman citizenship indiscriminantly. Even in the 70s AD the Elder Pliny knew of various kinds of citizenship in Sicily (Plin., *NH* III, 88–91), and emphasized that the inhabitants of the interior still continued to enjoy only Latin rights. Diodorus too, who was most knowledgeable about conditions in Sicily, gave no clear information as to which rights were granted by Caesar and which by Augustus (Diod. XIII, 35, 3; XVI, 70, 6). We thus align ourselves with the sceptics in making the following statement: Julius Caesar prepared no *lex de civitate Siculis danda*; he granted the Sicilians only *Latinitas*, whereas the extension of rights reported by Diodorus as eye-witness was not activated until the time of Augustus.

14 LEX JULIA DE INSULA CRETA (44 BC)?

Similar doubts arise in connection with the authenticity of this law. Cicero spoke not of a law but only of a decree, and simply did not believe Antony's statement that Caesar had arranged to abolish Crete's status as a province when Brutus' period of office as governor ran out (Cic., *Phil.* II, 97; cf. Dio XLV, 32, 4; XLVI, 23, 3).

The sources at our disposal only emphasize the existing doubt. The Cretans must, in fact, have been freed from *vectigalia*, yet this relief is far from constituting removal of its provincial status. Antony appeared to have 'stumbled', in creating an anachronism which Cicero cleverly utilized: Caesar could not have made any decision about Crete in relation to Brutus' period of office. He had appointed Brutus to Macedonia, and here Cicero played his trump card – Brutus was not designated for Crete until June 5, two and a half months after Caesar's death! The query is, therefore, more than justified.

15 LEX JULIA DE REGE DEIOTARO (44 BC)?

Deiotarus was king of Galatia and one of Pompey's loyal clients. When he was accused of plotting Caesar's murder, his possessions were sequestered. The trial, at which Cicero appeared for the defence, took place in Rome, but Caesar was in no hurry to pronounce judgment. Deiotarus' fate was thus uncertain, until it was settled by the thrust of Brutus' dagger. Antony – apparently in Caesar's name – suggested returning the confiscated possessions to Deiotarus (*Phil.* II, 93-4; *ad Att.* XIV, 12, 1; 19, 2).

These four measures – the general amnesty, citizenship for the Sicilians, citizenship for the Cretans and the restitution of Deiotarus' property – all share a common denominator: they were apparently put forward by Antony in Caesar's name. Among other things, Antony undoubtedly wanted to establish his political position through the acquisition of a new *clientela*. On the other hand, it is clear that Caesar granted the Sicilians, and perhaps also the Cretans, *ius Latii*. Did the man who granted Gauls and Spaniards citizen rights also become convinced that others also deserved these rights? In his *Philippics*, Cicero does his utmost to defame and slander his enemy Antony, and to leave no hair on his head unsinged. Therefore, should we believe Cicero? His demagogy is transparent. He attacked his enemy of the moment, and never ceased to laud his enemy of yesterday. In his attacks on Clodius he was full of praise for Catiline; in his onslaught on Antony he attempted to prove that the connection between Antony's proposals and Caesar's intentions was purely coincidental.

And yet Cicero forces us to reconsider our opinion. As we read in Suetonius, 'he conferred citizenship on all who practised medicine at Rome, and on all teachers of the liberal arts, to make them more desirous of living in the city and to induce others to resort to it' (*Div. Jul.* 42, 1). It follows that Caesar did not distribute citizen rights with senseless lack of discrimination. His attitude was extremely selective and certainly not revolutionary. Others before him had acted in the same way, and Cicero's 'regrets' that the provincials streaming to Rome lack a sense of humour (*ad fam*. IX, 15, 2) is not to be taken seriously. At Cicero's request, Dolabella applied to Caesar on behalf of the Sicilian Demetrius Megas and obtained citizenship for him (*op. cit.* XIII, 36). Perhaps Demetrius' sense of humour was more highly developed, but one cannot reproach Caesar for demanding different criteria.

CHAPTER THREE

ADMINISTRATIVE MEASURES (OF A POLITICAL CHARACTER)

16 RELIEF FOR THE PROVINCE OF ASIA (48 OR 47 BC?)[1]

After the battle of Pharsalus Pompey withdrew to the East and Caesar followed in pursuit. Many historians doubt whether he found time to bother with the problems of the province of Asia at this point; it is thus plausible to assume that he did not issue his regulations for the province until after the Egyptian campaign. It is possible that he published most of his regulations on his first visit, and the rest on his second, but the exact chronology cannot be established. His activity can, therefore, be described only in general terms: he visited Troy, the city of Aeneas (the son of Venus), exempted it from taxes, granted it autonomy, and gave it an additional strip of land along the coast as far as Dardanus. Alexander had dealt with Granicus in precisely the same fashion after his victory (Strabo XIII, 593-5; Lucan, *Pharsalia* IX, 964-99). Caesar also declared Cnidus a free city (Plut., *Caes.* 48, 1), treated Pergamum extremely generously, and was recognized by its people as *Soter Euergetes* (*IGRRP* IV, 305, cf. 304); he remitted one-third of the taxes for the other inhabitants of Asia.

Julius Caesar rescued the people of the province from the machinations of the *publicani*, who ruthlessly exploited them (Dio XLII, 6, 3). He commented on this exploitation in *Bellum Civile* (III, 31-32). Antony visited the province after Caesar's death, and Appian (*BC* V, 4) put into his mouth a speech from which some features of Caesar's reforms can be discovered: Antony reminded the people of Asia that when Attalus bequeathed his kingdom to the Romans, they did not collect taxes by the same ruthless methods that were common under the Attalids. Instead of demanding a fixed quota of tax (*pars quarta*), without reference to income, they demanded a tithe on the harvest. When it became known that the *publicani* cheated the provincials, Caesar permitted repayment of a third of the taxes and handed over their collection to local residents (cf. App., *BC* II, 92). This is evidence of a later period, and cautious scholars prefer not to rely on it, but there is no doubt that some reliefs were granted. Caesar was not acting merely from romantic or humanitarian motives. Lucullus also thought it vital to lighten the tax burden on the people of Asia to regain their loyalty.

Nor did Cicero deny the deceitful practices of the *publicani* and their exploitation of the natives. He was not surprised that in times of crisis they turned their backs on Rome and looked to the Parthians (*ad fam.* XV, 1, 5). When Caesar arrived in Asia Minor, he found that his enemy Metellus Scipio had imposed heavy taxes on the province, and had ordered the *publicani* to collect them for two years in advance, while permitting the contributions for a third year to be advanced as a loan on favourable terms (Caes., *Bell. Civ. loc. cit.*).

Therefore, one cannot lay all the blame on the *publicani*, but by and large one must agree with Badian that those responsible for the exploitation of the provinces belonged to the ruling élite. Governors such as Appius Claudius and Lentulus (Cic., *ad. fam.* III, 7, 5) did not exactly distinguish themselves by their generous conduct towards the provincials, and although there is no abundant proof that senators held unregistered shares in *societates publicanorum* (cf. e.g. Cic., *In Vat.* 29), this may safely be assumed. As far as the exploitation of provincials was concerned, *concordia ordinum* always worked.

Thus the question arises of the political significance of Caesar's administrative measures in Asia Minor. Was he prepared to renounce his alliance with the *publicani* (who had certainly supported him in Italy in 48 BC)? It would be a mistake, however, to draw conclusions about Caesar's general attitude to the *publicani* exclusively from his measures in Asia Minor. Circumstances dictated by the severity of the civil war determined his attitude. He was concerned that Pompey's loyal supporters in Asia Minor were so numerous – a reminder of the latter's activity there in the 60s (Dio XLII, 2, 1).

Caesar arrived in Ephesus at the beginning of 48 BC, a short while after the Pompeian Titus Ampius had gone, leaving the district without supervision, and without taking any steps to preserve normal conditions. The inhabitants appeared before Caesar anxiously, wondering how he would treat them (*Bell.*

Civ. III, 105, 1-2). Caesar refrained from expressing anger at Pompey's followers; he sought out a few important men, who might be prepared to support him in his campaign, and attempted to win their loyalty. Thus we hear of a wealthy man called Mithridates, who worked for him in Pergamum, and of a certain Caius Julius Theopompus in Cnidus. The provincials thought first of their own good, and guarded against becoming involved in the struggles of the Roman dynasts. They usually changed sides and joined forces with the victor of the day, just as the people of Rhodes had initially supported Pompey, but deserted to Caesar as soon as they learned of his victory (*loc. cit.* 106, 1; App. *loc. cit.* 89).

At first Caesar was probably not in a position to bolster his standing. Apparently he was in such a hurry to pursue Pompey to Egypt that he handed over Asia minor to his henchman Cn. Domitius Calvinus. However, the latter not only failed to tighten his grip on the province and finally win it over for Caesar, but was also unable to withstand Pharnaces' attack. Caesar was, therefore, obliged to return hastily from Egypt to Asia Minor and to defeat Pharnaces at Zela (47 BC) in a spectacular victory. His political and administrative measures after this victory are no less impressive.

He won the trust of Tarcondimotus, pardoned Ariobarzanes of Cappadocia for his support of Pompey and thus won him over, and began to plan a series of colonies throughout the district (see pp. 143 ff.). In the meantime he needed money. Obviously, his first step was to see that the funds intended for Pompey flowed into his own coffers (Dio XLII, 49, 1). He also imposed heavy taxes on the province, but exacted them selectively, especially from Pompey's supporters, even if he continued to give the impression that loyalty to Pompey was not in itself a ground for punishment.

It was also clear to Caesar that those who had seen which way the wind was blowing and changed sides accordingly, required more cautious treatment (Dio XLI, 63, 2-6, cf. also XLII, 3). It is in this context that his tax reforms must be understood. Apart from the renunciation of one-third, the change in the system is itself significant – that the communities now collected the taxes themselves, and took them to the quaestor of the province. Obviously the influence of the *publicani* was thereby undermined, but Caesar solved this problem in his typical fashion by means of a compromise.

Only direct taxes were taken to the quaestor; indirect taxes, such as *portoria*, stayed in the hands of the *societates*, who consequently remained faithful to Caesar. As Badian said, 'Treated with courtesy and assured of their reasonable profits, the publicans would co-operate . . .' (p. 117). This was one of the reasons why numerous *equites* also remained in Caesar's service.[2]

Caesar did not neglect the concerns of the provincials for even a moment. To ensure the continuation of his policies even after his return, he appointed loyal followers as his representatives. They held the real power in their hands, so that the *publicani*, much to their dislike, were unable to carry out their schemes.

In 47 BC Vibius Pansa was sent to Bithynia and P. Servilius Isauricus to Asia. The latter even won the *cognomina Soter* and *Euergetes* because he restored to the Pergamenes 'the democracy and laws of their fathers' (*ILS* 8779). It is hard to believe that these honours constituted mere lip service – an inseparable accompaniment of *adulatio graeca*. We hear of a definite sympathy for Caesar in Mytilene, Cos and Ephesus as well. We learn of a delegation from Mytilene to Rome, to request the right to renew the friendship between the two cities, and even to be permitted to make sacrifices to Jupiter Capitolinus (*SIG*[2] 764 = Abbot and Johnson, no. 25). Caesar replied briefly, assured them of his goodwill, gave them the right to enjoy all the revenues from their territory, and promised that no resident of Mytilene should enjoy the privilege of immunity (not even Roman citizens).

The promise of religious freedom for the temple of Aphrodite in Aphrodisias[3] and the temple of Apollo in Didyma is conclusive proof that Caesar's liberal policies in the provinces were not accidental, even if all these provisions could be ranked as the purely administrative measures of a Roman proconsul concerned for his subjects; one should nevertheless not lose sight of the obvious political intentions behind these provisions. Caesar's regulations in Judaea can also be considered from this point of view.

JUDAEA[4]

The alliance that Caesar intended to conclude with Pompey's opponents in Judaea was never put into practice. Aristobulus was poisoned, and his son Alexander brutally murdered by Metellus Scipio. After Pompey's defeat at Pharsalus, Hyrcanus and Antipater did not hesitate to join the victor. Caesar was apparently much impressed with Hyrcanus' influence over the Jews of Egypt, who joined Caesar's camp only after the intervention of the Hasmonaeans. There were rewards. After his final victory in the Alexandrine war, Caesar turned his attention to Syria (in 47 BC) without paying any attention to the despairing complaints of Antigonus, Aristobulus' second son. 'While confirming Hyrcanus in the high-priesthood, he granted Antipater Roman citizenship and exemption from taxation' (Jos., *Ant.* XIV, 137; *Bell. Jud.* I, 194). In fact, Caesar did restore Hyrcanus to his rightful position: he named him ethnarch of the Jews, and appointed Antipater *epitropos* of Judaea. When Flavius Josephus wanted to demonstrate that the kings of Asia and Europe held the Jews in high regard and recognized their courage and loyalty (Jos., *Ant.* XIV, 186), he took the trouble to cite the original text of the Senate's decrees in relation to Hyrcanus and the Jews in the days of Caesar (*op. cit.* 190 ff.).

Severe confusion of text and chronology gave rise to tedious debates in the modern literature on this question. Momigliano brought chronological order to the complicated text of Josephus,[5] and suggested that the passages should be read in the following order:

Ant. XIV, 190 = Oct.-Dec. 48; XIV, 192-5 = Spring 47; XIV, 197-9 = Autumn 47; XIV, 205-10 = Dec. 47; XIV, 202-4 = Dec. 47-Apr. 46; XIV, 211 = 9 Feb. 44; XIV, 200-1 = Feb. 44; XIV, 219-22 = Apr. 44

No one knows the legal significance of the title *epitropos* (procurators were never appointed in Caesar's time), but there is agreement on the fundamental facts; in 44 BC Hyrcanus was given the right to rebuild the walls of Jerusalem that had been razed to the ground by Pompey (*Ant.* XIV, 200-1). Caesar's attitude can be derived from the following passage,

It is my wish that Hyrcanus, son of Alexander, and his children shall be ethnarchs of the Jews and shall hold the office of high priest of the Jews for all time in accordance with their national customs, and that he and his sons shall be our allies and also be numbered among our particular friends; and whatever high-priestly rights or other privileges exist in accordance with those laws, these he and his children shall possess by my command. And if, during this period, any question shall arise concerning the Jews' manner of life, it is my pleasure that the decision shall rest with them. Nor do I approve of troops being given winter-quarters among them or of money being demanded of them.

(*Ant.* XIV, 194 f.)

One of the most important provisions concerned the return of Joppa to Judaea:

Gaius Caesar, Imperator for the second time, has ruled that they shall pay a tax for the city of Jerusalem, Joppa excluded, every year except in the seventh year, which they call the sabbatical year, because in this time they neither take fruit from the trees nor do they sow (*ibid.* 202).

Therefore, the change made by Caesar was that Joppa paid its taxes to Jerusalem, and not directly to Rome, as it had in Pompey's time. This was expressly stated in paragraph 205,

It is also our pleasure that the city of Joppa, which the Jews had held from ancient times when they made a treaty of friendship with the Romans, shall belong to them as at first; and for this city Hyrcanus, son of Alexander, and his sons shall pay tribute, collected from those who inhabit the territory, as a tax on the land, the harbour and the exports, payable at Sidon in the amount of twenty thousand six hundred and seventy-five *modii* every year except in the seventh year, which they call the sabbatical year, wherein they neither plough nor take fruit from the trees. As for the villages in the great plain (Jesre'el, the plain of Esdraelon) which Hyrcanus and his forefathers before him possessed, it is the pleasure of the Senate that Hyrcanus and the Jews shall retain them with the same rights as they formerly had.

Caesar was assured of the Jews' lasting loyalty and esteem. Suetonius appropriately noted (*Div. Jul.* 84, 5), that after Caesar's murder 'a throng of foreigners went about lamenting each after the fashion of his country, above all the Jews, who even flocked to the place for several successive nights'.

From ancient times the Jews were grateful to their bene-factors, but it must be said that in his conduct towards the Jews Caesar did not deviate in any way from the norms customarily applied to the 'friends and allies' of Rome.

The rebellious activities of the Galilean Heskiah prove that not all Jews were content with Caesar's measures. Josephus called Heskiah an arch-robber (*archilestes*), and stressed that the Syrians rejoiced over his death (*Bell. Jud.* I, 204; *Ant.* XIV, 159). Yet the Jews never forgave Herod for permitting the execution of Heskiah without lawfully bringing him before the Sanhedrin for sentence (*Ant.* XIV, 167), and, according to the Hebrew sources, his memory was held in honour and esteem (*Kohelet Raba* I, 1). A more balanced evaluation of Caesar's attitude to Judaea and the Jews is in order.

A brief glance at Antonius' law of 71 (?) proves that the Pisidian city of Termessus obtained exactly the same rights as Caesar had granted to Hyrcanus. The inhabitants of Termessus, likewise 'friends and allies of the Roman people', were given the right to live according to the laws of their forefathers, on condition that these laws did not contradict the *Lex Antonia*. Among other things, the law stated,

The people of greater Termessus in Pisidia are to be free, and to be friends and allies of the Roman people and are to use their own laws. And so all the inhabitants of greater Termessus are to be allowed to use their own laws in so far as not contrary to this law.

(*ILS.* 38 [6–10] = Riccobono, *FIRA* I, pp. 135 ff.)

Caesar's liberal conduct towards Judaea deserves some praise. It was far more favourable to Judaea than that of Pompey, Gabinius or Cassius (Pompey's settlement lasted from 63 to 57 BC, Gabinius' from 57 to 47 BC, and Cassius' from 44 to 42 BC). Jerusalem did not become one of the *civitates liberae et immunes*. It continued to pay taxes to Rome, and thus remained a *civitas stipendiaria*, in whose affairs the governor of Syria could continue to interfere. Massilia was more fortunate. In Strabo IV, 181 it is clearly stated that Caesar preserved its autonomy, and its citizens were not subjected to interference by the generals sent out to the province. On the other hand, autonomy was promised to Hyrcanus, and Judaea was released from the obligation to supply Rome with *auxilia*, just as the Jews were freed from military service (*Ant.* XIV, 228). Further, the establishment of a garrison in Judaea was forbidden, according to *Ant.* XIV, 204,

. . . No one, whether magistrate or pro-magistrate, praetor or legate, shall raise auxiliary troops in the *territoria* of the Jews, nor shall soldiers be allowed to exact money from them, whether for winter quarters or on any other pretext, but they shall be free from all molestation.

If we consider the return of Joppa to Judaea and the special honour accorded to the ethnarch and his companions of attending gladiatorial shows (*Ant.* XIV, 205-10), it is not surprising that Hyrcanus believed himself to be a *socius et amicus populi Romani*. Antipater, however, must have understood the limits of this honour.

17 LEX JULIA DE PROVINCIIS (46 BC)

Julius Caesar learned from his own experience that long tenures of provincial governorships, such as his own in Gaul, nurtured ambition and self-esteem. Therefore 'he limited by law the term of propraetors to one year, and that of proconsuls to two consecutive years, and enacted that no one whatever should be allowed to hold any command for a longer time' (Dio XLIII, 25, 3). When the dictator presented this proposal to the *comitia centuriata*, Cicero praised him highly (*Phil.* I, 19),

What better law was there, what more useful, what more often demanded in the best period of the Republic, than that the praetorian provinces should not be held longer than a year, nor consular longer than two years? (cf. *ibid.* 24)

Thus Cicero, too, categorically demanded the retention of the law after Caesar's death (*ibid.* III, 38), if only to prevent a five-year governorship for Antony (*ibid.* VIII, 28).

It is not easy to understand the legislator's real intention, yet in this case it may be supposed that Cassius Dio was correct. Caesar wished to prevent the concentration of power in the hands of governors. By shortening the period of office, he severed the knot linking the close ties between the governor and his *clientela*, without renouncing his own right to make arrangements for the praetorian provinces (Dio XLII, 20, 4; Cic., *Phil.* III, 38). He disposed of governorships according to his own assessment of the candidates, without resort to the lot (Dio XLIII, 47, 1); yet it is doubtful whether he acquired this privilege by law; probably it was simply a matter of *usus*.

Caesar had more than the well-being of the provincials in mind when he hit on this arrangement. A governor who had only a short term was frequently inclined to fill his pockets quickly because he knew that such an opportunity might not come his way again. This could not have been Caesar's aim. The Emperor Tiberius, on the other hand, wanted to lengthen the period of office in the provinces. He had a clear policy and in his mind the good shepherd should certainly shear his sheep but not flay them (Suet., *Tib.* 32, 2). He therefore left his governors in the provinces for longer periods. (A distinction must also be made between Tiberius' views and the proposals of the tribunes under Antony, who wanted to establish a period of office of six years for governors (Cic., *Phil.* V, 7).)

Caesar cannot be said to have been ignorant of the problems of the provincials. The *Lex Julia de pecuniis repetundis* of his first consulship in 59 BC proves the opposite[6] and his treatment of the people of Asia Minor, Syria, and Judaea is also an indication (pp. 104 ff.). but in this case the question was rather different, for it was a matter of buttressing his own rule.

18 LEGES JULIAE DE MAGISTRATIBUS CREANDIS (47–44 BC)[7]

'He increased the number of praetors, aediles and quaestors as well as of the minor officials' (Suet., *Div. Jul.* 41, 1; cf. 76, 2). This enlargement of the body of magistrates, begun in 47 BC, continued until 44 BC. The number of praetors was first raised to ten (Dio XLII, 51, 3), later to fourteen, and eventually to sixteen, and that of the aediles to six (full details in Dio XLIII, 47).

Dealing with a man like Caesar, the usual explanation that state business had increased, and therefore demanded a larger number of magistrates, is insufficient. The ulterior motive is more attractive: Julius Caesar promised so much to so many that the only way to reward them for their services was by appointments to positions of influence (Dio XLIII, 47, 2). Since there were not enough offices available he did not hesitate to increase them, thereby devaluing the magistracies (Cic., *ad fam.* X, 26, 2; Gell., *Noctes Atticae* XVI, 7, 12). Cicero was infuriated at the very idea that it could even occur to a man like M. Curtius Postumus to stand for the consulship (*ad Att.* XII, 49), and that is only one of many examples. In this respect we can take it for granted that Caesar did not trouble himself with all the details, since, even in his time, aides were involved in every transaction. Thus, the need to create new offices is not to be traced back merely to Caesar's whim. We read in the so-called *Lex Julia municipalis*, for instance (pp. 117–22), of *III viri viis in urbem purgandis, II viri viis extra propiusque urbem Romam passus M. purgandis*, etc. Did Caesar add another element to the *collegia*, from which the vigintivirate was constructed in the principate? There is no proof, yet our assumption about the extension of the praetorship is securely based. Why, then, not agree with the explanation, to which Mommsen alluded years ago, that the development of the Roman provinces was closely connected with that of the praetorship? The number of praetors is readily understandable in this case, since, apart from the ten Sullan governorships, there were eight others: 1 Sicily, 2 Sardinia, 3 Hispania Ulterior, 4 Hispania Citerior, 5 Macedonia, 6 Africa, 7 Asia, 8 Gallia Narbonensis, 9 Cilicia, 10 Gallia Cisalpina, 11 Bithynia, 12 Cyrene, 13 Crete, 14 Syria, 15 Illyria, 16 Gallia Comata, 17 Africa Nova and 18 Achaea.

19 LEX JULIA DE SACERDOTIIS (47 BC)[8]

'He added one member each to the pontifices and to the augurs . . . and also to the Quindecemviri' (Dio XLIII, 51, 4). Details of this law are unknown. It is mentioned only once in contemporary sources, in a letter from Cicero to Brutus (I, 5, 3), 'est etiam lege Julia, quae lex est de sacerdotiis proxima, his verbis, QVI PETET CVIVSQVE RATIO HABEBITVR' (whosoever shall make application or be taken into consideration). Since Cicero, like Caesar, was an augur (*ad fam.* XIII, 68, 2), there is no doubt that there was such a *Lex Julia* as affirmed by this explicit statement.

Sacral office raised the *dignitas* of the incumbent, murder of a Pontifex Maximus was counted sacrilege (Ovid, *Fasti* III, 697), and in the administration of the cult, the pontifices played a particularly significant role. Possibly the priestly offices were more important in the eyes of the masses than in those of the aristocrats, but no over-riding political significance should be attached to them. Caesar himself was a Pontifex Maximus from 63 BC onwards. Yet, after the crossing of the Rubicon, this gave him no advantages over Pompey. In any case, he never emphasized in his works that he was Pontifex Maximus. He never once was able to influence the other pontifices such as Metellus Scipio, Domitius Ahenobarbus and Lentulus Spinther (Caes., *Bell. Civ.* III, 83, 1). One point is clear: the only reason for the increase in the number of priestly offices was to make room for the followers to whom Caesar felt he had an obligation (Dio XLII, 51, 9). It is questionable to what extent this law was part of a far-reaching religious reform; and the fact that Granius Flaccus and Varro dedicated their works *de indigitamentis* and *Antiquitates rerum divinarum* (*ad Caesarem pontificem*) to Caesar, gives us no further help. As far as the *Lex Julia de sacerdotiis* is concerned, even Weinstock, who considered Caesar a great religious reformer, confessed ignorance.

The similarities or differences between this law and Sulla's reforms in the same area remain obscure (Livy, *Per.* 89), yet it is clear that Caesar's law, inter alia, was concerned with the candidates' right to be elected in their absence.

20 REFORM OF THE CALENDAR[9]

Suetonius reported that Caesar reorganized the calendar, 'which the negligence of the pontiffs had long since so disordered, through their privilege of adding months or days at pleasure, that the harvest festivals did not come in the summer nor those of the vintage in the autumn' (*Div. Jul.* 40, 1).

Plutarch, too, underlined the urgency for reform, and explained that Caesar not only reorganized the calendar with admirable ingenuity, and corrected discrepancies in the regulation of the seasons, but also provided for a system that proved extraordinarily useful,

For not only in very ancient times was the relation of the lunar to the solar year in great confusion among the Romans, so that the sacrificial feasts and festivals, diverging gradually, at last fell in opposite seasons of the year, but also at this time people generally had no way of computing the actual solar year; the priests alone knew the proper time, and would suddenly and to everybody's surprise insert the intercalary month called Mercedonius . . . But Caesar laid the problem before the best philosophers and mathematicians and out of the methods of correction which were already at hand compounded one of his own which was more accurate than any. This the Romans use down to the present time . . . (Plut., *Caes.* 59).

Caesar appeared to be genuinely interested in problems of reckoning time (*Bell. Gall.* VI, 18, 2). The Elder Pliny mentioned the astronomer Sosigenes, who helped Caesar to carry out successfully this great task (Plin., *NH* XVIII, 211). Macrobius added that the new calendar was brought to the public's attention by means of an edict (*Saturnalia* I, 14, 10; 13: 'edicto palam posito').

The calendar reform was made legal and the Senate was informed (Bern. *Comm. ad Lucan.* X, 187), 'Est autem liber fastorum divi Julii Caesaris qui ordinationem continet anni secundum auctoritatem compositus Chaldaeorum quem in senatu recitavit'. Mommsen ascribed the authorship to Caesar himself, and praised 'the light touch of the practitioner who does not belie his profession in minor matters either'.[10]

Before the calendar was changed, the Roman year had 355 days, with 31 days each in March, May, July and October, 28 days in February, and 29 in the other months. In order to fit the lunar month to the astronomical year, every two years there was an intercalary month, sometimes of 27 and sometimes of 28 days, which fell at the end of February. But in these leap years February had only 23 days. So a period of four years had $4 \times 355 = 1,420$ days, and, together with the $28 + 27 = 55$ days of the two intercalary months, it totalled 1,475, less the $2 \times 5 = 10$ days subtracted from February in leap years, making 1,465 days altogether. This number, however, did not agree with the number of days in four astronomical years.

The object of Caesar's reform was to make the calendar year agree with the astronomical year and take away from the priests the right to insert days and months at will. They had been given this right by the law of Acilius in 191 BC (Censorinus XX, 6; Macrob., *Sat.* I, 13, 21), and since then had been persuaded to shorten or lengthen the year by tax farmers and influential magistrates (Macrob. *loc. cit.*). There are many examples. When Cicero was governor of the province of Cilicia, he asked Atticus to make sure the priests did not extend the year, so that he did not have to stay in the province any longer than necessary. Curio went over to the *populares* because his proposal to extend the year was unsuccessful (*ad fam.* VIII, 6, 5).

In any case, determination of the length of the year became a potent political weapon. Between 65 BC and 45 BC, only five intercalary months were inserted, not ten. As a result, the calendar was so disorganized that 'the harvest festivals did not come in summer nor those of the vintage in the autumn' (Suet., *Div. Jul.*, *loc. cit.*). Caesar attempted to solve these problems, and, to make the year 45 BC into a regular astronomical year with 365¼ days, he was obliged to distort the year 46 BC into a very odd unit of 445 days (Macrob., *Sat.* I, 13, 3).

Mommsen found the solution to the problem as he

explained in his *Römische Chronologie*, published 1859, 'the reform achieved a twofold object: to restore the months to their proper time of year and to bring the magisterial year into line with the calendar year' (p. 277).

Caesar went a step further. The days of the year had long been divided into *fasti*, on which court proceedings and everyday occupations were allowed, *nefasti* days, on which they were forbidden, and, finally, a limited number of *dies comitiales* suitable for assemblies of the people. Caesar ordained that the additional days resulting from the reorganization of the calendar should be designated *fasti*. The magistrates were to be prevented from using the changes for their own purposes, or from improperly postponing public occasions (Macrob., *Saturnalia* I, 13, 12; Censorinus XX, 7; Dio XL, 62, 1).

Caesar's reform was not final. 'Inasmuch as the calendar, which had been set in order by the deified Julius, had later been confused through negligence, he restored it to its former system' (Suet., *Div. Aug.* 31, cf. Plin. *NH* XVIII, 211; Censorinus XX, 10–11; Solinus I, 46–47; Macrob. *Saturnalia* I, 14, 6; 13–15). The technical details of the change cannot be explored here, but attention must be drawn to the fundamental work of Laffi, which discusses epigraphic evidence from Priene, Apamea, Eumenia and Dorylaeum, and argues convincingly against Radke. Eventually, in 1582, Pope Gregory XIII bridged the gap of eleven days that still existed between the astronomical year and the Julian year.

In *Divus Julius* (p. 197), Weinstock proposed the theory that the regulations made in 46 BC after the reform of the calendar were to keep Caesar's victory and birthday for posterity, and for naming a month Julius. Ultimately a calendar was devised which included a number of Caesar's festivals and those of the gods.

Attractive as this view may be, it conceals an error: the reform of the calendar was decided on in 46 BC, the *mensis Julius* not before 44 BC, and there is not the slightest evidence that these two proceedings were part of a plan conceived in 46 BC.

To sum up, it may be said that the reform of the calendar itself belongs to cultural history, but that Caesar's changes were not innocent. Their political and administrative intentions were very obvious, and gave his enemies an opportunity to attack him. When someone said to Cicero in a speech that the constellation *Lyra* would appear on the morrow, the latter answered 'Yes, to order', as if Caesar had imposed this, too, on the general public (Plut., *Caes.* 59, 3), an illustration of the well-known Ciceronian humour and wit.

Caesar reformed the calendar in his capacity as dictator rather than as Pontifex Maximus: as dictator he had the authority to issue *edicta*, but as Pontifex Maximus he could provide only for *intercalatio*. Intercalation, the invention of which was attributed either to Romulus Numa or Servius Tullius (Macrob. *Sat.* 1.13.20) tended to be neglected by the pontiffs of later periods (Cic. *de leg*, II, 29). Then as reported by Macrobius (1.14.2),

. . . since there was thus no consistency in the marking of the times and seasons but all was still vague and uncertain, Caius Caesar introduced a clearly defined arrangement of the calendar with the help of a clerk named Marcus Flavius, who provided the dictator with a list of the several days so arranged that their order once found, the position of each day would remain constant.

Hence we have further proof that the reform was the work of the dictator rather than of the Pontifex Maximus.

21 LEX JULIA DE VIIS URBIS ROMAE TUENDIS ET PURGANDIS (46 BC?)[11]

There is no clear-cut evidence for this law. Modern scholars ascribe a concern for order and cleanliness in the city of Rome to Caesar. That is possible, although not certain, and a conclusion based solely on a few lines from the inscription of Heraclea (24-26) is not clear proof. In modern times lines 20-82 of the *Tabula Heracleensis* would be included in a municipal ordinance. It mentions streets in Rome and its environs, and the duty of the aediles to maintain a street by deputing its upkeep to those living in it. It was the responsibility of the residents to prevent great puddles from making the streets impassable. The curule and plebeian aediles had to share the responsibility determined by lot for the different districts of the city, and there were penalties for residents who failed to comply. The aedile must have been entitled to delegate compulsorily the matter of dealing with transgressors to the *quaestor urbanus* or officials responsible for the *aerarium*. The proceeds must have been entered in the *tabulae publicae*, and the residents obliged to contribute pro rata for their portion of the street (lines 32-38).

The law also applies to householders who refused to pay their share (lines 41-45). Lines 50 ff. deal with the responsibility for the footpaths leading past houses (*semita*). Then follows a reference to the prohibition on bringing heavy goods vehicles (*plostra*) into the city of Rome during daylight hours (lines 56–61); vehicles with teams of horses or oxen were only permitted to enter the city at night (line 66). Provisions are made for ensuring free access to public places (*loca publica*), and forbidding any building on them (lines 68–72). Further, in lines 50–53, 'IIII vir(ei) vieis in urbem purgandeis' are mentioned. The question, therefore, arises, why was a special *lex de viis urbis Romae tuendis et purgandis* necessary? Are lines 20-82 of the *Tabula Heracleensis* relevant?

A second theory presents itself. In 45 BC, Cicero referred in several letters to a measure *de urbe augenda*, initiated by Caesar and proposed by a tribune of the plebs named Caecilius or Pomponius (Broughton, *MRR* II, 307); whether he meant a *Lex Caecilia* or a *Lex Pomponia* cannot be established. But since Cicero was writing in 45 BC, it should be assumed that the orders had already been issued in 46 BC (*ad Att.* XIII, 20, 1, and also 35, 1).

Is there a connection between this notice and the passage of Suetonius (*Div. Jul.* 44, 1-2), in which he described in detail the plans for extensions and public works? It is probable that some of this took place, but it is doubtful that it was laid down by law. But it is unthinkable that the *cura viarum* did not begin until the time of Augustus (Suet., *Div. Aug.* 37). It is true that Suetonius maintained that it belonged to the *nova officia*, but, as it turns out, he was none too exact about the prefecture either. Therefore, it is probable that in this case, too, Caesar was the precursor of Augustus.[12]

22 LEX JULIA DE ABSENTIBUS (46 BC?)

Evidence is also lacking for this law. According to Suetonius,

> Moreover to keep up the population of the city, depleted as it was by the assignment of eighty thousand citizens to colonies across the sea, he made a law that no citizen older than twenty or younger than forty, who was not detained by service in the army, should be absent from Italy for more than three successive years. (*Div. Jul.* 42, 1)

There is no mention in Plutarch, Appian or Cassius Dio of any such law, and not one hint in contemporary sources to support Suetonius' version. A large question mark would be appropriate here, especially as Lange's supposition (*Röm. Alt.* III, 49) that some *Lex Julia militaris* is in question is unfounded.

23 LEX JULIA IUDICIARIA (46 BC)

In his stirring plea for Marcellus, Cicero turned to Caesar and requested the reconstitution of the courts (*Pro Marcello* 23). And, in fact, Caesar altered the *Lex Aurelia* of 70 BC, whereby senators, knights, and *tribuni aerarii* each formed a third of the jury. 'He limited the right of serving as jurors to two classes, the equestrian and senatorial orders, disqualifying the third class [*tribuni aerarii*] (Suet., *Div. Jul.* 41, 2). When Cassius Dio wrote that the *tribuni aerarii* were men of the people, he should not be taken literally (XLIII, 25, 1). They were fairly wealthy persons, but did not have the status of knights.

In general, every attempt to broaden the social basis of the judiciary met with devastating criticism from the oligarchy (Cic., *Phil.* I, 19; XIII, 3; V, 12-16). Cicero (*Phil.* I, 24) praised Caesar's reform, and attacked Antony's proposal to restore the *status quo* and build up the courts to three *decuriae*, so that centurions could be appointed jurors.

What is the significance of Caesar's reform? In Eduard Meyer's view (p. 418), that Caesar was not fulfilling the aims of the Gracchi, but was trying to increase the power of money and create an undisguised plutocracy, this law is decisive. In filling up the jury places Caesar passed over the third class, the *tribuni aerarii*, and only appointed senators and knights. A different conclusion is possible, however, on the basis of the text: Suetonius did not say that the *tribuni aerarii* were excluded. He reported only that 'from now on the courts were to be composed of two kinds of jurors'. We cannot believe that Caesar intended to injure the *tribuni aerarii*, who were wealthy and influential in Roman society. Perhaps he simply promoted them to knights and only abolished their *decuria*? So Mommsen supposed, by reason of Caesar's policy of promoting even centurions to equestrian rank (*Staatsrecht* III, 192, n. 4; 489; 535).[13]

24 LEX JULIA MUNICIPALIS (45 BC)?[14]

We place the question mark in the heading because neither is the date certain, nor is it at all clear whether Julius Caesar ever brought in such a law. Hardy characterized the inscription on which this law is based as 'a mysterious document', while Mommsen doubted whether the lapicide had a sufficient knowledge of Latin (*CIL* I, 119: 'a sculptore incurioso sane nec fortasse Latini sermonis satis gnaro').

The inscription was discovered at Heraclea in southern Italy on the back of a bronze tablet (there was a Greek inscription of the fourth century on the front). Hence the name by which it is known in modern literature, *Tabula Heracleensis*. The text is in *ILS* 6058 = Riccobono, *FIRA* I, 13. The law established *inter alia* regulations for elections to city offices in Italy, defined the qualifications required of a candidate for the local senate and the rules for the organization of a local census.

It is a remarkable document because it relates to more than one subject. In fact, only lines 83-141 deal with municipal elections, and lines 142-58 with the census. The first two parts are concerned with quite different subjects, i.e. lines 1-19 deal with corn distribution in Rome (see pp. 156 ff.), and lines 20-82 with the duties of the aediles and other officials in Rome to take care of the upkeep and cleansing of the streets (see pp. 114-15).

The second part of the law, that forbids heralds (*praecones*), gravediggers, actors and pimps to serve as municipal magistrates, concerns us here. Can regulations of this kind be interpreted as innovations of Caesar's day? It is hard to say, yet it is quite possible that this law merely made official what was already common local custom, in the same way, for instance, that proof was demanded from applicants over the age of thirty that they had served time in a legion, either as cavalry or infantry.

There are also references to this law in a contemporary source. Cicero told his friend Lepta (*ad fam.* VI, 18, 1, cf. XIII, 11, 3) that Balbus, when questioned about the right of erstwhile heralds (*praecones*) to be elected decurions, replied that a working herald could not be a member of the council in a *municipium*, although a retired one could. It is intolerable, Cicero added, that today's practising soothsayers could sit in the Roman Senate tomorrow, while former heralds did not have the right to become decurions in municipalities.

From the date of this letter it can be inferred that in January 46 BC similar considerations were being put forward by people in Caesar's entourage; perhaps even a preliminary proposal had been put down in writing, though the public was not made aware of this, and Cicero was just trying to collect trustworthy information about details as he did not want to depend on rumour. It is not clear why he was so interested in the fate of the *praecones*, who were not particularly respected in Rome (Juv., *Sat.* III, 157).

F. C. von Savigny, in 1838, connected Cicero's letter with lines 94 ff. of the *Tabula Heracleensis*. He interpreted Cicero's question, 'quid esset in lege', in such a way that it could only refer to a *Lex Julia municipalis*, and came to the conclusion that this law and the *Tabula Heracleensis* were identical, dating from the year 45 BC. Mommsen agreed with Savigny until 1894. Then he changed his opinion after the discovery of the Tarentum inscription (*Lex municipii Tarentini* Riccobono, *FIRA* I, 18), and not only backed away from the theory identifying the Heraclea inscription with the *Lex Julia municipalis*, but doubted the existence of such a *lex* altogether. (So did H. Hackel, who proposed to drop the term.) In fact, an inscription from Patavium (*CIL* V, 2864 = *ILS* 5406) exists concerning a certain M. Junius Sabinus, *quattuorvir aed. pot.*, in which the *Lex Julia municipalis* is also mentioned by name, but it is difficult to come to any conclusion because the reference may be to a *Lex Julia* of Augustus. It is also possible that this law referred only to Patavium, as there is no evidence that a general municipal law is meant. It is even more to the point that no inscriptions have so far been found in which local magistrates boast that the *Lex Julia municipalis* helped them win elections.

The framework of this study is too narrow to permit an exhaustive survey of the research into this *lex*. It is sufficient to say that scholars like Savigny, and Mitteis after him, categorize it as a *lex satura*, a law that covered a whole series of disparate matters. Premerstein, among others, believed that there was no question of codification of a *lex municipalis* before 42 BC, while in Caesar's time there were only incomplete drafts. Yet Savigny's influence continued to make itself felt into the twentieth century; Eduard Meyer still spoke of a comprehensive municipal law (p. 425). But the sharpest controversies arose after H. Rudolph's book was published in 1935.

Rudolph came to the conclusion that there was a fundamental difference between Caesar's municipal policy and
everything that preceded it, since, in his opinion, the *Lex Julia
municipalis* signified the beginning of a standard reorganization
of the nature of municipal office. For various reasons the
reform was postponed after the end of the Social War. Cinna
failed in his plan to make the *quattuorvirate* a standard system in
those *municipia* that had recently obtained the vote. The
administration of the country remained in a state of suspense,
because here too the Senate was unable to make a positive
decision. The system remained the same: in areas inhabited by
old citizens the prefectures remained, and in areas where new
citizens lived the original system of administration by Rome
was reintroduced. All new citizens were under the praetor and
they had to live under laws made in Rome. This impossible
situation could not last. Drastic steps had to be taken to solve
the problem, and Caesar decided to act. A beginning was
made in 55 BC with the *Lex Mamilia-Roscia-Peducaea-Alliena-
Fabia*. Rudolph did not believe that the legislators had mainly a
lex agraria in mind, but rather that the origin of a *lex municipalis*
is here at issue. Its authors were all supporters of Caesar, and
their intention was to give *praefecturae, fora*, and *conciliabula* the
status of *municipia*.

The second stage occurred in 49 BC, with the grant of
Roman citizenship to Gallia Cisalpina (see pp. 66 ff.); yet consequently the construction of a comprehensive local jurisdiction.
This emerged from the *Fragmentum Atestinum* (see p. 66); yet
Rudolph considered this legislation no accident. It was the
forerunner of the great *Lex Julia municipalis*, which was then
passed in 47 BC or 46 BC, granting legal authority to the
magistrates of the Italian *municipia*.

Rudolph found his proof in the inscription from Patavium
(see p. 69): from that time onwards, all chief magistrates of
colonies, who until then were simply *duoviri*, became *duoviri
iure dicundo*, and those of the *municipia*, who had simply been
quattuorviri, were called *quattuorviri iure dicundo* or *quattuorviri
aediliciae potestatis*.

In 45 BC, Caesar planned a rider to the *Lex Julia municipalis*,
but it was only after his death that Antony carried it through.
According to the passage of the *Tabula Heracleensis*, the rider
concerns the qualifications of candidates for the local senate
and regulations for the census.

To sum up: the praetor's exclusive authority in judicial affairs was abolished by the *Lex Julia municipalis*; the independent jurisdiction of the cities took its place; the Roman power to administer the law was divided into a state and city jurisdiction. Rome renounced some of her judicial supremacy and handed it over to the cities. Thus it was a delegated authority regulated by purely administrative limits. In this way, Caesar ended the overall supremacy of Rome and founded the Italian municipal system.

Rudolph's book aroused lively interest. For those who were already convinced that Caesar was the first 'Caesar' and the true founder of the Roman Empire, this book appeared to answer their wish. Sceptics and Minimalists were not especially enthusiastic, but there was unanimous praise for the imaginative and incisive approach to the unsatisfactory and dry material. In 1937 Strasburger could still write, 'Certainly, the book's significance is in no way exhausted by its factual results, but the outstanding method and mastery of the material it reveals assures it an unquestionable value, even if there remains disagreement on matters of opinion' (*Gnomon* XIII (1937), 191). And Strasburger was right. Even as late as 1973 there were many pages devoted to a discussion of Rudolph's views in Sherwin-White's new edition of *The Roman Citizenship*, and the debate still continues.

In general, twentieth-century scholars are not prepared to admit that so fundamental and comprehensive a municipal reform could be conceived and carried through by an individual. Strasburger also rejected as exaggerated Rudolph's view that it was no accident that municipal administration was not tackled under the Republic, but was taken up only by the first Emperor. Autonomous jurisdiction was not born a fully developed concept. Rather, it developed step by step over many years before Caesar's time. Finally, no one can say that the grant of jurisdiction alone was the guiding principle in shaping the nature of municipal offices. Many arguments were put forward against Rudolph. Sherwin-White (p. 164) does not believe that the addition *iure dicundo* had as great a significance as Rudolph attributed to it. Jones and Cary showed that there were *duoviri* and *quattuorviri iure dicundo* in Rome before the years 55 BC and after 44 BC *duoviri* still appear in inscriptions without the addition *iure dicundo*. Rudolph's statement that all the inscriptions in the first volume of *CIL* originated from the period before Caesar's murder is not valid when they are examined in detail: Degrassi even refused to include the Sabinus inscription from Patavium in his collection of Republican inscriptions.

Most Sceptics find it difficult to accept the idea that there was a far-sighted plan for municipal legislation, on which Caesar must have embarked as early as 59 BC. Therefore they will totally reject any suggestion that considers the *Lex Julia municipalis* as an integral component of a pronounced imperial policy. Thus Rudolph maintained that even the *Lex Rubria* (see p. 68) was modelled after the *Lex Julia municipalis*. 'when it extended the measures designed for the rest of Italy to Gallia Cisalpina'. Yet even Bruna, in his careful analysis (see p. 69), could not find so much as a hint to prove that the *Lex Rubria* may go back to a more comprehensive law such as the *Lex Julia municipalis*.

It was precisely the slow development of the Roman municipal system that Sherwin-White (p. 164), Taylor and Sherk succeeded in demonstrating; this development went back to ancient Italian tradition, and they rejected the idea that it came suddenly into being as a result of a provision initiated by Caesar.

With regard to the census (to which lines 142-58 of the Heraclea inscription are devoted) Brunt (pp. 35-43) also proved that before Italy received the right to vote, the local authorities conscripted men for the legions, and that in the period before Caesar the census was also taken locally, so that people did not have to travel to Rome.

The *Tabula Heracleensis* must not be identified with the *Lex Julia municipalis*; perhaps this somewhat fragmentary inscription is a selection of ordinances from different Roman laws that pertained only to the inhabitants of Heraclea. That is Frederiksen's carefully considered suggestion, and, if we agree with him, we need not date all the individual items to the same period. In 1910 De Sanctis expressed a similar opinion, 'It deals with a collection, probably in chronological order, of excerpts of Roman laws from various sources published in the time of Caesar by the city of Heraclea' (cited in Tibiletti, p. 726). Through careful study of the works of Italian scholars (Degrassi, Sartori, Tibiletti), we discover that immediately after the Social War the authorities in Rome were already beginning to simplify the municipal system; that this was a protracted and gradual process (cf., e.g. Cic., *Pro Cluent.* 25), and that Caesar's involvement was in no way revolutionary or unusual. Conclusive proof is to be found in Gabba's comprehensive article, 'Urbanizzazione e rinovamenti urbanistici', which not only contains the source material, but also references to modern academic works. Gabba is a Moderate. Caesar did not create the municipal system, 'But this does not signify that the process of urbanization was spontaneous.' This view also frees us from having to reject every notion of Caesar's involvement with ideas for the *municipia*; that would show too minimalistic a tendency, and be no less extreme than Rudolph's interpretation. Caesar's Senate is unimaginable without the influence of the aristocracy of the Italian *municipia* (Syme, *RR*, p. 92, cf. Wiseman). Caesar could not consider his rule secure without buttressing it with the loyalty of a reorganized Italy; this fact is independent of any interpretation of the *Lex Julia municipalis*. Therefore it is meaningless to employ empty phraseology such as 'Caesar changed the city state into an empire', for which there is no support of any kind in contemporary sources. On the other hand, on the basis of the *Lex de Gallia Cisalpina*, we must agree with Laffi about the *Fragmentum Atestinum*, the *Lex Ursonensis* and parts of the *Tabula Heracleensis*, 'Caesar increased in a decisive manner the spread of communities of jurisdictionally autonomous type in the districts of the ancient ager Romanus originally under the control of the prefectures' (p. 51).

Thus Caesar's work, too, was unfinished, and after his death, *fora* and *conciliabula* were given the higher rank of *municipia*. It is doubtful whether the whole system was ever standardized. *Forum Clodii* was still a prefecture in the second century AD, and Peltuinum as late as the third (*ILS* 6584, 6110).

25 APPOINTMENT OF PREFECTS (45 BC?)[15]

The notice in Suetonius is, as usual, so vague that it cannot be the basis for far-reaching conclusions,

He held his third and fourth consulships in name only, content with the power of the dictatorship conferred on him at the same time as the consulships. Moreover, in both years he substituted two consuls for himself for the last three months, in the meantime holding no elections except for tribunes and plebeian aediles, and appointing praefects instead of the praetors to manage the affairs of the city during his absence (Suet., *Div. Jul.* 76, 2)

It is regrettable that there is no further support for this one notice to be found in the writings of Caesar's contemporaries, particularly as no clear conclusions can be made from the numismatic material to which Alföldi devoted so much research. What were Caesar's real intentions when he made these changes? Was it an *ad hoc* measure to solve a pressing administrative problem, or was this the basis for far-reaching reform? A remark attributed to Caesar by Titus Ampius 'that the state was nothing; a mere name without body or form' (Suet., *Div. Jul.* 77), could indicate that he meant it was high time to put an end to administration by elected magistrates, and that a new system of appointment of prefects loyal to the dictator should be introduced

O. E. Schmidt (*Der Briefwechsel des Cicero*, p. 48), at any rate, tended to think that before his departure from Rome in 46 BC, Caesar did not have the time or patience to convene the voting assemblies, and preferred to be chosen sole consul after his departure under the supervision of his *magister equitum*, Aemilius Lepidus. In place of other magistrates he appointed a number of city prefects who were subordinated to Cornelius Balbus and C. Oppius. Schmidt relied on references in Cicero (*ad fam.* VI, 8, 1) and Tacitus (*Ann.* XII, 60), from which he concluded, 'Thus for the first time a government elected by the people was replaced by cabinet government, a privy council such as characterized the absolutism of the seventeenth and eighteenth centuries' (*loc. cit.*). Yet here again we cannot make simplistic assumptions, and so close a connection between the sole powers of Oppius and Balbus on the one hand, and the appointment of prefects on the other, is not proven.

Tacitus (*Ann.* VI, 11) ascribed the creation of the *praefectura urbis* to Augustus, not Caesar, and sketched the origins of the office,

For previously, to avoid leaving the capital without competent authority, when the kings – or later, the magistrates – had to absent themselves from home, it was usual to choose a temporary official to preside in the courts and deal with emergencies.

Eventually, with the election of the *praetor urbanus*, the office of prefect became superfluous, but the name was retained and given to the officials who remained in the city when the consul went to the Mons Albanus for the Feriae Latinae. Such a prefect was called *praefectus urbi Feriarum Latinarum*, yet Tacitus also knew that this was no more than a shadow (*simulacrum*) of the oldest prefecture; the young Octavian, the future princeps, had also held this meaningless office (Broughton, *MRR* II, 292). In the above-mentioned chapter Tacitus did not refer to the prefects of the time of Caesar, but proceeded directly to Augustus, and mentioned Maecenas, who certainly held the office but not the title, and Messala Corvinus, who was appointed *praefectus urbi* to 'overawe the slaves and that part of the population which, unless it fears a strong hand, is disorderly and reckless'. The fundamental difference between the *praefectus urbi* of Augustus and those of former times must be considered, and it is no coincidence that in his life of Augustus (*Div. Aug.* 37) Suetonius grouped this office under the *nova officia*, together with the *cura viarum*, *aquarum*, *operum publicorum* etc. Suetonius found some confirmation in Dio's rhetoric (LII, 21, 1),

It should be the prefect's duty, not to govern merely when the consuls are out of town, but in general to be at all times in charge of the affairs of the city, and to decide the cases which come to him from all other magistrates . . . and his jurisdiction should extend, not only to those who live in the city . . .

This raises the question of who, in fact, were Caesar's prefects. Under the year 47 BC Cassius Dio described an official who might be viewed as a kind of *praefectus urbi* (XLII, 30, 1). He reported that Antony – then the dictator's *magister equitum* – felt obliged to travel to Campania on account of the unrest that had broken out in the army, and appointed the dictator's uncle, L. Julius Caesar, a highly respected consular (consul 64 BC) as *poliarchos*, but he was too old to cope with the problem.

These moves did not break the law, for, in the absence of other magistrates with imperium, Antony was legally obliged to make this appointment, even if the scrupulous could point out that there was no precedent for the appointment of a *praefectus urbi*; but no one else was available to take the appointment, and the situation recalls that of the early Republic as described by Tacitus.

For the years 46 and 45 BC Cassius Dio also mentioned *praefecti urbi* (Dio XLIII, 28, 2). In this case they were appointed directly by Caesar, the dictator, to support Lepidus, the *magister equitum* (away in Spain). This time they are not *poliarchoi* but six to eight *polianomoi*. Another passage of Dio's is illuminating.

In addition to these measures carried out that year, two of the city prefects took charge of the finances, since no quaestor had been elected. For, just as on former occasions, so now in the absence of Caesar, the prefects managed all the affairs of the city, in conjunction with Lepidus as master of the horse. And although they were censured for employing lictors and the magisterial garb and chair precisely like the master of the horse, they got off by citing a certain law which allowed all those receiving any office from a dictator to make use of such trappings. The administration of the finances, after being diverted at this time for the reasons I have mentioned, was no longer invariably assigned to the quaestors, but was finally assigned to ex-praetors. Two of the city prefects then managed the public treasuries, and one of them celebrated the Ludi Apollinares at Caesar's cost. The plebeian aediles conducted the Ludi Megalenses in accordance with a decree. A certain prefect, appointed during the Feriae, himself chose a successor on the following day, and the latter a third; this had never happened before, nor did it happen again (Dio XLIII, 48, 1-4)

This passage completely agrees with the vague statement of Suetonius cited at the beginning, 'praefectos pro praetoribus constituerit'.

Thus, the prefects of the year 46-45 BC were appointed as aides to Lepidus (Broughton, *MRR* II, 313). But why were the other magistrates incapable of administering the affairs of the city? These prefects are totally different from those appointed by L. Julius Caesar in the emergency of 47 BC, and from Messala Corvinus appointed under Augustus to keep order in the city. Perhaps Cassius Dio wished to emphasize something unusual when he distinguished between *poliarchoi* and *polianomoi*, a striking, but unintelligible, differentiation. Vitucci unsuccessfully attempted to prove that, despite all, a gradual development of the *praefectura urbi* did take place from Caesar to Augustus. Cadoux, who preferred to leave the question open, took issue with Vitucci, '. . . his fault lies in not perceiving that the difficulties are insuperable' (p. 154). Cadoux thinks that it is simply impossible to prove that the prefecture of Augustus developed from Caesar's. The prefect of the year 47 BC was a temporary necessity, and did not violate any tradition. The prefects of 46-45 BC aroused sharp public criticism, and further efforts in this direction were abandoned. Augustus' prefect, on the other hand, was a new, independent phenomenon. Cadoux's sceptical explanation might suffice, for there is no need to look for a clear line of progress in every political development.

The fact remains that Dio expressly reported opposition to this office (XLIII, 48, 1-4), which was caused by the prefects' use of their lictors and *sellae*; although, he added, the prefects cited certain laws as the basis for their behaviour. In any case, it must be supposed that legalities were not the real reason for opposition. More fundamental factors were involved.

The senatorial aristocracy suspected that Caesar was planning to fill gradually all offices with his own men, and to destroy the traditional power-base that they had carefully constructed. Perhaps there is a connection between the appointment of the prefects and the information in the following passage of Suetonius (*Div. Jul.* 76, 3), 'He assigned the charge of the mint and of the public revenues to his own slaves, and gave the oversight and command of the three legions which he had left at Alexandria to a favourite of his called Rufio, son of one of his freedmen.' But, as in so many other situations, Caesar seemed to be far less perturbed than we often try to make him. He, too, understood that the appointment of prefects in Rome aroused opposition, and therefore they are not mentioned in his reorganization of the list of the officials that he made before departing on his Parthian campaign (Dio XLIII, 51, 1-5).

26 LEX CASSIA DE PLEBEIS IN PATRICIOS ADLEGENDIS (45 BC)[16]

'As for the nobles, to some of them he promised consulships and praetorships in the future, others he appeased with sundry other powers and honours' (Plut., *Caes.* 58, 1). Among the 'sundry other powers and honours' must be reckoned the promotion of plebeians to the patriciate. It is not clear whether the *Lex Cassia* was a law of the tribune Lucius Cassius Longinus, or a praetorian law (*lex*) of Caius Cassius Longinus; it cannot be assumed that the right to appoint patricians can be traced back to an old royal prerogative. *Cooptatio in patres* (e.g. Livy IV, 4, 7; Suet., *Tib.* 1) is also unlikely. It should be supposed that Caesar as Pontifex Maximus took care to fill up the ranks of the patricians which had been decimated by the civil wars. Many years later, the Emperor Claudius was able to cite this measure as a precedent: '. . . and even those selected to fill the void under the Cassian law . . . by the dictator Caesar . . . were exhausted' (Tac., *Ann.* XI, 25). Suetonius reported that 'he enrolled additional patricians' (*Div. Jul.* XLI, 1), and Dio added the word 'many' (XLIII, 47, 3). This action was conceived to embarrass all those who looked upon Caesar as a revolutionary dictator attempting to shake the traditional foundations of the Republic, but it does not necessarily support the statement that Caesar was the last of the patricians, and in every respect a conventional Roman senator.

These new patricians were probably well aware to whom they owed their power and position, and from then on were alert to Caesar's every nod. For small favours (e.g. Dio XLIII, 23, 6) they renounced their freedom, that aristocratic freedom whose fundamental principle was not to serve the just ruler, but not to serve any ruler at all (Cic., *de republica* II, 43). Thus the *Lex Cassia* is to be viewed as a measure to strengthen Caesar's position as sole ruler.

27 LEX ANTONIA DE CANDIDATIS (44 BC)?[17]

The popular assemblies in Rome, the *comitia tributa* and the *comitia centuriata*, were not exactly bulwarks of democracy but the view that they had some influence should not be brushed aside. In the critical years of the Late Republic they formed the chief arena for power struggles. Their significance is evidence that the *nobiles* could neither ignore the assemblies nor refuse to interest themselves in their *clientes* there. The Roman people never functioned as a single unified body, and it was precisely in the assemblies that the special relationship between patron and *clientela* was illustrated. For Caesar's period, however, there are no relevant sources, and nobody knows how magistrates were elected. Nor is the process by which an assembly ratified the laws, adequately depicted by a contemporary.

The accounts of Cassius Dio and Suetonius are unclear. Both leave room for all sorts of interpretations, which in turn often lead to diametrically opposed opinions among modern scholars. Many believe that Caesar received overriding authority in the popular assembly only after the battle of Munda, or even not until the beginning of 44 BC, and that by means of a 'binding *commendatio*' (Mommsen). Other scholars suppose that his influence derived solely from his *auctoritas* (Herzog), but L. R. Taylor's blunt statement cannot be refuted *in toto*, 'The arch-manipulator Caesar, while moving the rostra to a place which could accommodate great throngs at the *contiones*, and while continuing his plans for the great marble *saepta*, actually destroyed both: the legislature and the electoral *comitia*' (p. 113).

Actually, the popular assembly became gradually weaker by a process that began as early as 48 BC, which had already been pointed out by Stobbe in an article published in 1868. Most recently R. Frei-Stolba persuasively dealt with the problem in her investigations of the elections under the Roman Empire.

Some of the most important problems still remain. As early as 49 BC, Caesar, in his capacity of *dictator comitiorum habendorum causa*, presided over the elections, and not only had himself elected consul for 48 BC, but also saw to it that his own followers were elected to all the remaining magistracies. (Broughton, *MRR* II, 272.) Cassius Dio (XLI, 36, 2) made no bones about it: 'He . . . filled all the offices for the ensuing year', using the ambiguous verb *apedeikse*. It cannot be established how these elections were actually carried out. Did Caesar succeed in imposing his will through his *auctoritas*? Did he somehow silence the electors with the help of the army, or should *apedeikse* perhaps be translated by *nominavit*, i.e. he proposed the candidates, and his proposal in some sense signified a binding recommendation?

The passage in Cassius Dio referring to the elections of 48 BC is no less problematic. It stated (XLII, 20, 4), 'All the elections except those of the plebs now passed into his hands, and for this reason they were delayed till after his arrival and were held toward the close of the year.' An exact translation of the words *ep' auto egenonto* is difficult. We know that Caesar was in Egypt that year, and returned to Rome in September 47. Was it perhaps decided in his absence in 48 BC to wait for his return, and should the following passage of Cassius Dio (XLII, 51, 3) be read under the year 47 BC by reason of the decrees passed in 48 BC? 'Upon the senators he bestowed priesthoods and offices, some of them for the rest of that year and some for the next. Indeed in order to reward a larger number, he appointed ten praetors for the next year.' Further, the significance of *apodeiknumi* remains obscure: is a process based on a legal norm intended here, or one resulting from a *de facto* exercise of influence?

In his description of the honours bestowed on Caesar after the battle of Thapsus (46 BC), Cassius Dio reported that the Senate voted 'that he should have the appointment of the magistrates and whatever honours the people were previously accustomed to assign' (XLIII, 14, 5). It is possible that Dio was being more exact here, both when he used the word *demos* and not *plethos* for people, and when he referred only to patrician offices (as though the elections to the plebeian offices had already taken place as usual). Suetonius (*Div. Jul.* 76, 2) may perhaps be introduced as additional proof of such an assumption, 'holding no elections except for tribunes and plebeian aediles, and appointing praefects instead of praetors'. Perhaps Caesar believed that 'appointing prefects' was preferable to the appointment of curule magistrates without election.

In 45 BC, after the battle of Munda, a further step was taken, 'For they (sc. the Senate) offered him the magistracies, even those belonging to the Plebs' (Dio XLIII, 45, 2). Here, too, the terminology is obscure. Did Dio mean that Caesar was authorized to appoint even tribunes, or to make recommendations for their appointment, or is this perhaps a hint at a grant of *tribunicia potestas*? The question becomes even more complex, since Dio himself admitted that Caesar refused this honour (XLIII, 47, 1), 'The remaining magistrates except the consuls were nominally elected by the plebs (*plethos*) and the whole people (*demos*) in accordance with ancestral custom since Caesar would not accept the right of appointment of them.'

However, in preparing for his great campaign against Parthia, Caesar was obliged to consider the magistrates that remained in Rome. In this connection we have an unambiguous statement from Cassius Dio (XLIII, 51, 2),

In order that the city should neither be without officials in his absence, nor, again, by attempting to choose some on its own responsibility, fall into strife they decided that the magistrates should be appointed in advance for three years, this being the length of time they thought necessary for the campaign . . . Nominally (*logo*) Caesar chose half of them, having a certain legal right (*en nomo tini*) to do this, but in reality he chose the whole number.

Everything in this passage is doubtful, and the other sources nowhere mention an appointment of magistrates for three years in advance. Cicero knew only of appointments two years in advance (*ad Att.* XIV, 6, 2), Appian mentioned five (*BC* II, 128; 138), Suetonius an indefinite number (*Div. Jul.* 76, 3): 'with the same disregard of law and precedent he named magistrates for several years to come', and Hirtius gave similar indications in his letter to Cicero (*ad Att.* XV, 6, 2).

On the other hand, the degradation of the consulship by the appointment of *consules suffecti* doubtless met with opposition from various quarters. It is reported that when Fabius Maximus (45 BC), consul three months, entered the theatre, and the lictor, as was the custom, called for attention, everyone cried out that he was no consul (Suet., *Div. Jul.* 80; Cic., *ad.fam.* VII, 30). Certainly Caesar's influence on the choice of candidates was a powerful one, even if we are prepared to tone down Cicero's bitter words to the effect that Caesar pledged himself to arrange Dolabella's election, 'Dolabellam consulem esse iussurum' (Cic., *Phil.* II, 80, 82). Yet there is no proof that such influence was rooted in any kind of binding legislation. Neither is the passage in *Phil.* VII, 16 conclusive proof of the assumption of a *Lex Antonia de candidatis* introduced by Lucius Antonius, nor does the confused passage in Varro (*RR* III, 2, 1) support the existence of a *Lex Antonia*, as Stobbe supposed in the nineteenth century.

Therefore, we can only make do with the passage of Suetonius (*Div. Jul.* 41, 2), 'He shared the elections with the people on this basis: that except in the case of the consulship, half of the magistrates should be appointed by the people's choice, while the rest should be those whom he had previously nominated.' The brief formulaic note he sent to each of the tribes ran, 'Caesar the dictator to this or that tribe. I commend to you (*commendo vobis*) so and so, to hold their positions by your votes.' Suetonius did not mention any law, and the pertinent sentence in Eutropius (VI, 20), 'cum ergo et honores ex sua voluntate praestaret, qui a populo antea deferebantur' makes us none the wiser. It is useless to continue the discussion about whether Caesar had a right of appointment, and we should accept the view that the operation of Caesar's *commendatio* was based on his *auctoritas*. We know, too, that he paid scant attention to a *certus ordo magistratuum* and the *aetas legitima* of the candidates (Willems I, 590).

How matters actually proceeded at the elections we shall never discover. Nevertheless, we must cite the ingenious observation of R. Frei-Stolba 'that Caesar immediately read out the names of those candidates he had determined on, without in the meantime setting in motion the process of voting'. This view is based on a passage in Cicero's letters (*ad fam.* X, 32, 2), which described how Balbus conducted himself in Gades. Asinius Pollio confirmed that Balbus, in addition to his thefts and robberies, demanded the quattuorvirate for himself, settled the election of magistrates for a period of two years in two days, and took it upon himself to declare that the ones he approved of were elected, thereby boasting that he was following Caesar's example.

Thus, regarding the differences between Barbara Levick and Staveley, it may be observed: Caesar the dictator, in his capacity as magistrate conducting the elections, could deny *renuntiatio* to those candidates to whom he had given no *commendatio*; under these circumstances it was doubtful whether anyone would persist in his candidacy against Caesar's will (cf. Staveley, p. 262, n. 433).

The path has indeed been somewhat circuitous, yet it brings us back to the conclusion of L. R. Taylor (p. 130), which is confirmed in an almost contemporary source: Nicolaus Damascenus stated that Caesar perceptibly weakened the power of the people (*F.Hist.Gr.* 130, 20, 67).

The process of the decline of the popular assembly was a gradual one, and there is no question of its sudden disappearance (Cic., *Phil.* II, 82; Suet., *Div. Jul.* 80). The tendency was clear, however, and it is no coincidence that many years later Lucan called the popular assembly a fiction,

> *Fingit solemnis campus*
> *Et non admissae divinit suffragia plebis,*
> *Decantatque tribus et vana versat in urna*
> (Luc., *Phars.* V, 392, cf. App., *BC* IV, 93)

The interesting question still remains: to what degree were the Roman masses annoyed that the little power they still retained in the various popular assemblies was now taken from them? We do not have any evidence of such feeling, for there was no popular literature of protest. Yet a consideration of Augustus' conduct implies that control over the popular assembly could be preserved without completely sweeping aside its traditional form (Suet., *Div. Aug.* 56, 1), 'Whenever he (*sc.* Augustus) took part in the election of the magistrates, he went the round of the tribes with his candidates and appealed for them in the traditional manner.'

Caesar, however, had no patience for this; he was content to issue a written recommendation for election, and thus possibly incurred the animosity of many lesser citizens, especially those of the *clientelae* of nobles opposed to him. Probably most of the citizens were indifferent to the problem, yet it is certain that the senatorial aristocracy, accustomed to contending for power and influence in the popular assembly, had to stand by powerless at the loss of its influence over its *clientes* while 'a single man acquired more personal power from day to day to the detriment of the old Republic' (*Ep. ad Caes.* II, 6, 2).

If our analysis is correct, it becomes clear that little remained of Caesar's claim that 'free elections and the whole control of the republic be handed over to the senate and the Roman people' (libera comitia adque omnis res publica senatui populoque Romano permittatur *Bell. Civ.* I, 9).

CHAPTER FOUR

ECONOMIC AND SOCIAL MEASURES

28 SETTLEMENT OF THE QUESTION OF DEBTS (49–46 BC)[1]

Caesar explained the regulations of 49 BC on debts, 'He considered that this was the most suitable method at once of removing or diminishing the fear of that general repudiation of debts . . . and of maintaining the good faith of the debtors' (*Bell. Civ.* III, 1).

Was the problem of debts really so pressing as represented in the ancient literature? The answer is certainly yes. The burden of debt was most oppressive to those 'whose debts were greater than their possessions'. A Roman magistrate received no salary. His expenses in the campaigns for election to high office were enormous (presentation of games, entertainments for the people and bribes), and he could only hope to recoup them by governing a wealthy province after his term of office in the capital. He gambled on these expectations by borrowing enormous sums, usually at interest.

Velleius Paterculus mentioned the penurious Quintilius Varus, who went on to govern the rich province of Syria. At the end of his term Varus was rich and Syria poor (II, 117, 2). In the 60s Caesar himself was in debt to the tune of 25 million sesterces (Plut., *Caes.* 5, 4; Dio XXXVII, 8, 1-2), but he was fortunate enough to become consul and later proconsul: he was thus able to rob and plunder the Gauls, and pay back not only his own debts but those of his friends too. This is how he guaranteed the allegiance and service of ambitious young men and of politicians up to their ears in debt and unable to settle their obligations. The Roman law of credit was severe, and people unable to pay their debts on time became bankrupt (their possessions were compulsorily auctioned off). Catiline's slogan, 'abolition of debts', lured many young politicians to his side.

Thus the view developed that cancellation of debts (*tabulae novae*) was a particular catchword of indebted aristocrats, for the masses did not own any assets, had no credit, and therefore no debts (*CAH* IX, 491–94). A thorough examination of the sources proves, however, that it was not only indebted aristocrats that had an interest in the abolition of debts; there were also the small farmers, and working shopkeepers (*tabernarii*). Anyone wishing to open a *taberna*, pay rent for it, renew his stock from time to time, and perhaps even keep one or two slaves, required working capital and credit. In times of crisis all these people willingly supported any demagogue who promised cancellation of debts, and especially abolition of rent.

In 49 BC Rome was on the brink of such a crisis. Cicero feared above everything 'all the criminal and social outcasts . . . nearly all the younger generation; all the lowest city rabble . . . all the insolvent, who are more in number than I imagined' (*ad Att*. VII, 3, 5). The wealthy were panic-stricken that Caesar might seize private property (*ibid*. IX, 7, 4; X, 8, 2) and announce the general abolition of debts. The debtors took advantage of the situation and stopped paying. 'No one pays his debts', wrote Cicero in March 49 BC (*ad Att*. VIII, 7, 3; 10, 1) and repeatedly complained that money was disappearing from the market (*ibid*. VII, 18, 4; IX, 9, 9; X, 11, 2).

At that point Caesar was too busy to settle financial problems. After making himself master of Rome and Italy, he went to Spain. It was not until his return that he decided to remedy the credit squeeze and, once and for all, end the anxiety about a general abolition of debts, particularly, as it turned out that the lowering of the interest rate, carried out by the tribunes in his absence, was insufficient (Dio XLI, 37, 2). Radical measures were necessary.

Whether Caesar the dictator made use of a so-called (by Mommsen) *lex data*, or put through a *lex rogata* in the popular assembly, cannot be definitively established. But it is probable that he forced creditors to take not only land, and at its pre-war value, but also moveables, in payment for outstanding loans (App., *BC* II, 48). To avoid arbitrary action and profit-making, special arbitrators were appointed to value land and property at its pre-war price, and to settle possible disputes between the parties. Caesar thereby proved that he did not intend to make an arbitrary abolition of all debts and thus probably won the additional support of the moneylenders. Apart from this, as a matter of principle, he published an ordinance that would put money into circulation. 'Since also many were said to possess much wealth but to be concealing it all, he forbade anyone to possess more than sixty thousand sesterces in silver or gold . . . his object was . . . that those who were owing money should pay back a part of their debt to the lenders and the latter should lend to such as needed . . .' (Dio XLI, 38, 1-2).

The small borrowers were the main beneficiaries of this ordinance, as they were the first to be hit by the credit squeeze, and, in times of crisis, were unable to get credit from the moneylenders.

Suetonius also confirmed all these details, 'As to debts, he disappointed those who looked for their cancellation, which was often agitated, but finally decreed that the debtors should satisfy their creditors according to a valuation of their possessions at the price which they had paid for them before the civil war' (*Div. Jul.* 42, 2). But Suetonius added a rider, according to which Caesar deducted 'from the principal whatever interest had been paid in cash or pledged through bankers; an arrangement which wiped out about a fourth part of their indebtedness' (*loc. cit.*).

The question arises whether Caesar acted on the measures concerning interest as early as 49 BC. Mathias Gelzer said that he did, Eduard Meyer dated this measure to a later period, while M. W. Frederiksen was inclined to the year 48 BC.

It is difficult to answer this question. Suetonius cannot be relied on in matters of chronology. He admitted that he wrote 'not in chronological order, but by topics (*Div. Aug.* 9). When he reached the subject of debts, he put all the material he had collected in his 'file' into Chapter 42. Cassius Dio dated the abolition of all interest that had accrued since the outbreak of the civil war to the year 47 BC (XLII, 51, 1), and added a detail of the greatest significance: Caesar increased the value of possessions with which the debts were to be equated; hence the attractive attempt to connect Caesar's provisions concerning debts with a *Lex Julia de bonis cedendis*, and to date a *senatus consultum* on usufruct (Cic., *Top.* III, 17) to the year 46 BC (G. Crifò, p. 112).

There are no reasonable grounds for completely rejecting Cassius Dio's evidence. In 49 BC Caesar resigned the dictatorship, only eleven days after he had assumed it, and set off in pursuit of Pompey. But tempers in Rome did not cool. The slogans 'abolition of debts' and 'abolition of rent' were still written on the banners of those organized by Caelius in 48 BC and by Dolabella in 47 BC. Only after Caelius' removal and the suppression of Dolabella's revolt could Caesar become generous and give further relief to debtors. This is consistent with his nature and his policy.

This does not, however, solve the chronological difficulties. In describing an economic crisis under the Emperor Tiberius, Tacitus noted 'a law of the dictator Caesar, regulating the conditions of lending money and holding property within the boundaries of Italy' (*Ann.* VI, 16). G. Rotondi (p. 420) ascribed this law to 46 BC under the title *Lex Julia de modo credendi possidendique intra Italiam*. Its content may to some extent be inferred from a similar regulation issued under the Emperor Tiberius, which obliged moneylenders to put two-thirds of their property into land, while debtors had to pay a corresponding portion of their debts, and it should probably be assumed that this regulation went back to the *Lex Julia*.

In conclusion, Caesar's policy on debts was not especially revolutionary. It was designed to moderate the strict law of credit in force in Rome, to promote a certain measure of relief for both large and small debtors, to reassure citizens that the government was permanent and reliable, and that it was worthwhile returning to business as usual. When Balbus began to build houses, even Cicero was soothed (*ad. Att.* XII, 2, 2), and when it became clear that Caesar was not encouraging slaves to spy on their masters and betray them, the moneylenders calmed down.

Cancellation of the debts of a whole city, such as Dyrrachium's debts to C. Flavius (*ad. Brut.* I, 6, 4 (XII, 4)), was not a basis for a permanent policy and has only few parallels. Money circulated on the market again, and anxiety about cancellation of debts disappeared. This development was protracted, and in 46 BC Cicero still reminded Caesar in the *Pro Marcello* (23) 'revocanda fides . . .'. By and large there is now general agreement that Caesar's measures on debts are consonant with his generally moderate line of policy: his aim was to ally himself to the propertied classes in Rome, Italy and the provinces, without damaging his reputation with the masses. Cicero recognized this tendency earlier, and in 49 BC unambiguously wrote to his friend, 'Is it the tax collectors who have never been loyal and are now very friendly with Caesar? Or is it the financiers or the farmers whose chief desire is peace? Do you suppose they will fear a king when they never declined one so long as they were left in peace?' (ad Att. VII, 7, 5). For Caesar, it was worthwhile to win the allegiance of such influential classes and to reject the support of the few aristocrats who lived riotously, dissipated their money, and were deeply in debt. Thus it mattered little to him that he was deserted by Caelius, who in 48 BC wrote in bitterness, and therefore with exaggeration, that everyone except the money-lenders had supported Pompey (ad fam. VIII, 17, 2).

29 LAND DISTRIBUTION[2]

Land distribution was a social requirement of the first order. It was brought up in the days of Tiberius and Caius Gracchus, by Saturninus, the younger Livius Drusus, and less celebrated tribunes such as Rullus (in 63 BC) and Flavius (in 60 BC). Demands for it were made mainly by army veterans, most of whom had been recruited from the country districts of Italy, and on their return after long years of service expected to be rewarded with land. The city plebs had no special desire for land. These landless city-dwellers wanted to improve their lot among the comforts and bright lights of the city and were totally unenthusiastic about settling in remote and lonely areas. This attitude explains the failure of Rullus' proposal in 63 BC.

When Pompey returned to Italy from his successful campaign in the East (62 BC), the picture changed completely. The Senate's stubborn refusal to ratify grants of land to Pompey's soldiers, among other things, paved the way for the alliance between Pompey, Crassus and Julius Caesar that was to hasten the end of the Republic. The problem of Pompey's veterans was solved by a land distribution scheme promoted by Caesar during his consulship of 59 BC (Gruen, p. 402).

How did Caesar treat the land question after 49 BC? He took care of his soldiers first, and is alleged to have addressed them one day as follows, 'And when the wars are ended I will give lands to all, not as Sulla did by taking it from the present holders . . . but I will give the public land, and my own, and will purchase the necessary implements' (App., *BC* II, 94). It is risky to rely on Appian's rhetoric here, especially as in the same book (II, 140) he put into Brutus' mouth a speech that is quite different in tone: Caesar plundered and robbed Italy without mercy, as if she were enemy country, drove the inhabitants out of their houses and confiscated their possessions. It is thus advisable to rely on contemporary sources.

Unfortunately, we have no reliable evidence for a *Lex Julia agraria* during Caesar's dictatorship between 49 BC and 44 BC. Suetonius does mention veteran settlements 'e lege Julia' in Capua a few months before Caesar's murder (*Div. Jul.* 81, 1), but we cannot offer a convincing counter-argument to the view that the reference was to a *Lex Julia* of Caesar's consulship of 59 BC. Whether Cicero (*Phil.* V, 53) referred to a *Lex Julia* of 46 BC, as Eduard Meyer believed, remains equally questionable. That is why we have omitted a reference to a *Lex Julia agraria* in the title of this section. We have made do with the general title 'distribution of land', on the firm assumption that settlements of veterans were undertaken during the years between 49 BC and 44 BC.

We referred previously (pp. 66; 119 ff.) to the complicated law known as the *Lex Mamilia-Roscia-Peducaea-Alliena-Fabia* (MRPAF), which was thought to have originated in 109 BC. Later, it was credibly dated after 55 BC. Not long ago, in an excellent article, Hinrichs suggested dating the law to 49 BC, and thus connected it with the land distribution initiated by Caesar. Hinrichs did not accept Fabricius' view that the MRPAF constituted a law extending the great *Lex agraria* of the year 111 BC, or the usual theory, which dates the law to 55 BC. He explained 'constituere municipia, praefecturas, fora et conciliabula' as 'the restitution of already existing communities and their reorganization, and not the establishment and founding of new ones' (Broughton, *MRR* II, 21; cf. (Riccobono, *FIRA* I, 12), on which see Gabba, p. 101).

It is precisely the reconstruction of derelict communities that Caesar had in mind, as may be concluded also from Dio XLIII, 50, 3, 'This was a source of pride to him, as was also the fact that he had restored again Carthage and Corinth. To be sure, there were many other cities in and outside Italy which he had either rebuilt or founded anew; still other men had done as much. But in the case of Corinth and Carthage, more ancient, brilliant, and distinguished cities which had been laid in ruins, he had not only colonized them, in that he regarded them as colonies of the Romans, but also restored them in memory of their former inhabitants, in that he honoured them with their ancient names; for he bore no grudge, on account of the hostility of those peoples, towards places that had never harmed the Romans.'

Hinrichs suggested proceeding by identifying the five legislators to whom the MRPAF law is attributed. The identity of four can be established without difficulty, and they can all be connected with the year 49 BC: L. Roscius Fabatus, A. Allienus and Sex. Peducaeus were praetors in that year, while Q. Fabius Maximus, together with Q. Pedius, was legate in Spain in 48 BC, which leads to the logical assumption that he, too, was praetor in 49 BC. Thus, there remains only the question of Mamilius: reference, however, is not to him, but to Aemilius, in fact Marcus Aemilius Lepidus. Hence, the law which should be called the *Lex Aemilia-Roscia-Peducaea-Alliena-Fabia* was nothing more than Caesar's legal pledge of land in 49 BC.

At first glance Hinrichs' theory is persuasive, since the dating of the MRPAF to 55 BC is based on the gap in the list of known tribunes for that year. As seven names are missing, it was easy to suppose that they were Mamilius, Roscius, Peducaeus, Allienus and Fabius, the tribunes of 55 BC. In that case, why not suppose that the name Mamilius was a corruption for Aemilius? Hinrichs could see no reason for a land distribution in 55 BC because at that time Pompey and Caesar were busily recruiting troops and not discharging them. There was no reference to any land settlement at the conference of Luca, and not a single text relating to this conference mentioned the MRPAF.

And yet it is doubtful whether Hinrichs' theory should be accepted without question. The Sceptics could always argue that there is no trace of the MRPAF in contemporary sources. The only text comes from the *Corpus Scriptorum Gromaticorum* (*FIRA* I, 138–40), and no one will ever know why this law was never mentioned in connection with land distribution of 55 BC and 49 BC. Does it perhaps concern a law supplementary to another law? Brunt (p. 712) adduced a further reason for doubt: the fact is that in *Phil.* V, 53 there is an explicit reference to a *Lex Julia* and not a *Lex Aemilia*; surely Cicero would not have been mistaken in such a detail.

A further weighty argument against Hinrichs' view lies in its assumption that there were ten praetors in office in Rome as early as 49 BC, an impossible premise, since such a drastic constitutional change could not have been adopted in the stormy year 50 BC without arousing considerable opposition.

A further query: it must be assumed that Caesar did not personally initiate all the laws issued during his dictatorship, and that, after giving his approval, he allowed some of them to appear under the names of his followers (for instance, the *Lex Antonia*). But would the man who carried the *Lex Julia* in favour of Pompey's followers in 59 BC, and thereby earned their firm support, have permitted so important a law on land distribution to have been called after Aemilius Lepidus? The affair remains unexplained, and we can only state that Caesar's veterans did acquire land. And, even if we do not know the details of the statement 'lex agraria quam C. Caesar tulit' (*Dig.* XLVII, 21, 3, cf. *Lex col. Genet.* 79, Riccobono, *FIRA* I, 189), we glean from a letter of Cicero an echo of the problems that resulted. In 46 BC he wrote to his friend Papirius Paetus that Caesar's men were exploring and measuring out estates around Veii and Capena not far from Cicero's holdings in Tusculum (*ad fam.* IX, 17, 2), and alluded to arbitrary confiscations. In 45 BC, Cicero addressed Valerius Orca, one of Caesar's legates who was delegated to carry out the distribution of the plots promised to the soldiers (*ad fam.* XIII, 4). Cicero asked him to spare the people of Volaterrae in Etruria, and not to force them to give up their land. Doubtless the landowners asked Cicero to plead on their behalf, and he cited the precedent of 59 BC, the year of Caesar's consulship, when they were not disturbed.

In another letter (*ibid.* 5, 2), he interceded in favour of C. Curtius, who had been appointed to the Senate by Caesar, but whose estates were nonetheless to be divided among new settlers on Caesar's orders. Cicero asked that he be spared, since, if his land were taken away, he could not remain in the Senate because of his lowered census.

Estates in Gallia Citerior belonged to the Campanian city of Atella, and Cicero pleaded with C. Cluvius to leave them alone. He was indeed well aware that Cluvius did not have the authority to make such an important decision, but begged him to put the matter to Caesar, and promised him that if he was successful he would get all the credit (*ad fam.* XIII, 7). Cicero could rely on precedent here too: a similar request had been granted to Regium. In another letter Cicero intervened on behalf of the senator C. Albinius, pointing out to Rutilius (apparently a legate) that no one should oppose Caesar's express intention (*ad fam.* XIII, 8).

What can be learned from all these examples? First, that Caesar handed over the distribution of land to his legates (praetors by rank), and not to a special committee of the Senate.

Second, Caesar was careful not to offend the landowners. As he had been similarly cautious about debts, it may be said that he was well aware that a ruthlessly executed distribution of land and cancellation of debts could shatter the foundations of the Republic ('labefactant fundamenta rei publicae', Cic., *de off.* II, 78). He preferred to distribute public land from the little at his disposal, or land for which compensation had been paid or land confiscated from incorrigible Pompeians (Dio XLII, 51, 2). It is not quite clear from Cassius Dio XLIII, 47, 4 and Appian, *BC* II, 140 whether temple property was also sold for this purpose. Caesar was often in financial straits and, when there is reference in the sources to public auctions, it is not necessarily true that he organized them only to compensate his retired veterans. He needed money for other purposes too.

Third, it must be stressed that it was impossible to make such an extensive distribution without seizing some public and private property. There are references to this: the settlement in Capua a few months before Caesar's murder (Suet., *Div. Jul.* 81, 1) led to unrest, and several very ancient tombs were destroyed. Yet it is no exaggeration to say that Caesar's treatment of the matter of land distribution was distinguished for its extreme consideration for the rights of private property. If a landowner felt that he had been treated unfairly, he could still hope for relief, even after the publication of instructions for confiscation. Cicero's recommendations are reliable proof. It is known that Balbus permitted Lentulus' interests to be put forward even though he was a political enemy (*ad Att.* VIII, 15 a; IX, 7 b, 2).

Caesar's distribution of the land is described in two passages, one from Suetonius and one from Appian, 'He also assigned them (the veterans) lands, but not side by side, to avoid dispossessing any of the former owners' (*Div. Jul* 38, 1), and from the same (dubious) speech of Caesar in Appian (*BC* II, 94) it emerged that he would not allow the veterans to settle in the immediate neighbourhood of the old landowners, to avoid 'hereditary enmity' between them. There are indications that removal of boundary stones by force or deception was severely punished, although this measure was not always strictly observed (Riccobono, *FIRA* I, 12; *Dig.* XXI, 3; Dion. Hal. II, 74, 5; Hor., *Carm.* II, 18, 23-6).

There is a further supposition: Caesar avoided settling his veterans in concentrated groups to prevent them from terrorizing their neighbours, and, when opportunity offered, from plotting revolts (as happened later, Tac., *Ann.* IV, 27). We learn, too, of the new settlers' other difficulties, especially with rights of access (Sen., *Benef.* V, 24). Perhaps this is why he preferred to scatter them in small groups throughout Italy (Dio XLII, 54, 1).

Thus we arrive at the most complex problem – Caesar's intentions. Regarding the land distribution of 59 BC (the year of his consulship), Cassius Dio (XXXVIII, 1, 1) wrote, 'The swollen population of the city, which was chiefly responsible for the frequent rioting, would thus be turned towards labour and agriculture; and the greater part of Italy, now desolate, would be colonized afresh, so that not only those who had toiled in the campaigns, but all the rest as well, would have ample subsistence' (cf. also App., *BC* II, 10; Suet., *Div. Jul.* 20, 3).

Was this the aim Caesar also had in mind between 49 BC and 44 BC? The inference should be permitted as the circumstances were basically similar to those in 59 BC. However, in an age of power politics such a 'naïve' intention may not be acceptable. Another explanation seems more attractive; Caesar's true reason was to strengthen his *clientela* in rural areas, and this was assured through the *beneficium* of land distribution.

Yet, from a quantitative point of view, the settlement was not particularly widespread. In order to preserve existing rights and possessions, Caesar was satisfied with viritane assignments (Suet., *Div. Jul.* 38, 1), and then only three colonies in Italy, Capua, Casilinum and Calatia, where the seventh and eighth legions were settled (the sixth and tenth were settled at Arelate and Narbo (Nic. Dam. 31; Cic., *Phil.* II, 102). This indicates that Caesar's aim to spread his veterans throughout the whole of Italy was not always viable, because it is always easier to colonize areas where there are no complicated legal problems to solve first. Actually, the number of settlers in 47 BC, and 46 BC was not very large. Caesar was not in a position to relinquish the services of too many soldiers, for he still had much to do on the battlefield. In fact, land distribution to Caesar's veterans did not begin in earnest until 41-40 BC. Brunt does not believe that Caesar's distribution of land reveals a system of social privilege. Perhaps he had such a purpose in mind, but at the time of a brutal civil war it was difficult to carry through with any degree of consistency. It was also possible that some of Caesar's adherents feathered their own nests; in Brunt's words, 'one set of great proprietors were replaced by another' (p. 322). Dio's statement (XLII, 51, 2) was probably true that after confiscations from the Pompeians there was plenty of land on the market. Antony grasped the opportunity to improve his own financial position (Cic., Phil. XIII, 10), and he was certainly not the only one.

Yet a policy is clearly recognizable: above all, Caesar wanted to avoid the rapid break-up of any of the new settlements once they were firmly established. Therefore, he avoided the haphazard settlement of troops after outbreaks of mutiny; rather, his first selections were those who had chosen to be farmers and would, hopefully, remain settled on their land (Dio XLII, 55, 1). To prevent them from converting their land into money and then streaming to Rome in rootless hordes (as happened before the Catilinarian conspiracy), Caesar forbade the settlers to sell their land for a period of twenty years. This regulation was repealed by Brutus and Cassius only after his murder (App., BC III, 2, 5).

Perhaps Caesar thought of colonization on a larger scale, but there was not enough land in Italy to carry out such a policy. To gain extra land for distribution and cultivation, Caesar planned to drain marshes (Suet., Div. Jul. 44, 2; Dio XLIV, 5, 1), but these were long-term projects. Meantime, he found another solution: the foundation of overseas colonies, which he carried out with great energy.

30 COLONIZATION AND POLICY WITH REGARD TO CITIZENSHIP (AFTER 46 BC)[3]

The settlement of Roman citizens in overseas territories was nothing new in itself – Caius Gracchus had made use of this device some eighty years earlier. But the scale of Caesar's activity is so impressive that even Sceptics and Minimalists, with raised eyebrows, ask yet again whether an action of this kind could have been purely coincidental, without a political purpose behind it. The section heading has been chosen because we consider F. Vittinghoff's book, *Kolonisation und Bürgerrechtspolitik*, to be a fundamental contribution to the many problems associated with this subject. Even if there are scholars who dismiss the idea that a master plan formed the basis of all Caesar's actions in this sphere or who in any case did not accept Vittinghoff's method of identifying the colonies, at least they must admit that this is the most stimulating and challenging book written on the subject in the last fifty years.

Let us begin with two statements by Brunt, who has devoted particular attention to this subject:

(a) Caesar's efforts in the area of colonization did not begin before 46 BC, and only few of the planned settlements were set up in his lifetime (p. 101; 255); Narbo, Curubis and Sinope are the only colonies that can be authenticated as having been founded during his life;

(b) it is extremely difficult to establish which colonies and *municipia* owed their status to Caesar and which to his adoptive son (p. 234); epigraphic and literary sources on the founding of colonies rarely refer to their dates, and the name Julia is not conclusive proof that a colony was really founded by Julius Caesar.

Before launching into actual argument, let us take Brunt's cautious view as an indisputable starting point, for neither Vittinghoff's list of thirty-two colonies and twenty-seven *municipia* (p. 148), nor H. Bögli's, with thirty-one *municipia*, is certain.

Brunt stated that of all the so-called Caesarian sites overseas eighteen at most can certainly be said to have been Caesarian (p. 236):

1 Narbo (new foundation); 2 Arelate; 3 Baeterrae; 4 Lugdunum; 5 Raurica; 6 Hispalis; 7 Urso; 8 Celsa; 9 Carthage; 10 Curubis; 11 Clupea; 12 Corinth; 13 Buthrotum; 14 Cassandrea; 15 Dium; 16 Lampsacus; 17 Heraclea and 18 Sinope.

But subsequently Brunt was led into demographic speculations: he was prepared to accept Suetonius' statement (*Div. Jul.* 42, 1) that Caesar settled 80,000 Roman citizens in overseas colonies. In Brunt's view, 10,000 of them were veterans settled in Italian colonies, leaving 70,000 (mainly resourceless people) for the overseas colonies. If 2–3,000 inhabitants are allowed for each colony, then the total of eighteen colonies established as certain is obviously too small. Thus Brunt arrived at 'colonies which may be Caesarian', of which there are sixteen: 1 Ucubi; 2 Tarraco; 3 Carpis; 4 Neapolis; 5 Hippo; 6 Thabraca; 7 Uthina; 8 Turris Libisonis; 9 Dyrrachium; 10 Pella; 11 Philippi; 12 Dyme; 13 Byllis; 14 Cnossus; 15 Apamea and 16 Parium.

Alföldi, on the other hand, counted Salona as a double foundation (that is, Caesarian and Augustan), and Narona and Epidaurum as purely Caesarian.

It may be assumed that the source material on colonization and policy with regard to the citizenship – apart from discussion about Caesar's efforts to be king or god or both at the same time – supplied Minimalists as well as Revisionists and Sceptics with their major arguments. First, let us take the easy path for once, and begin with what we know from the *Lex Coloniae Genetivae Juliae Ursonensis* (*ILS* 6087 = Riccobono, *FIRA*, I, 21). From the inscription it is learned that the colony was founded on the dictator's decree. Its name recalls Venus Genetrix, whom Caesar considered the ancestress of his *gens*. A statue of Venus was erected at Urso next to those of Jupiter, Juno and Minerva, and together they embodied the divinities of the colony. According to its constitution, freedmen could also serve as magistrates. Freedmen as well as Roman *proletarii* settled in Urso – that much is clear.

Yet, a regulation appears (in lines 130–31 of the inscription), expressly prohibiting the choice of a Roman senator or senator's son as patronus, except by secret ballot of all the *decuriones* and then by a three–quarters majority. Perhaps when making this provision Caesar had in mind Sextus Pompey, with his numerous Spanish connections. It may certainly be assumed that there was a similar clause in the constitutions of the other colonies – and a regulation of this kind would certainly not have been published without a precedent.

Ever since the days of the Gracchi senators had feared the formation of private *clientelae* by their political opponents. Opposition to the resettlement of Junonia by Caius Gracchus was well founded, and when Saturninus, who had planned to set up colonies in Africa, Sicily, Achaea and Macedonia, had been killed, there was a general sigh of relief. Settlers from the lower classes of society were inclined to become the clients of a powerful man (the founder of the colony, for instance), and it was no coincidence that it was Caesar and Augustus particularly who set up numerous overseas colonies where they could build up their political strength without opposition. Meanwhile, reports of Caesar's generous distribution of the rights of citizenship spread rapidly, but here, too, his good intentions were abused. His favourites sold citizenship for money. When this news reached the dictator, he had the tablets that had been erected with the names of the new citizens removed for revision (Cic., *ad fam.* XIII, 36, 1). In this instance, too, his intentions will never be ascertained. Did he act from motives of principle and integrity, and because he was concerned that citizenship should be conferred only on those whose claims had been confirmed by the central administration? Or did he act to prevent his favourites, who were selling the *beneficium*, from acquiring power that might endanger his sole rule by means of new citizens?

Brunt (p. 256) also saw in Julius Caesar's conduct here a continuation of C. Gracchus' policies, but mainly discussed the dictator's social and economic attitudes.

In this respect Caesar's colonies were much more than *propugnacula imperii*. Caesar developed a policy of controlled emigration abroad, while at the same time forbidding all those capable of carrying arms from leaving Italy. Freedmen were not only settled in Urso, but also in Curubis, Carthage, Clupea and Corinth. However, members of a single stratum of society were never concentrated in one place. Caesar attempted to mix slaves and freedmen, who were for the most part merchants and artisans, the city proletariat and discharged soldiers, and thus rid himself of 80,000 'superfluous persons'. Brunt made no attempt, from the known source material, to arrive at any far-reaching conclusions about Caesar's future intentions regarding colonization.

Vittinghoff, on the other hand, was unwilling to concur with such a sober attitude. In his view, Caesar's measures pursued his social, economic and political aims (p. 57). He agreed that Caesar attempted to rid the city of superfluous elements, and that Caesar had in mind the same objective as Plutarch ascribed to Pericles (11, 5): 'All this he did by way of lightening the city of its mob of lazy and idle busybodies, rectifying the embarrassments of the poorer people . . .'

Bögli went into even more detail. He accepted Colonia Julia Felix Sinope, Colonia Heraclea Pontica, Colonia Julia

Concordia Apamea and Colonia Julia Genetiva Lampsacus as Caesarian colonies, and maintained (p. 7) that it was no accident that they formed a line from the Propontis along the southern coast of the Black Sea. They were located there to serve as supply bases for the projected Parthian war.

In the colonization of the East Bögli detected economic interests; in the colonization of Hispania Ulterior and Narbonensis an effort to Latinize that area. A tendency to place sentry posts at strategically important points and development as an end in itself are detectable everywhere. Corinth, for instance, must have been extended to enlarge its potential as a trading centre, and the city's position was further improved with the opening of the isthmus (Suet., *Div. Jul.* 4, 3; Plin., *NH* IV, 4, 10).

Vittinghoff, however, was not satisfied with all these historical reconstructions. He wanted more, and attempted to look at the whole subject against a broader background; the ponderous machinery of the Senate, the operation of cliques among the families of the *nobiles*, the mistrust of any success, the corruption, the power wielded in the streets and the exploitation of the subject peoples. After centuries of conquest, the Republic was incapable of settling pressing problems in the Empire; the governing class failed to give the *imperium* a new political form, and the size of the Empire eventually demanded a monarchical system of government. Vittinghoff, of course, agreed that Caesar's colonization policy reinforced his position as ruler, but at the same time he wanted to provide a long-range policy for the Empire. The Rhine was supposed to be the boundary, and Caesar envisaged greater Italy beyond the Po as citizen territory. That is why he founded *municipia*[4] and granted citizenship very cautiously. His policy on citizenship was not designed to destroy its personal value or cheapen the privilege of being a citizen of the ruling people, but to extend and fortify the circle of Roman citizens, and, in particular, introduce untapped sources of strength to the Roman state.

Vittinghoff emphasized that not only were all of Caesar's measures designed according to a logical and consistent plan, but that behind them all stood a single man. Like other distinguished scholars of the nineteenth century, Vittinghoff judged personalities by their vision. Thucydides showed that this must be an essential trait of every great man of history, and the idea was further developed by Hegel, Carlisle, and especially by Plechanow. Herzog, who was usually much more reserved than Mommsen, and who was particularly concerned with the difficulties that a change of constitution brings, wrote, 'Far ahead of his time, Caesar had already endeavoured to produce internal unity within the Roman Empire as rapidly as possible, more rapidly, in fact, than his successors believed or found possible, even when they followed the same path.'

A theoretical discussion on the problem of personality in history would be inappropriate here and, in any case, those who deny that Caesar had the statesmanlike insight of the first Emperor in Rome will never be convinced by Vittinghoff. Therefore, let us return to the facts: what can be inferred from the settlement of 80,000 Roman citizens in overseas colonies? A passage in Dionysius (IV, 24, 8), may reflect the prevailing atmosphere: 'discreditable characters, the foul and corrupt herd should be expelled from the city.' We know who gained from it. Were there also victims?

There are no doubts about Caesar's policy towards the cities of the Roman Empire. He increased the *territoria* belonging to the cities that had supported him, remitted their taxes, and even generously distributed citizenship among their inhabitants (see pp. 66 ff.). He reduced the *territoria* of cities that had opposed him, imposed heavy taxes and fines on them, and frequently planted settlements on their land (Dio XLII, 49, 2; XLIII, 39, 4). And, just as he avoided infringing on the rights of Roman citizens in Italy, he did the same in the provinces. The affair of Buthrotum in Epirus indicates his methods: he wished to punish the city because its taxes had fallen into arrears, and the most effective way to show his iron hand was to establish a new colony there. But as it happened, Atticus owned extensive property in the neighbourhood, and so influential a millionaire was a force to be reckoned with. Atticus prevailed upon all his friends and acquaintances in Rome (Cicero among them, of course) to intervene and ask Caesar to halt the foundation of the colony. Atticus pledged himself to pay all the city's fiscal debts, and Caesar agreed, but took the precaution of concealing from the prospective settlers the fact that he had given in to the 'moneybag', so as not to spoil his image as a popular ruler. He waited until the settlers set out from Rome on their journey overseas, and then put other territories for settlement at their disposal (Cic., *ad Att.* XVI, 16a, 4-5). This behaviour is consistently repeated in all his measures, and a clear intention begins to emerge.

Could all this activity be accidental? Of course Caesar's words, 'the tranquillity of Italy, the peace of the provinces, the safety of the empire' (*Bell. Civ.* III, 57, 4) can be dismissed as pure rhetoric, but his colonization policy has a certain significance. Even if the details were not worked out in advance, and even if Caesar acted intuitively and not according to sober political considerations, he did achieve notable results. He solved the problem of land scarcity in Italy without running up against the great landed proprietors. He removed unruly elements from the city, thereby reducing the over-population in Rome, and, at the same time, made it possible to attract more acceptable elements to the city (A. Momigliano, *JRS* XXXI, 1941, p. 162). He granted citizenship to all practising doctors in Rome and to teachers of the liberal arts (*grammatici*, rhetoricians, and philosophers, Suet., *Div. Jul.* 42).

We do not know whether Caesar had a specific plan for romanizing the Empire and balancing the differences between Italians and provincials, although there are scholars who are convinced of this (Felix Stähelin). In any case, it became a reality in the course of time.

Gelzer believed that extensive colonizing did, in fact, deal the *coup de grâce* to Rome's republican structure, and was a significant aspect of the monarchical policy that made the popular assembly in Rome a mere fiction (p. 276). This point was also grasped by the writer of the celebrated letter to Caesar, who attempted to make it plain that the spread of citizenship threw the *nobilitas* into a state of panic, and, because so many depended on the favour of a single individual, it necessarily changed the Republic into an empire (*Ep. ad Caesarem* 6, 1): 'regnum denique ex libera civitate futurum ubi unius munere multitudo ingens in civitatem pervenerit'.

In this instance we must, up to a point, agree with Vittinghoff, 'Like the great forerunners of history, Caesar, too, straddles the ages' (p. 49). With him, an epoch both begins and ends. 'Nothing was finished with his death, but, quick as a flash, a new order sprang into being' (p. 95).

Obviously, Caesar did not invent the policy of colonization, and he was not the first to begin the process of granting citizenship, but in his case quantity evolved into quality, a fact reflected by the third Cyrenean edict, a reference I owe to Professor Fergus Millar (Riccobono, *FIRA*, I, 408).

31 LEX JULIA DE MERCEDIBUS HABITATIONUM ANNUIS (46 BC)[5]

'He also remitted a year's rent in Rome to tenants who paid 2,000 sesterces or less, and in Italy up to 500 sesterces' (Suet., *Div. Jul.* 38, 2). The scarcity of accommodation in Rome and the unrest organized by Caelius and Dolabella in 48 BC and 47 BC have already been described (pp. 79; 136). Even Caesar agreed that in 48 BC Caelius won great favour with the masses when he suggested that rents be abolished for a whole year (Caes., *Bell. Civ.* III, 21), and that when no solution to the problem was found, Dolabella promoted violent uprisings in 47 BC, to Cicero's shame and consternation (*ad Att.* XI, 12, 4; 14, 2). Exact details are lacking, and even if it might perhaps be concluded from Suetonius that Caesar laid down maximum limits for rent, Cassius Dio's evidence appeared to contradict him (XLII, 51, 1): Caesar remitted a whole year's rent to all who paid an annual rent of 2,000 sesterces. This was not a permanent provision but an attempt to obtain cheap accommodation for poor tenants. Cicero, as a householder, was angry even about this moderate measure, and reproached Caesar for making it possible for tenants to live gratuitously in houses that they did not own (*de off.* II, 83). But, in fact, Caesar was extremely moderate. He supported the needy, who, despite their troubles, did not want to leave the bustle of the city though, at the same time, he was cautious about taking any action that would be detrimental to householders.

This device is in keeping with Caesar's main political line. For that reason Cassius Dio's version is to be preferred to that of Suetonius, especially as it also finds confirmation in *CIL* XIV, Suppl. 4531.

32 PROMOTION OF INCREASE IN THE BIRTH-RATE (46 BC)[6]

The Elder Pliny claimed that there were 1,192,000 victims of Caesar's wars. So precise a number gives rise to doubt, but clearly many people, including numerous Romans, lost their lives. Cassius Dio (XLIII, 25, 2) also spoke of a serious reduction in population in 46 BC, which was equally reflected in the census count, at which Caesar was present as though he, too, were censor.

Julius Caesar guaranteed special rewards for families with a large number of children (Dio, *loc. cit.*); in Cicero's opinion the encouragement of an increase in the birth-rate was an essential measure to restore the Republic, which had been ravaged through protracted wars (Cic., *Pro Marcello* 23).

A welfare policy in the modern sense was foreign to Roman ideas. Corn distributions were made not only to hardship cases, but to all Roman citizens, rich and poor. Only in the days of 'enlightened' emperors, Nerva and Trajan, was special consideration given to the needy, and it is precisely for this reason that Caesar's attitude needs emphasizing. In the agrarian law of 59 BC (the year of Caesar's consulship), special attention was paid to families with numerous children and to impoverished tenants in the law on rent. Chance? Perhaps, but worth mentioning. It might be argued that Caesar merely provided for 'cannon fodder'; hence the promotion of an increase in the birth-rate. Yet that is not a convincing argument, for Pompey also had the same interest in maintaining a large army but it never occurred to him to take steps to increase the birth-rate.

There was already an awareness of the problem in the time of Lucilius (678M = 644W), and in 131 BC the censor Q. Metellus proposed that every unmarried man be obliged to take a wife and produce children (Livy, *Per.* LIX). His speech is preserved in Gellius I, 6, and was the basis of Augustus' proposals about marriage and an increase in the birth-rate (Suet., *Div. Aug.* 89, 2). If Caesar did put forward similar suggestions, he had no more success than his predecessors or successors.

33 LEX JULIA DE PORTORIIS MERCIUM PEREGRINARUM (46 BC)[7]

'He imposed duties on foreign wares' (Suet., *Div. Jul.* 43, 1), but no more is known about this matter. There are historians who believe that this regulation was part of the *leges censoriae*. This is possible. *Lex* is sometimes synonymous with the contract concluded by the authorities with a contractor (*leges contractus*), where the magistrate always stated his conditions in advance (Cic., *Verr.* II, 1, 143; III, 16).

These *leges contractus* constituted standard business practice, and only possible variations from the common form merit particular attention in the *leges censoriae* (*RE* XII, 2, 2317).

Whether this particular *Lex Julia* formed part of the *leges censoriae* cannot be established. It can, however, be assumed that Caesar reintroduced the *portoria* that had been abolished some fifteen years earlier by a *Lex Caecilia* (Dio XXXVII, 51, 3; Cic., *ad Att.* II, 16, 1).

The reason why Caesar wanted to reintroduce the customs dues remains obscure. Carcopino's view (*César* p. 960), that Caesar wanted to introduce a protectionist policy to shield Italian goods against the influx of foreign imports, was convincingly demolished by de Laet (p. 61). So it may only be assumed that a supplement to the *leges sumptuariae* was somehow involved, the purpose of which was to restrict extravagant modes of life in Italy or, at the very least, restrict the import of luxury articles.

Admittedly, there is no proof for this interpretation. Suetonius' words are too general and too ambiguous. We do not know whether a *portorium maritimum* or a *portorium terrestre* is in question (cf. *CIL* I, 204, l. 31). There is no indication of a date for this law (if it may be considered as such at all) or of the circumstances of its introduction. We only know that Caesar's exchequer was perpetually empty, and that any additional levy of tax was acceptable. Only the extremely rich would possibly have been incensed about such a law; the *publicani* would certainly have called it a blessing, while the masses would probably not have been affected at all. This attitude to the various social classes was clearly perceptible throughout Caesar's whole political career (Dio XXXVIII, 7, 4; Cic., *Pro Planc.* 35 with *Schol. Bob.* Stangl 159).

34 LEX JULIA DE RE PECUARIA? (46 BC)

'He made a law ('sanxit') . . . that those who made a business of grazing should have among their herdsmen at least one-third who were men of free birth' (Suet., *Div. Jul.* 42, 1). There is a similar provision in the *Lex Licinia-Sextia* (App., *BC* I, 8), traditionally ascribed to 367 BC, although recently there has been a tendency to redate it to the pre-Graccian era (second century BC).

It was the task of these free workers to superintend the slaves and report what was going on amongst them. Whether this was also Caesar's intention in making this provision cannot be ascertained. It is generally debatable whether a law, in the true sense of the word, is involved here, but the question is important for those who are interested in the role of free labour and slave labour in the Roman economy. Yet source material is lacking, and we must be very careful not to make unsound conjectures.

Caesar saw a potential danger in the large number of slaves employed as herdsmen. It was these same slave herdsmen of southern Italy who had played such a significant role in the unrest fomented by Caelius and Milo the previous year as attested by contemporary sources (Caes., *Bell. Civ.* I, 24, 2; III, 21, 4). It could be said that the free citizens who worked in the fields were not exactly peaceful elements of society – they took part in almost all of the slave uprisings, including that of Spartacus. Likewise, slaves were not the only segment of society who tended toward crime (Cic., *Brut.* 85). On the other hand, the herdsmen were armed to defend themselves against wild beasts (Varro, *RR* II, 10), and seemed to be a warlike, and therefore dangerous, group. An extant fragment of Cicero's speech *In toga candida* (Asc. 87, Clark) reported that the vendor of a property retained his herdsmen so that he could recruit them for an armed uprising at any time ('Alter pecore omni vendito et saltibus prope addictis pastores retinet, ex quibus ait se cum velit subito fugitivorum bellum exitaturum').

Even if Caesar passed a *lex de re pecuaria* or made an ordinance on this occasion, it is doubtful whether it actually came into effect. Varro, writing on the subject ten years later, adduced the fact that the *pastores* were slaves (*RR* II, 10). Even under the Principate we hear of such slave revolts (Tac., *Ann.* IV, 27; XII, 65), and as late as 29 BC a consul was despatched 'ad servos torquendos' (*ILS* 961). Therefore, it is probable that this social problem, which posed questions of security, was likely to attract Caesar's attention. But whether he was interested in the relationship between the free and the slave herdsmen is indeed a difficult question. Did he believe that the employment of slaves could endanger free workers? Doubtless free men and slaves worked on the *latifundia* side by side. Cato (*RR* 5, 4 and 13), Varro (I, 17, 2) and Columella (I, 7) talked about *operarii*, *mercenarii* and *politores* in addition to slaves, and even Seneca mentioned free-born shepherds (*Ep.* 47, 10). Yet the employment of slaves as herdsmen was probably more usual than the appointment of an *operarius*, who was hired merely as a *saisonnier* (Frank, *ESAR* I, 384-85).

Even Chester G. Starr,[8] who underestimated the value of slave labour to the Roman economy, allowed that the number of slaves employed in breeding cattle and sheep was considerable, even more than that of free men. Did Caesar wish to alter the proportions between free and slave labour?

35 LEX JULIA SUMPTUARIA (46 BC)

In his capacity of *praefectus moribus* Caesar restricted the expenditures of the wealthy, which had reached prodigious proportions. He took draconian measures to curb their desire to squander (Dio XLIII, 25 2). However, Mommsen was right in questioning that Caesar was *praefectus morum* (*Staatsrecht* II, p. 685). When Cicero spoke of Caesar as 'noster hic praefectus moribus' (*ad fam.* IX, 15, 5; 26, 4; *ad Att.* XII, 7, 1), he should not be taken too seriously. He was merely having a joke at Caesar's expense, just as he made fun of Pompey in referring to him as 'ille Hierosolymitanus' and, on another occasion, 'Sampsiceramus'. Nevertheless, Caesar did pass *leges sumptuariae*, and Cicero said that even when he himself had guests he spent far less on his dinners than the law allowed (*ad fam.* IX, 26, 4). Suetonius went further and described Caesar's interference in people's personal affairs,

He annulled the marriage of an ex-praetor, who had married a woman the very day after her divorce, although there was no suspicion of adultery . . . He denied the use of litters and the wearing of scarlet robes or pearls to all except those of a designated position and age, and on set days. In particular he enforced the law against extravagance, setting watchmen in various parts of the market, to seize and bring to him dainties which were exposed for sale in violation of the law; and sometimes he sent his lictors and soldiers to take from a dining room any articles which had escaped the vigilance of his watchmen even after they had been served (*Div. Jul.* 43)

Here, too, Caesar was no innovator. The dispute concerning the *leges sumptuariae* during the time of Cato the Elder[9] (early second century BC) comes to mind, as does a letter, probably of 57 BC, in which Cicero frivolously enumerated the list of vegetables banned on account of Aemilius' law of 115 BC (*ad fam.* VII, 26, 2). Further, *leges sumptuariae* were not restricted to the luxuries of the table, but were also concerned with other subjects. It is known from a contemporary source that the law reduced extravagance in the construction of buildings, and taxed the use of columns and sumptuous funerary monuments (Cic., *ad Att.* XIII, 6, 1; cf. XII, 35, 4; 36, 1). A further reliable notice from Jerome, *Chron.* 46, mentioned the use of sedan chairs, and jewellery such as pearls and shells, especially in the case of unmarried or childless women.

None of these laws were particularly strongly enforced. The Emperor Tiberius, wise from bitter experience, said, 'It is better . . . to leave vigorous and full-blown vices alone, rather than force matters to an issue which might only inform the world with what abuses we were powerless to cope' (Tac., *Ann.* III, 53). Caesar himself was compelled to change the law and modify the passage on extravagance in private building (Cic., *ad Att.* XIII, 6) when he realized that no one took any notice of it (*loc. cit.* XIII, 7, 1).

As always it is difficult to establish what Caesar had in mind when he advocated this legislation, yet one cannot follow Eduard Meyer's view (p. 422) that it was of an entirely aristocratic character, and that the unattainable pattern Caesar strove to emulate was the Sparta of the Lycurgus legend.

Nothing could be further from Caesar's mind than the Sparta of Lycurgus. Caesar was no model of frugality – he was a spendthrift – and it is doubtful that moral considerations prompted him to advocate this legislation. His policy was not to elevate the upper classes, as Meyer believed, but rather the reverse. He denied others what he allowed himself, and feared that the showy banquets in the houses of influential senators could be politically hazardous. He had no objection to senators meeting and dining with their friends in private. But enormous parties for large groups indicated an intention to curry favour with masses of people, and this was precisely what Caesar tried to avoid. In *Comm. Pet.* 44 we read, 'see that banquets are celebrated both by yourself and your friends (*amicis*) and in each tribe (*tributim*)' and in *Pro Mur.* 72, 'stands were erected for whole tribes (*tributim*) and crowds were invited to feasts (*ad prandium*)'.

After Caesar's death, when pseudo-Marius (Amatius) wished to smooth his path to power he held a fiesta in his gardens which he opened to the public. Antony interpreted the charade correctly, and destroyed him without a qualm, only one example of many. The senatorial aristocracy, recognizing Caesar's intentions, contemptuously disregarded the law. It would be interesting though to know what Cicero meant by the *libidines* he asked Caesar to curb (*Pro Marcello* 23). Could he have had in mind the licentiousness depicted in his speech against Piso (*In. Pis.* 67)?

36 LEX JULIA FRUMENTARIA (46 BC)[10]

Appian (*BC* II, 48) vaguely mentioned a corn distribution to the hungry population, which took place in 49 BC, immediately after Caesar's entry into Rome. There is a more detailed report on the year 46 BC,

> He made the enumeration of the people neither in the usual manner or place, but from street to street aided by the owners of blocks of houses, and reduced the number of those who received grain at public expense from three hundred and twenty thousand to one hundred and fifty thousand. And to prevent the calling of additional meetings at any future time for purposes of enrolment, he provided that the places of such as died should be filled each year by the praetors from those who were not on the list (Suet., *Div. Jul.* 41, 3)

To interpret this passage properly one must go back to 58 BC when Clodius had first introduced distribution of free corn to the people of Rome. Subsequently the number of recipients grew so large that the distribution became a heavy burden on the exchequer. Many people freed their slaves, presenting the state treasury with the bill for their keep, and the number of illegal recipients of the free corn also continually increased (Dio XLIII, 21, 4; cf. XXXIX, 24, 1; Dion. Hal. IV, 24, 5). Thus the fact that the number of corn recipients rose to 320,000 is understandable. In this connection, it should be explained that slaves were not usually freed by *iusta manumissio*, and that Caesar intended to curb the enormous growth in the number of recipients (in 70 BC only 50,000 enjoyed price reductions, Cic., *Verr.* II, 3, 72), and to prevent those who were not eligible from obtaining any corn.

Therefore, the phrase from Livy's epitome (CXV) 'recensum egit' can be taken literally, even though from both Plutarch (*Caes.* 55) and Appian (*BC* II, 102) it might appear that the total population of Rome had sunk to 150,000. There had been many deaths and the total population had decreased, and it is no coincidence that Cassius Dio spoke of an *oliganthropia* (XLIII, 25, 2). There is no reason, however, to associate this reduction in population with the figure 150,000. Rather, we can rely on

Suetonius, who mentioned that this number concerned only the recipients of corn. Meyer (p. 417) and Brunt (p. 104, n. 3) stressed that Livy's account referred only to a *recensus* of the *plebs frumentaria*, and not to a general census of the population (*census populi*).

Nicolet (p. 270) contributed a new theory, by ingeniously connecting the topic with Cic., *Pro Mil.* 73 who reported how Clodius' gangs set fire to the temple of the Nymphs in order to destroy the lists of recipients of corn that were stored there (*publica recensio*). These lists referred to Pompey's distribution of corn in 57 BC, which was resented by Clodius' followers.

The best description of the *leges frumentariae* can be found in Nicolet's book (especially pp. 250–78) in which there are a plethora of new ideas. He had serious doubts about those sections of the *Tabula Heracleensis* that treat the corn distributions as originating in the time of Caesar, and ascribed them to a period closer in date to the *Lex Terentia*, 'Even the practical aspect of distribution eludes us for the Republican period' (p. 271). Nicolet also attempted to illuminate the Republican period from epigraphic evidence from the time of the Emperor Claudius.

In this connection, we would, however, submit that a few particulars of the rules for corn distribution in Caesar's time can be inferred from the first nineteen lines of the notorious *Tabula Heracleensis*. According to this law, anyone who wanted to be a Roman citizen had to make a formal declaration before the consul – or, in his absence, the *praetor urbanus* or *praetor peregrinus*, or in their absence, the tribune (lines 1–12).

The law obliged the magistrate in charge to see that the citizen's name was duly registered, along with his declaration and the date of the declaration ('in tabulas publicas referundas curato') and that the (white) tablets (hence 'album'), on which the names of the legally entitled recipients of corn had been engraved in black letters, were daily displayed at a prominent place in the forum (at the spot where the corn distributions took place), so that each of the names was clearly readable.

Many problems remain unresolved. How should we interpret 'it must be possible to read (the names) at ground level', [(u)nd(e) p(lano) r(recte) l(egi) p(ossit)]? How could thousands of names be written so that this was possible? Did this provision refer to all citizens or only those included in the census? We do not know the ways and means of testing the truth of the declarations made by applicants for the corn dole. Was a bona fide declaration, 'civis Romanus sum', sufficient, or were the *domini insularum* responsible for each *vicus* employed expressly for this purpose, as Suetonius reported (*Div. Jul.* 41)? Did the applicant have to present the praetor with a *tessera*, and did this serve as a basis for a *subsortitio* to establish who was to take the place of a dead person on the list?

Magistrates who distributed the corn unlawfully were liable to a fine of 50,000 sesterces (line 17), but the penalty imposed on anyone else who managed to get himself put on the lists illegally is not mentioned. One thing is clear: this law is not in any way to be viewed as providing for the poor on a large scale, as Meyer believed (p. 417). Nothing is said about a possible investigation of the economic circumstances of the applicant or the number of his dependent children. Each Roman citizen – not only the poor – had a claim to *frumentum publicum* (Cic., *Tusc. disp.* III, 48). In this respect Caesar made no changes (*contra*, Elmore). He merely saw to it that non–citizens could not participate; he prevented black-market dealings with the *tesserae* of deceased citizens, and made sure that no one broke the law.

The actions to decrease the number of corn recipients cannot be seen as a move against the city plebs. Consider that about 80,000 needy people left Rome to settle in overseas colonies (pp. 143–50), and that the civil war claimed many victims. It is always dangerous to rely on the figures given in ancient sources. When Caesar reported that 15,000 of the enemy fell at the battle of Pharsalus, while he lost only 200, he was probably exaggerating, but there is no doubt that the population was considerably reduced as a result of the many wars. And so Caesar did not lose his popularity with the plebs urbana: quite the reverse: their loyalty grew, and Roman citizenship became a proud and valuable possession. In addition, the reform would have pleased the *boni*, who were likely to see in its provisions a step towards achieving some semblance of order in a matter that they had viewed since the days of Caius Gracchus as detrimental, as superfluous, as encouraging the plebs to indolence, and as exploiting the *aerarium* to the last farthing (Cic., *Pro Sest.* 103).

37 LEX DE URBE AUGENDA?

(Building and plans for development in and outside Italy)

Cicero knew that Caesar had great plans for city improvement, but even he had no knowledge of the details (*ad Att.*
XIII, 20, 1). Most of our information comes from later
sources, even if there is no reason to question their credibility.
He was not a member of the planning committee, and thus
discovered a few details merely by accident; Sallust was not
writing about this period, and the subject was not relevant to
Caesar's own works. Other contemporary sources are not
available. At a later date Pliny also referred to such plans (*NH*
IV, 10), but some scholars believe that too much of the credit
has been given to Caesar. It is possible that the *Lex Caecilia de
urbe augenda* refers in part to Caesar's activity in this sphere,
but not much is known about it either. Even the title is questionable: perhaps the law was known as the *Lex Pomponia* (Cic.,
ad Att. XIII, 35, 1).

Caesar also had plans for areas outside Rome which
included the draining of the Pomptine marshes and the Fucine
Lake (Dio XLIV, 5, 1; Plut., *Caes.* 58; Suet., *Div. Jul.* 44, 2-3).
To reduce traffic and encourage trade, he planned to build a
road from the Adriatic over the Apennine ridge up to the Tiber
(Suet., *loc. cit.*) and cut a canal through the Greek isthmus of
Corinth (Plut., *Caes.* 58; Dio, *loc. cit.*). This canal would have
been of great strategic and economic importance; in fact, the
idea was conceived while planning the campaign against
Parthia (Plut., *Caes.* 58).

That Caesar took a personal interest in building and
development projects is mentioned in Nicolaus Dam. 22, 78.
He called in experts (*technitai*) to advise him, and became
personally involved with the building contracts. Suetonius
(*Div. Jul.* 44) declared that fresh plans for the improvement
and enhancement of the city piled up from day to day.
Gabriela Giglioni[11] accepted the *Lex Julia de urbe augenda* as
fact, and in this context enumerated all the building plans for
Rome.

An urge to build is frequently a characteristic attributed to
an autocrat, and Caesar was no exception. Like many a patron
he must have liked to make presents and build.[12] The people
were enthusiastic about it: it offered the poor the possibility of
employment and sources of income, and the aesthetes reason to

find fault. If they could put the blame on a Greek architect, so much the better. The temple of Felicitas was built on the foundation of the Curia Hostilia, and a new Curia Julia dedicated to Mars was planned for the Forum Julium (Cic., *ad Att*. XIII, 42, 3; cf. *Caes.*, *Bell. Afr.* 83; Dio XLIV, 5, 1-2; 49, 2). A temple was designed for this god, the like of which the world had never seen, and other gods, too, were not neglected (Venus Genetrix, Clementia Caesaris, Libertas, Quirinus, Concordia Nova). Later, there were plans for the construction of a large theatre near the Tarpeian rock (Suet., *Div. Jul.* 44; Dio XLIII, 4, 1; 49, 2). Caesar also erected a new building for the Senate (Dio XLIV, 5, 1), instead of the old one, burnt down during the unrest after Clodius' murder, and named it after himself, the Curia Julia.

The bed of the Tiber from the Pons Mulvius to the hills on the far side of the Mons Vaticanus must have been diverted already, and the resulting broad flat area of the Campus Vaticanus must have taken over the function of the Campus Martius (Cic., *ad Att*. XIII, 33a, 1).

For all these reasons the *lex de urbe augenda* cannot simply be dismissed even if there is no conclusive proof for it, but the question is raised because, in the final analysis, one does not require laws to build. Caesar intended to remove the sand-banks and rocks from the Bay of Ostia to construct suitable berths for the many ships that anchored there. Apparently he even began the work, but had to abandon it later because of technical difficulties (Suet., *Div. Claud.* 20). Caesar wanted to make it easy for merchant ships to sail up to Rome. To do this he planned to divert the course of the Tiber by means of a deep canal in the direction of Cape Circeum, which would then reach the sea near Tarracina (Plut., *loc. cit.*; Cic., *loc. cit.*).

Gabriela Giglioni rightly doubted whether Caesar's building plans can be pin-pointed in detail. She rejected Carcopino's statement that 'Caesar worked for the masses, that he intended the masses for their part to be worthy of his beneficence and to work for the state'.[13] She emphasized that Caesar's 'desire for glory, is an element not to be underestimated in the ancient world'.

'Full employment' was obviously not exactly the slogan of a Roman senator.

CHAPTER FIVE

INTERIM STATEMENT

Even when the scope and limits of the subject of an historical monograph are precisely sketched out, and the reader warned not to look for what the author initially decided to omit, the danger still exists that a distorted picture may emerge. The reader who studies all of the thirty-eight measures discussed in the previous chapters might get the impression that Caesar was first and foremost an important legislator. He would thus lose sight of the fact that Caesar was, among his other talents, one of the greatest soldiers in history.[1] Whether or not Machiavelli had Caesar in mind when he wrote in Chapter 12 of *Il Principe* that the foundations vital to any state are good laws and a good army is difficult to say. Caesar produced both. However his legislation be judged, there is almost universal agreement on his expertise as a general.

For a proper understanding of Caesar's regime from 49 BC to 44 BC, we must keep in mind that from 58 BC to the time of the crossing of the Rubicon he was in charge of extremely difficult and complicated military operations in Gaul. The man appointed dictator in 49 BC was not only a tried and tested politician with as much experience in the workings of the forum as in the intrigues of the Senate, but also the man who had conquered Gaul, to whom 'command came easier than persuasion' (Schmitthenner). It is not our intention to treat Caesar the general in a comprehensive or exhaustive fashion. Rather, we shall concentrate on Caesar as a leader of soldiers.

In military history it is not difficult to find examples of strict and inflexible commanders, rigidly tied to certain rules, whose leadership is unhesitatingly accepted by their troops who are convinced that their commander will always act consistently according to his character and conscience. Soldiers will obey this commander more from awe than from promptings of duty, and will recognize his *severitas* as genuine. Yet there are other generals, who spontaneously win their soldiers' hearts by doing the unexpected. Their subordinates admire them precisely because they react differently in different situations, and their resourcefulness demands no less respect than consistent inflexibility. Such qualities are innate, and not to be learned from a *Handbook of Leadership*. A relevant passage of Xenophon is cited here, not to prove that Caesar would have followed Socrates' advice, but to show that the wise Greek's definition of the problem cannot be surpassed,

But then that (sc. tactics) is only a small part of generalship. For a general must also be capable of furnishing military equipment and providing supplies for the men; he must be resourceful, active, careful, hardy, and quick-witted; he must be both gentle and brutal, at once straightforward and designing, capable of both caution and surprise, lavish and rapacious, generous and mean, skilful in defence and attack; and there are many other qualifications, some natural, some acquired, that are necessary to one who would succeed as a general. It is well to understand tactics too . . .

(Xen., *Mem*. III, 1, 6-7)

Caesar was just such a general, and not only because he had the natural talent. There is evidence that he often pondered these matters, and once even expressed the view that a ruler wishing to maintain his position must take into consideration two factors, soldiers and money,[2] which, in the end, depend on each other (Dio XLII, 49, 4).

Military experts praise Caesar's outstanding qualities as a leader: he encouraged *esprit de corps* among his soldiers, and made fun of a council of war, in which cautious, staid (and often frightened) officers were usually in the majority. Caesar particularly approved of the personal initiative of the more audacious officers who could solve problems in an unconventional fashion. Caesar also promoted direct contact between soldiers and their immediate superior, and between officers and the commander-in-chief. The *legatus legionis* enjoyed a more important position in Caesar's army than the *tribunus militum*, but the centurions formed the real backbone of the army. It was they who, before the civil war, made it increasingly plain to the soldiers that it was more profitable to be a 'miles Caesaris' than a 'miles Pompeii' (Caes., *Bell. Civ*. II, 32, 14; *Bell. Hisp*. 17, 1, cf. Gabba, p. 66, n. 52 = *English trans*., 185, n. 52).

But even that was not the most important aspect of his leadership. From the beginning, Caesar knew how to command by personal example. Before each battle he instructed his soldiers personally, and impressed his recruits by behaving like a master with his young gladiators. At difficult times he could spur his troops on by his self-confidence, energy and humour (which cannot be valued too highly), and in the first charge of a battle he did not hesitate to be at the head of his troops. Caesar's soldiers loved and respected him, but he never abandoned his principles of rigid discipline. Throughout the Gallic war there was never a serious mutiny among his troops (but cf. Caesar, *BG* I, 38-9), and only isolated ones during the civil war. Even then the troops immediately returned to their duties, not, perhaps, on account of their commander's indulgence, but because of his stubbornness in never giving in to trouble-makers (Suet., *Div. Jul.* 69). Thus he court-martialled and severely punished deserters and mutineers (*ibid.* 67, 1; Dio XLII, 55, 3; Caes., *Bell. Afr.* 46, 4; 54, 8). At Placentia, the soldiers of the Ninth Legion mutinied in 49 BC. The troops accused him of uselessly prolonging the campaign, in order to withdraw their promised reward, and were incensed because he refused to permit them to rob and plunder. Caesar did not give in. He executed the ringleaders and dishonourably discharged the rest (Suet., *loc. cit.* 69; Dio XLI, 26-35; Lucan, *Pharsalia* V, 237 ff.). On another occasion, before the African campaign in 47 BC, the soldiers of the Tenth Legion demanded their pay and release with angry threats, and said they would not hesitate to intimidate Rome at a time when the war in Africa was spreading like wildfire. Despite warnings of friends, Caesar promptly confronted them and ended the mutiny with a single word. He addressed them, not as soldiers, but as *Quirites* (citizens), and their tempers immediately cooled down (Suet., *op. cit.* 70; App., *BC* II, 93-4; cf. Gabba, p. 61, n. 40 = English trans., p. 184, n. 40).

These exceptional cases show that Caesar never attempted to purchase popularity the easy way. The same man who knew how to praise his soldiers generously, and to credit them with an honourable reputation for courage and initiative, was inflexible when it came to military discipline.

Caesar's versatility is woven like a golden thread through all his dealings. His chameleon-like qualities stood him in good

stead when he embarked on a civil war in 49 BC. All of the laws
we have described were passed in the intervals between Ilerda
and Pharsalus, Alexandria and Zela and Thapsus and Munda.
It comes as no surprise, then, that A. Ferrabino was enthusiastic, 'La luce della gloria tradizionale si è venuta riflettendo
molto più su Cesare che su Augusto, perchè in Cesare molto
più che in Augusto rifulge la energia della genialità personale,
in contrasto con la violenza della fortuna.' (If the light of glory
has, by tradition come to be reflected more by Caesar than by
Augustus, it is because the energy of personal genius, as
opposed to the violence of fortune, is reflected far more by
Caesar than by Augustus; *Cesare nel bimilleniario della morte,*
Rome 1956, p. 247).

Caesar's political genius is illustrated in his dealings with
officers and soldiers: a small episode shows his skill. In the
Spanish war he borrowed money from his higher-ranking
officers and distributed it to the common soldiers (Caes., *Bell.
Civ.* I, 39, 3-4). He admitted that this achieved two aims: the
centurions 'mortgaged' their loyalty to him in this fashion,
and at the same time he was assured of his troops' affection, a
method that was always one of his guiding principles. That
was the secret of his success as a young man, and, as we shall
see, a characteristic that would be reflected throughout his
entire political career.

On the other hand, all of Caesar's admirers seemed to speak
of him in superlatives, basically because they agreed with
Favorinus, who said that it is more shameful to be damned
with faint praise than to be severely and bitterly criticized
(Gellius, *Noctes Atticae* XIX, 3). That is why it is so difficult to
achieve a balanced picture of Caesar. His many-faceted
personality will trouble historians and psychologists, political
scientists and authors of historical novels for a long time to
come (e.g. Corradini's *Giulio Cesari,* 1902, and Bertolt Brecht,
Die Geschäfte des Herrn Julius Caesar, Berlin, 1949). He was the
warrior without fear or reproach, who appeared in the critical
theatre of war at the right moment, who managed to write
books, found time to love Cleopatra and Eunoe (the wife of
Bogud of Mauretania), to send letters of consolation to his
friends (see, e.g. Cic., *ad Att.* XIII, 20, 1), and to plan Greek and
Latin libraries of a large scale. He even commissioned Varro
about their construction and equipping, perhaps from a feeling
of regret that 400,000 scrolls were burnt in the Alexandrine war

(Suet., *Div. Jul.* 44, 2). He was the patron of philosophers and musical virtuosi (such as M. Tigellinus Hermogenes), a brilliant conversationalist, and such a grand host that he once threw his baker into chains for serving his guests with bread inferior to that served to himself (Suet., *Div. Jul.* 48). More of his unusual qualities could be enumerated and we could content ourselves with an interim evaluation of his activity based on the measures described in the previous chapters because these afford an insight into how Caesar's image was reflected by public opinion. This, however, would be only a part of the story. Caesar's relationship to the people and Senate was not merely expressed by laws and decrees, but in a series of political dealings, in which a distinct policy towards the people and the Senate ultimately emerged. This policy needs some attention before a comprehensive analysis of the laws themselves.

It would be wrong to assume that Caesar limited his relations with the people to a *lex frumentaria* (pp. 156 ff.), or a *Lex Antonia de candidatis*. Caesar never forgot *largitiones*.[3] 'The Roman plebs should not be robbed of the enjoyment it gets from games, gladiatorial shows and banquets, which were all established by our ancestors, nor should candidates be prevented from displaying an open-handedness, which is the token of liberality (*liberalitas*) rather than of bribery (*largitio*) (Cic., *Pro Murena* 77). *Largitio* was thus indicative of giving generously with the motive of bribery, and not from pure magnanimity. *Largitio* developed into one of those slogans which must be guarded against. Only one's opponent was branded with *largitio*; a decent man practised *liberalitas*, according to the principle 'inter bonos amicitia, inter malos factio'. Catullus, 29, 15, can be understood in this sense when he spoke of the 'sinistra liberalitas Caesaris'.

The means by which Caesar obtained the allegiance of influential men like Curio, Dolabella or Antony, who did not serve him without a *quid pro quo*, are well known. Sallust, too, joined him not for ideological reasons only (Dio XLIII, 9, 3). Caesar obtained office for some, for others he paid debts, and to the praetor Lucius Basilius he paid a large sum in compensation for not sending him to a province (*ibid.* 47, 5). Cicero himself owed Caesar money, a fact that greatly tempered his political decisions. When Julius Caesar once jokingly remarked to some young men who were deeply in debt that all they had to do was to undertake a civil war (Suet.,

Div. Jul. 27, 2), he was virtually repeating Cicero's joke to a similar group, that Sulla must be fetched back from hell (*In Cat.* II, 9, 20).

Caesar did not underestimate the influence of people in high places, but he never neglected the masses. 'And in the effort to surround himself with men's goodwill as the fairest and at the same time the securest protection, he again courted the people with banquets and distributions of grain' (Plut., *Caes.* 57, 5). This method of winning favour warrants our attention.

When his wars were over, Caesar did more than just distribute land to his veterans. 'To each and every foot-soldier of his veteran legions he gave twenty-four thousand sesterces by way of booty, over and above the two thousand apiece which he had paid them at the beginning of the civil strife' (Suet., *Div. Jul.* 38, 1). He gave corn, oil and meat to the poor, as well as public receptions, in addition to 300 sesterces a head, and a further 100 sesterces to compensate for delay. (He had already promised them the 300 sesterces in 49 BC, when he threatened the tribune Metellus and demanded that he open the *aerarium* for him.) He further provided food and drink, and, after his Spanish victory, two breakfasts: the first he considered too meagre, so five days later he gave them a second, more copious meal (*ibid.* 2; Dio XLIII, 21, 3; 22, 2-3; App., *BC* II, 102). He also realized that a government would be judged as much on the basis of the entertainments it provided for the people as on the basis of its serious actions (Fronto, *Princ. Hist.* 210, Naber). Plutarch reported that Caesar entertained the people with parties and shows. At mealtimes they sat together on 22,000 couches (Plut., *Caes.* 55, 2). Many triumphal processions (after the victories over Egypt, Pontus and Libya) and festivities lasting many days achieved their object of heightening the people's pleasure. (The triumph after the Libyan victory was officially held for the victory over Juba, king of Numidia, and not for the victory over the Roman Scipio.) No effort was too great and no expense was spared when it served to keep the people in a good mood. C. Hirrius provided 6,000 lampreys (*muraenae*) for the festivities, and, as he was not prepared to sell them, loaned them (Plin., *NH* IX, 171, Macrob., *Sat.* III, 15, 10). Suetonius (*Div. Jul.* 39) described these festivities in detail,

He gave entertainments of divers kinds: a combat of gladiators and also stage plays in every ward all over the city, performed too by actors of all languages, as well as races in the circus, athletic contests, and a sham sea-fight . . . For the races the circus was lengthened at either end and a broad canal was dug all about it; then young men of the highest rank drove four-horse and two-horse chariots and rode pairs of horses, vaulting from one to the other. The game called Troy was performed by two troops, of younger and of older boys. Combats with wild beasts were presented on five successive days, and last of all there was a battle between two opposing armies, in which five hundred foot-soldiers, twenty elephants, and thirty horsemen engaged on each side . . . The athletic competitions lasted for three days in a temporary stadium built for the purpose in the region of the Campus Martius. For the naval battle a pool was dug in the lesser Codeta and there was a contest of ships of two, three, and four banks of oars, belonging to the Tyrian and Egyptian fleets, manned by a large force of fighting men. Such a throng flocked to all these shows from every quarter, that many strangers had to lodge in tents pitched in the streets or on the roads, and the press was often such that many were crushed to death . . .

Even if none of these sources were contemporary, there is no doubt about the facts, although a few figures here and there appear to be exaggerated. Caesar knew the value of gladiators even before he crossed the Rubicon – they were a considerable source of income (e.g., Cic., *ad Att*. IV, 4a) and a splendid means of winning popularity with the masses. For these reasons he maintained a gladiatorial school in Capua which could provide 5,000 fully-equipped fighters.

Yet, it is doubtful whether Caesar ever thought of using these highly-trained gladiators in battle (Suet., *Div. Jul*. 31, 1). Their loyalty could not be relied on in war: Lentulus easily won over to Pompey's camp trainee gladiators from Caesar's school in Capua by promising them their freedom (Caes., *Bell. Civ*. I, 14). Caesar considered them principally as a source of income, and was prepared to risk his popularity with the masses by ordering that the lives of those gladiators condemned to death in the arena were to be spared, so that they could participate in other games of combat (Suet., *Div. Jul*. 26, 3).

To sum up, the festivities and games instituted by Caesar were indeed impressive but not unusual. Caesar did not discover any new means of dealing with the Roman masses – he only changed the scale. The scale, though not the principle, was gigantic. The consequent success of bringing elephants, lions and hippopotami to ancient Rome cannot be under-estimated. A hippopotamus was first displayed in Rome in 58 BC (Plin., *NH* VIII, 96; Ammianus Marcellinus XXII, 15, 24), an achievement not repeated in Europe until May 25, 1850. Ludwig Friedlaender described the event,

A whole regiment was occupied in capturing it; its transport from the White Nile to Cairo took five or six months . . . From Alexandria it was forwarded in a steamer especially constructed with a fresh-water tank containing 400 gallons, and daily renewed; whilst two cows and ten goats barely satisfied its requirements of milk.

There is no doubt about the aims of Caesar's exhibitions: 'that in return for small advantages the people would make greater concessions' (ut minoribus perceptis maiora permitteret) (Vell. Pat. II, 13, cf, Cic. *de off.* II, 21). Publilius Syrus made a typical comment: 'only wicked or foolish people think that bene-factions are granted for nothing' (93D) and Plutarch (*Caes.* 5, 4) confirmed that Caesar was buying things of the highest value at a small price. He must have known that men of humble means have only one way of repaying their benefactors: by accom-panying them to the forum and assisting them in the campaigns for office (Cic. *Pro. Mur.*, 70).

As to Caesar's relationship with the Senate,[4] this was not connected with any one reform based on law or decree, but was rather a process reaching back over several years and characteristic of Caesar's policy.

Tempers flared against Caesar in 46 BC for admitting unsuitable persons to the Senate (Dio XLIII, 27, 2), and later for his appointment of soldiers and freedmen's sons. This action increased the number of senators to 900 (*ibid.* 47, 3; cf. Cic., *ad fam.* XIII, 5, 2). The same tone is evident in Suetonius, 'He admitted to the House men who had been given citizen-ship, and in some cases half-civilized Gauls (*Div. Jul.* 76, 3)'. The cynical reaction of his opponents is not surprising, 'Caesar led the Gauls in triumph, led them to the senate house; Then the Gauls put off their breeches, and put on the laticlave' (*Div. Jul.* 80, 1–2; cf. also Cic., *ad fam.* IX, 15).

We know the names of a few of the men with whom Caesar 'packed' the Senate (Suet., *Div. Jul.* 41). One was Octavius the Marsian, about whom Cicero sarcastically remarked, 'this senator is unknown to me' (Cic., *Phil.* XI, 4), an indication that his origins were not respectable enough. Another was a certain Decidius Saxa from the far-distant mountains of Celtiberia, 'whom we saw tribune though we had never seen him citizen' (*Phil*. IX, 12; XIII, 27). On one of Cicero's visits to Pompeii his host Publius Mallius asked him to support his stepson's candidacy for the city council. Cicero quickly replied, 'In Rome he would get it (without further ado) if that is what you want, but here in Pompeii it is not quite so simple' (Macrob., *Saturnalia* II, 3, 11). A certain Sulla, who was a minor official (*scriba*) under the dictator Sulla, attained the rank of quaestor under Caesar and thus became a member of the Senate (Cic., *de off*. II, 29). And the career of Ventidius Bassus, born in Picenum of 'lowly origins', reached giddy heights. During the Social War he was imprisoned, but later managed to earn a meagre livelihood by providing vehicles and mules for officials sent to the provinces. This was how he met Caesar and jumped on his bandwagon. He first distinguished himself in the Gallic war and then in the civil war, and Caesar facilitated his promotion to the tribunate, the praetorship, and to an appointment as pontifex. Finally, in 43 BC, after Caesar's death, he rose to the consulship. Although this verse does not necessarily refer to Ventidius Bassus (cf. *Catalepton* 10 1-2), such promotions and careers prompted comic reactions,

> Assemble, soothsayers and augurs all!
> A portent strange has taken place of late;
> For he who curried mules is consul now[5]

(Gellius, Noctes Atticae XV, 4, 3)

And yet, by a twist of fate, Caesar was to be murdered by honourable men in the Senate that he had largely appointed.

The enlargement of the Senate apparently provoked the *homo novus* from Arpinum, who aired his misgivings about the new senators with such biting comments that they became part of Roman folklore. Once, one of Caesar's followers repaid him in the same coin: as Laberius passed Cicero's seat, the latter rudely addressed him, 'I would gladly give up my seat to you, were I myself not so squashed.' 'You are usually accustomed to take up two seats', answered Laberius, alluding to the open secret that Cicero knew how to curry Pompey's favour, but at the opportune moment had been quick to desert to the victor's side (Seneca Rhetor, *Controversiae* VII, 3, 9).

It appears *prima facie* that contemporary sources confirmed the versions of Suetonius and Cassius Dio that Caesar took persons of lowly origin into the Senate, and well-known modern scholars wholly accept these accounts. Dessau wrote that in Caesar's day slaves and actors entered the Senate and Friedländer, Meyer, Stein and Carcopino agreed. This view has now been abandoned. It was Gelzer who first rejected it. Münzer pointed out the close connections between Julius Caesar and the Aemilii and Servilii. Willems described the exact composition of the Caesarian Senate in two important chapters. But the most valuable contribution has been made by Sir Ronald Syme in two articles published in 1937 and 1938, as well as in a chapter of *The Roman Revolution* – now a classic.

Syme first explained why one should not take too seriously the type of slanders in the political dictionary of the Roman Republic. He pointed out that when a man was said to be of lowly origin, it merely meant that he was not of senatorial rank, but could very well have come from the equestrian class – a conclusion drawn from the slanders hurled at Sulla's new senators, who were highly respected knights. Caesar certainly reduced the influence of the traditional oligarchy, but did not abolish it altogether. Between 48 BC and 44 BC nine men served as consuls, of whom five belonged to distinguished families: P. Servilius Isauricus; M. Aemilius Lepidus; Quintus Fabius Maximus; Marcus Antonius, and P. Cornelius Dolabella. Four were 'new men' who earned their positions by military service in Gaul: Quintus Fufius Calenus, Gaius Trebonius, Publius Vatinius and Gaius Caninius Rebilus.

The centurions who were promoted after completing their period of service cannot be identified with mercenaries or beggars. Most of the centurions possessed equestrian census even before enlistment, and, according to law, all the magistracies were open to them. L. Decidius Saxa was no wild Celtiberian, as Cicero described him, but the son of a highly respected Italian family from one of the Roman colonies in Spain. Nor were the Gallic senators nameless nonentities; they were local notables whose ancestors had been given Roman citizenship by the proconsuls who served there. Nor did *scribae* belong to the poor – as early as the nineteenth century it occurred to some scholars that many of the *scribae* were extremely well-to-do. Sons of freedmen were not banned from membership of the Senate; some were members before Caesar's time, although they never constituted a substantial proportion of the new senators.

Caesar recruited his followers mainly from the equestrian class, and from the aristocracy of the Italian *municipia*. He maintained the closest connections with these classes even before the civil war, and it was not surprising that Pompey was compelled to leave Italy in great haste when Caesar crossed the Rubicon. Even Picenum left him in the lurch.

Caesar did not appoint Balbus, the millionaire from Gades, or Oppius, to the Senate. They served him better outside it. L. Cornelius L.f. Balbus the elder, content to remain an *eques*, was *consul suffectus*, and entered the *ordo senatorius* in 40 BC only after Caesar's death (Willems I, p. 607); L. Cornelius P.f.L.n. Balbus the younger became *quaestor* in 44 BC and *consul suffectus* in 32 BC. Typical of Caesar's new senators were L. Aemilius Lamia (*equestris ordinis princeps*) and C. Curtius (*fortissimus et maximus publicanus*).

Cicero's witty remarks were supposed to convince many people that Caesar's new senators were of low origin. But he himself came from the equestrian class, and never denied it. At one time he even hoped that Caesar would fulfil the dream of his life, *concordia ordinum*, but when his hopes were dashed, in addition to other criticisms, he sneered at the origins of the new senators who were loyal to Caesar, a common trick. After Caesar's death he had to change his tactics. Antony violently objected to the origins of young Octavian's mother, who came from Aricia; at this point, Cicero let fly at Antony, and made a stormy defence of Octavian, 'we all come from *municipia*' (*Phil.* III, 15).

Syme thus explained that Caesar's enlargement of the Senate was not as revolutionary as it might appear, and Cassius Dio was wrong in supposing that men who succeeded in entering the Senate did not traditionally belong there (XLII, 51, 5). Likewise, it does not follow that the Senate's membership was increased to 900, but apparently only to 800, as at least a hundred members were quaestors appointed between 48 BC and 44 BC. Nineteenth-century historians discovered the names of about half the members of the Senate, and the picture proved to be very different from the one sketched in the propaganda, from which Cassius Dio and Suetonius took their information. So much for matters elucidated by Syme.

It is, of course, true that Caesar, who paid due respect to *nobilitas* and *dignitas hominum* (*ad fam.* IV, 8, 2) should not be considered a revolutionary even if he was not just another traditional senator. His nominees to the Senate, however, constituted a thorn in the flesh to the old oligarchy, even if objectively viewed they were not of so 'inferior' an origin as their opponents maintained. The new senators were severely criticized because, like neophytes everywhere, they tried to imitate the ways of the old aristocracy, and always to behave more 'senatorially' than senators. On the other hand, one senator, Fulvius Sepinus, appeared as a gladiator in the arena (Dio XLIII, 23), and it is thus not surprising that such examples of unseemly conduct were blamed on Caesar and led to unwarranted generalizations about their behaviour.

No one knows why fifty-five *nobiles* joined Caesar and only about forty sided with Pompey. Most historians agree that there was more than just ideology at work in Rome. Caesar made it easy for those who joined him by issuing a proclamation calling for peace and tranquillity. While Pompey threatened to treat as enemies those who did not take up arms for the Republic (i.e. for him), Caesar let it be known that those who were neutral and did not belong to either party would be numbered among his friends (Suet., *Div. Jul.* 75, cf. Cic., *Pro Lig.* 33). Shackleton Bailey rightly pointed out that uncertainty about Pompey's intentions *vis-à-vis* Caesar provoked much doubt and soul-searching among senators; in the end, 'accidents of circumstance' and purely personal connections determined with whom they would side. But the explanation does not lie only in terms of *amicitia, adfinitas* and *cognatio* and not every marriage had political significance. Even amid the corruption near the end of the Republic there were senators who took pride in their standing, remained loyal to the old system of government, and were deeply hurt when Caesar treated the highest institution of the Republic with obvious disdain. Yet it was he they looked to for the reformation of the Republic.

Caesar rarely summoned a full meeting of the Senate (Stein, pp. 43-68), and did not often consult with its leading members (Dio XLIII, 27, 1). It soon became clear to the Senate that he only presented it with matters for formal confirmation that had already been settled (such as the ratification of treaties, Jos., *Ant.*, XIV, 189), or let them carry out plans he had already made (Dio XLIV, 5, 1). That he made his most important decisions in meetings with his reliable friends L.

Cornelius Balbus, C. Oppius, C. Matius, A. Hirtius and C. Vibius Pansa was an open secret. His private secretary Faberius (App., *BC* III, 5) was also a confidant, although he was better known for using his position for personal gain than for contributing to policy planning.

It was already clear to Cicero in 46 BC that any actions taken by Balbus and Oppius in Caesar's absence were subsequently treated as legally valid (*ad fam.* VI, 8, 1; Suet., *Div. Jul.* 52). However, when Tacitus (*Ann.* XII, 60) wrote that Caesar authorized C. Oppius and Cornelius Balbus to make arbitrary decisions about conditions of peace or declarations of war, the statement appears somewhat exaggerated. Caesar never delegated general supervision and effective control (*ad fam.* IV, 9, 2), but he had such a large staff of collaborators and advisers that modern scholars detect beginnings of cabinet government in his working methods. His aides were in continual correspondence with him (*ad fam.* IX, 6, 1; *ad Att.* XI, 14, 2; 18, 1), and a code was devised to preserve its secrecy (Gell., *Noctes Atticae* XVII, 9). Doubtless they kept him informed about all the important events in the various circles of Roman society. They acted as his lobbyists before meetings of the Senate (*ad Att.* XIII, 47a, 1), and, being well aware of Caesar's wishes and taste, advised senators (Cicero among them) on the kind of memoranda they should submit to the dictator (*ad Att.* XIII, 27 and 28). They organized the games (*ad fam.* VI, 19, 2; *ad Att.* XIII, 37, 4), and even became involved in Caesar's private affairs.

In spite of their considerable power, Oppius and Balbus were tactful enough not to push themselves too far forward ('Balbus semper tectus'). They described themselves as 'homines humiles' (*ad Att.* IX, 7a, 1), and preferred to remain in the wings. But for all their 'good conduct', the traditional aristocracy never liked them. Their tact could not outweigh the appointment of a freedman's son to the command of three legions in Egypt (Suet., *Div. Jul.* 76, 3), although the appointment of freedmen to high office was the exception rather than the rule under Caesar (Treggiari, p. 185). Nor could it provide any solace against the concentration of power ('nimii honores') in Caesar's hands.

Did the Senate perhaps turn away from Caesar because he strengthened the popular assembly? The answer to this question must be negative because he weakened the popular

assembly as much as, if not more than, the Senate. Those who
label him the man 'annointed with the oil of democracy' are
just as mistaken as those who call him the 'last patrician'.

It is the usual practice, and rightly so, to base the distinction
between Caesar and Sulla on Caesar's *clementia*. Yet it must be
emphasized that, even if we believe in a general amnesty (pp.
96 ff.), such *clementia* appeared arbitrary to the *nobilitas*.[6]

In reality, Caesar pardoned some of his former enemies for
boldly political reasons but at other times pardoned people
quite simply because he was goodnatured. His *clementia* could
sometimes be bought for cash, as can be proved in the case of
P. Vestrius in Africa. The compensation paid by the latter's
brother in Rome 'helped' to strengthen Caesar's acceptance of
Vestrius' apologia and to pardon him. Curio once said that
Caesar was inclined to be brutal by nature (*ad Att.* X, 4, 8), and
that, when the tribune Metellus once angered him (Plut., *Caes.*
35), he had almost decided to start a blood-bath, but controlled
himself at the last minute. Indeed, Cicero mentioned occasionally the 'insidiosa clementia Caesaris' (*ad Att.* VIII, 16, 2)
or 'simulatio mansuetudinis' (*ad Att.* X, 8, 6). A despairing
Caelius once related that Caesar had dark and fearful thoughts
and also expressed them (*ad fam.* VIII, 16).

Caesar was too clever a politician to let his true feelings
become public. His target was to carve out the political image
of one who wanted to rout 'armed enemies without resort to
arms' (*Ep. ad Caes.* II, 2, 4), and he would let nothing stand in
his way. Cicero was incensed and wrote to Atticus, 'Is there a
more wretched spectacle than that of Caesar earning praise in
the most disgusting cause (*causa*), and of Pompey earning
blame in the most excellent; of Caesar being regarded as the
saviour of his enemies, and Pompey as a traitor to his friends?'
(*ad* Att. VIII, 9, 3).

'Parcere subiectis et debellare superbos' was one of the
earliest principles in Roman political theory and practice, and
Virgil enshrined it in memorable poetry.[7] Caesar did not
hesitate to make brutal sport of the enemies of the Roman
people in Gaul (Caes., *Bell. Gall.* 8, 44; Plin., *NH* VII, 91-4)
when he thought it necessary, and in the civil war he was not
always guided by humanitarian considerations (*Bell. Civ.* III,
80, 7). But the moment it occurred to him that *clementia* was
the most rewarding path (*ad Att.* X, 4, 8), because hearts could
be won by taking it (*ibid.* IX, 7c), he never changed course.

Beneficium and *gratia, amicitia* and *fides* made Caesar popular (*Cic. Phil.* II, 116) and he must have known that when you forgive an enemy you win several friends at no cost (*Publ. Syr.* 143 D.). Whether *clementia* was defined already in Caesar's time as 'lenitas superioris versus inferiorem' as it was later in the time of Seneca, is doubtful. Concepts like *lenitas* and *mansuetudo* (esp. Sall. *Cat.* 54, 1) were indeed more current under the Republic, but, perhaps, one should not stray into hair-splitting and sophistry, as far as the difference between *clementia* and *mansuetudo* is concerned.

Clementia soon became a watchword. It was taken to mean that Caesar put aside political rivalries in order to simulate a god-like benevolence that enveloped all his subjects. In order to work, however, it had to be the answer to a misdeed on the part of his opponents ('poenam sceleris praetermittere'). Apparently the younger Cato understood this, preferring suicide to the indulgence of the all-powerful Caesar. He resisted a ruler who acted contrary to the law in pardoning those over whom he had no right to rule (Plut., *Cat. Min.* 66). Even if Plutarch's wording is not an exact quotation there can be no doubt of Cato's attitude. According to a contemporary report, Cato described the condition of a Roman citizen under Caesar's regime as 'arrogantiae, superbiae dominatusque unius mandatus' (*Anticato* fr. 5, Klotz). Cicero leaves no doubt: 'For all who were your enemies either lost their lives through their own pertinacity, or have been saved through your mercy (*misericordia*) so that they either do not exist any more or have become your devoted friends' (Cic. *Pro Marc.* 21).

Only now can we turn to a comprehensive analysis of the thirty-eight measures in the political, administrative, social and economic fields. The majority of laws and measures fall in the four months of the year 46 BC after Thapsus, and in the period between September 45 BC and March 44 BC, when Caesar was in Rome – an indication that he was personally concerned with the legislation. Not all of these measures were laws (*leges rogatae*), and not all of them originated with Caesar, but even the most sceptical historians must agree that the following ten at least were defined laws, 1 *Lex Antonia de proscriptorum liberis* (pp. 62–63); 4 *Lex Julia de civitate Gaditanorum* (pp. 70 ff.); 17 *Lex Julia de provinciis* (pp. 108–9); 18 *Leges Juliae de magistratibus* (pp. 109–10); 19 *Lex Julia de sacerdotiis* (pp. 110–11); 23 *Lex Julia iudiciaria* (p. 116); 26 *Lex Cassia de plebeis in patricios adlegendis* (pp. 126–27); 31 *Lex Julia de mercedibus habitationum annuis* (p. 150); 35 *Lex Julia sumptuaria* (pp. 154–56), and 36 *Lex Julia frumentaria* (pp. 156–58).

In thirteen other cases it is not certain that we are dealing with *leges*. Yet there is no doubt that these measures, at least, can be traced to Caesar: 2 *Leges de restituendis damnatis* (pp. 64–66); 3 *Lex Roscia de Gallia Cisalpina* (pp. 66 ff.); 6 *Lex Hirtia de Pompeianis* (pp. 75–76); 7 *Lex Julia de legationibus liberis* (pp. 76–77); 10 *De collegiis* (pp. 85 ff.); 21 *Lex Julia de viis urbis Romae tuendis et purgandis* (pp. 114–15); 27 *Lex Antonia de candidatis* (pp. 127 ff.); 28 Regulation of the question of debts (pp. 133 ff.); 29 Land distribution (*Lex Julia agraria?*) (pp. 137 ff.); 30 Colonization and policy with regard to citizenship (pp. 143 ff.); 33 *Lex Julia de portoriis mercium peregrinarum* (pp. 151–52); 34 *Lex Julia de re pecuaria* (pp. 152–54) and 37 *Lex de urbe augenda* (pp. 159–60).

Seven examples, which are certainly not laws, concern measures which can, without hesitation, be connected with Caesar: 5 *De agris Massiliensium* (pp. 73–74); 11 Re-erection of the statues of Pompey and Sulla (p. 96); 12 General amnesty for political opponents (pp. 96–97); 16 Relief for the province of Asia (pp. 109 ff.); 20 Reform of the calendar (pp. 111 ff.); 25 Appointment of prefects (pp. 122 ff.); and 32 Promotion of increase in the birth-rate (pp. 151–52). Thus thirty laws and measures can be ascribed to Caesar, which is itself impressive.

Two cases are ambiguous: the *Lex Julia de vi* and the *Lex Julia de maiestate* (pp. 77–79). (I am inclined, at least as far as the latter is concerned, to trace it to Caesar.) But in five additional cases there is no evidence of Julian legislation: *Lex Julia de civitate Siculis danda* (pp. 97–98); *Lex Julia de insula Creta* (pp. 98–99); *Lex Julia de rege Deiotaro* (pp. 99–100); *Lex Julia de absentibus* (it is uncertain whether there ever was such a *lex*) and the so-called *Lex Julia municipalis* (pp. 117 ff.).

There are hints that Pompey planned to codify laws, but gave up the idea for fear of opposition (Isid., *Orig.* V, 1, 5). We also know that Caesar intended to collect all the scattered individuals laws into a few volumes but never found the time (Suet., *Div. Jul.* 44). However, the value he attributed to legislation should not be doubted.[8]

Cicero had good reason to remark in the *Philippics* (I, 18), 'If you were to enquire of Caesar himself what were his acts in the city and as a civilian, he would reply that he had introduced many excellent laws.' But our attempt at an analysis of Caesar's legislation is not made to express positive or negative views on his actions but to test whether there is a fundamental difference between Caesarian legislation and senatorial legislation in the period between Sulla's death and the crossing of the Rubicon. Gruen[9] recently attempted to demolish the traditional view that the aristocrats themselves brought about the revolution by neglecting internal reform. He tried to prove that reform measures initiated by the Senate were double the number of those proposed by the tribunes and analysed nearly fifty laws and measures on electoral reform, criminal procedure, criminal law and administrative regulations. His task was not easy: the sources are defective, and sometimes conclusions must be reached about a law, that is more than a hundred paragraphs long, merely on the basis of a few lines that have accidentally been preserved. The *Lex Julia repetundarum* of 59 BC (Cic., *ad fam.* VIII, 8, 3) is a case in point.

In spite of these difficulties, Gruen presented a convincing case for the impressive amount of legislative activity in the period before Caesar's dictatorship. But, while attempting to prove that it is difficult to pinpoint a crisis in the government of the Republic right down to the moment of the crossing of the Rubicon, he had to admit that legislation alone could not produce fundamental reform, and, in fact, did more harm than good. 'A proliferation of statutory laws may have contributed to the Republic's undoing' (pp. 258–59).

If we compare the relationship between the legislation before Caesar's time and his own legislation, we would probably have to conclude, unimaginatively, that the picture is partly (as usual in history) one of change and partly one of continuity, but in most cases a mixture of both. What, however, is more important is that things were not functioning properly, and Tacitus' aphorism 'corruptissima republica – plurimae leges' ('when the state was most corrupt, laws were most abundant': *Ann.* III, 27) fits the context.

Many centuries previously Anacharsis had made fun of Solon for trying to put a stop to the citizens' unfairness and greed by means of written laws, 'which were just like spiders' webs; they would hold the weak and delicate who might be caught in their meshes, but would soon be torn in pieces by the rich and powerful' (Plut., *Sol.* 5). It is against this background that Caesar's rise to power and the attempt to consolidate his regime through more effective and enforceable legislation must be considered.

After the battle of Munda the skies began to clear for the Caesarians; the power of the *nobilitas* was broken and the Pompeians were crushed. Italy was peaceful, and, apart from the unrest stirred up by Caelius and Dolabella, the capital also adapted to the new regime. A sigh of relief went up in the provinces, and Caesar's glory stretched from Spain to Judaea (Gaul is a separate matter).

The ancients knew that political and military successes could not be ascribed to one individual. Without numerous energetic collaborators the statesman or general could not achieve success (Cicero, after Panaetius, *de off.* II, 16).

The detailed prosopographical examination by Syme proved that the so-called 'Caesarian party' was composed of senators, knights, centurions, businessmen, and prominent people from the *municipia* and provinces. We can draw the same conclusion in an examination of Caesar's legislation.

To describe his policy as one of restoration (cf. Francesco Arnoldi, *Cesare* (Milan, 1948), p. 160) would not convey an appropriate picture. Caesar was anything but an extremist. Just as he fostered the image of the indulgent ruler (p. 174 f.), he never hesitated to punish ruthlessly anyone who stood in his way (p. 175 f.). In distributing land, he was careful not to tread on the toes of the great landowners (pp. 137 ff.), and when he remitted debts he tried to keep the allegiance of the moneylenders. In 50 BC many were doubtful (Cicero among them) that the upper classes would support Caesar. At that time all the debtors, the city plebs, all accused and sentenced persons, youths and aggressive tribunes were on his side (*ad Att.* VII, 3, 5). In 49 BC the situation was reversed (*ibid.* VII, 7, 5), and in February 48 BC Caelius was of the opinion that no one apart from the moneylenders remained loyal to Caesar (*ad fam.* VIII, 17, 2). But Caelius was wrong. As Arnoldi pointed out, Caesar never based his support on a single stratum of society, and he knew how to establish his personal authority by complicated manoeuvres between groups who were often opposed to one another. In his earlier years, in any case, he never yielded to the pressure of a self-interest group. He tamed the *publicani* (pp. 101 ff.), and forbade unruly societies. He reduced the number of those on the corn dole (pp. 156 ff.), and increased the settlers in overseas territories. He bribed the people with gifts on a generous scale (pp. 165 ff.), but at the same time was careful not to give them any real political power. Moreover, he refused a popular request to add to one of his laws an invitation to slave informers, and swore never to trust a slave's denunciation (Dio 41, 38, 5).

That is the line of policy that was woven like a golden thread through all his dealings. It cannot be proved that they were the result of a predetermined plan: that is unnecessary. It is enough to assume that nothing occurred without due consideration. It cannot be denied that Caesar was motivated by desire for glory ('gloria et ambitio', Sen., *Ep.* 94, 65), and would not share power, although the state allowed two men to stand at its head. But men often succeeded in making great strides, even when driven by low, empty and self-seeking motives. Private vices may turn sometime into public benefits and Hegel coined this as *List der Vernunft*. Cardozo was more prosaic: 'Some principle, however, has regulated the infusion . . . a choice there has been, not a submission to the decree of fate, and the considerations and motives determining the choice, even if obscure, do not utterly resist analysis' (*The Nature of the Juridical Process*, 1921, p. 11).

It is only when each of Caesar's measures between 49 BC and 44 BC is analysed from the point of view of *cui bono* that the real picture emerges. Obviously there must have been some who were hurt by a particular measure, yet it is interesting to determine how, in every individual provision (even if one does not presuppose a general plan) damage was balanced by compensation. Thus the *Lex Antonia de proscriptorum liberis* and the *leges de restituendis damnatis* (pp. 64 ff.) were welcomed by all who had suffered under Sulla's or Pompey's legislation: they were only too eager to join Caesar's camp. Even those who doubt the authenticity of the legislation in Sicily and Crete must agree that in many provinces Caesar's popularity was beyond question, e.g. Gades (pp. 70 ff.), Asia Minor (pp. 101 ff.) and Judaea (p. 104). Of course, the Pompeians disliked Caesar and the Massilians never forgave him, but, in view of his enormous popularity, he could afford to reward his followers and punish his enemies.

We have shown how Caesar made certain that his economic measures were not too harmful to any one sector of the population. For instance, when he stung the Senate's pride by enlarging it, all of the newly-appointed senators, prefects and new priests (pp. 109 ff.) rejoiced. The Senate did not dare to complain about Caesar's measures – they allegedly served the good of the Republic. But Caesar 'proved' to the Senate by means of the good order he introduced in the *lex frumentaria*, and by the settlement of the proletarians and freedmen in overseas colonies that law and order was his prime intention. The senators were annoyed by the *lex de legationibus liberis* (pp. 76 ff.). But they must have recognized Caesar's concern for the common good, which was illustrated in his measures on reconstruction (pp. 159 ff.), concern for public order and security (pp. 79 ff.), ordering of military service and reform of the calendar, even if they did not always praise it.

Despite the cuts made by the *lex frumentaria*, Caesar gave soldiers and the man in the street a better life by settling them in overseas colonies, by giving them additional opportunities to earn a living and by caring for entertainments. Momigliano wrote (*JRS* XXXI 1941, pp. 158–65), 'If there is any royal road to the essential values of Roman history, it is the study of the Roman citizenship,' and we may revert to Caesar's policy on colonization and citizenship.

Obviously Caesar was not the first to award citizenship. Gaius Gracchus, Saturninus and Livius Drusus preceded him, and Pompey was also well aware that Rome was no mere *polis*, and that a Roman consul had to take care of the *urbs* as well as of the *orbis terrarum*.

No reference can be found to any general plan for a romanization of the state; it is much easier to place Caesar's measures against the background of his campaign to fight his internal political enemies. Yet if in this context, too, we judge Caesar by his acts and not by his intentions, we must also consider the historical significance of his colonization. In contrast to his predecessors, he ruled Rome for almost six years (49 BC to 44 BC). His feverish activity during that time builds up into a much more unified picture than that provided by the sporadic activity of earlier Roman statesmen. No one disputes that Caesar was the first to grant citizenship to an entire province, to recruit an entire legion from provincials, and that one of his Spanish followers (Balbus) was the first provincial to become consul. No one before him had conferred citizenship so generously (Caes., *Bell. Afr.* 28, 2; Cic., *Phil.* XI, 12; XIII, 27, etc.), or been more eager to improve the lot of slaves and freedmen (Suet., *Div. Jul.* 42; Strabo 381).

His friends refrained from stressing the positive side of his measures: increased self-respect for the thousands of inhabitants of the empire, who viewed their enfranchisement as a proud achievement, and in whom the hope of a better future was awakened; the economic advantages resulting from the policy of colonization, and the fact that it was fundamentally a Roman tradition to broaden the base of government from time to time, and constantly to widen the responsibility for the government of the Empire. On the other hand, Caesar's opponents always dwelt on his attempts to reinforce his personal rule. Thus his reputation suffered. It would be just as exaggerated to see him as a prophet as it would be small-minded to consider him as just another Roman politician whose sole aim was personal power.

It must be stressed that nothing in his extensive activity points to an intention to strengthen the Senate. Livius Drusus was more generous, and at least promised the Senate something, namely control of the law courts, 'Latinis civitatem, plebi agros, equitibus curiam, senatui iudicia permisit' (*Vir. ill.* 66, 4). In fact, Caesar never openly attacked the Senate or senatorial order as such, but asserted that he had struck only at a 'factio paucorum' (Caes., *Bell. Civ.* I, 22, 5). For, in spite of the weakening of the oligarchy, its influence was still great, and was capable of undermining his position. Many senators were convinced that all of Caesar's attempts for rapprochement with the Senate were mere hypocrisy. The re-erection of the statues of Sulla and Pompey (p. 96) strengthened his power more than it satisfied the *nobilitas*, and they saw in this an offence rather than a friendly gesture. His order forbidding senators and knights to appear in the arena as combatants did not help matters (Dio XLIII, 23, 5), and even if no more pungent expression of anti-senatorial feeling is preserved in the sources than that ascribed to Gaius Gracchus in a corrupt passage in Diodorus XXXVII, 9 ('Even though I perish I shall not cease . . . the sword wrested from the grasp of the senators'), there could be no *modus vivendi* between such a dictator and the traditional Roman aristocracy.

By the provisions of the years between 49 BC and 44 BC Julius Caesar strengthened his personal power beyond the authority granted to any annually elected Roman magistrate. He systematically and thoroughly built up his *clientela*, and willingly gave favours to friends, but not to the ones who were vain and self-seeking (Cic., *ad fam*. VI, 6, 8). The loyalty of Caesar's *clientes* was not one-sided – in return he never neglected a *cliens* (Gell., *Noctes Atticae* V, 13, 6), kept his promises, and remained loyal to them ('se Caesarem esse fidemque praestaturum', *Bell. Hisp.* XIX, 6).

The influence of the senatorial oligarchy languished slowly, but the process was not perceptible and evident even after Caesar's death. Within a very few years, his regime had destroyed any hope of turning back the clock of history. The Roman aristocracy would never be the same, and this was probably the reason why the upper classes looked on Caesar as their enemy and a friend of the rabble. 'Never have disloyal citizens had a better prepared man at their head', wrote Cicero (*ad fam*. XVI, 11, 3), and it is not difficult to deduce the reasoning behind Livy's description of the Romulus honoured by the people and hated by the Senate. Cicero's description of the situation, after Caesar's murder, was appropriate, 'He wasted all the power of his intellect . . . in pandering to popular humours ('levitas popularis'). Thus, having no regard to the Senate and to good men, he opened for himself that path to the extension of his power which the manly spirit of a free people could not endure' (*Phil.* V, 49).

Cicero was precise in his use of words, and they should not be interpreted as calling Caesar's regime a revolutionary one. *Levitas* is not revolution; 'haec commutatio reipublicae' (*ad fam*. XIII, 10, 2) likewise cannot be translated by 'revolution', and the terminology employed by Canali (p. 21), 'movimento democratico romano', or 'rivoluzione Caesariana', veils more than it reveals. A Marxist would probably not label Caesar a revolutionary because he never changed the existing law of property,[10] and never envisaged handing over real authority to the popular assembly. Syme was right in his brief and conclusive statement (*RR* p. 52) that 'Caesar was not a revolutionary.' During the unrest in 48 BC and 47 BC, there were probably many people to whom Caesar was not radical enough because he made compromises with former Pompeians and wealthy *publicani*. That his personality was so much more complex was beautifully recorded by Cicero,

In him there was genius, calculation, memory, letters, industry, thought, diligence; he had done in war things, however calamitous to the state, yet at least great; having for many years aimed at a throne, he had by great labour, great dangers, achieved his object; by shows, buildings, largesses, banquets he had conciliated the ignorant crowd; his own followers he had bound to him by rewards, his adversaries by a show of clemency: in brief he had already brought to a free community – partly by fear, partly by endurance – a habit of servitude (*Phil.* II, 116)

Thus, from Petrarch to Byron a real love-hate complex grew up around Caesar. Because he was not extreme in any one respect, every writer could see in him what he wished and be right. O. Seel (*Caesarstudien*, p. 57) maintained that a great man must always have a component of tragedy in order to move us; brightness and misery, good fortune and suffering, success and failure are closely bound together, and only the man who is neither a luminary nor a dark miscreant, but a mixture of both, serves as a tragic hero (according to Aristotle, *Poetica* 13, 2, p. 1453 a).

Such a Caesar would emerge if we restrict ourselves to a sober analysis of his legislation. He passed a series of laws which allied him to different groups and classes, without taking into account their varying interests. His personality had to be the cement that held them together, and Cicero correctly described this complex situation with the words 'se cum multis conligavit' (*ad fam.* IX, 17, 2).

Suetonius also understood this trait of Caesar's personality, and pointed out (*Div. Jul.* 27) that Caesar had tied people of every class to him with gifts, had not disdained lesser folk, and had extended his generosity to freedmen and favoured slaves, in proportion to their standing with their patron or master (*loc. cit.*, cf. Dio XL, 60, 4). It was no accident that *servi* and *egentes* especially mourned his death (*ad Att.* XIV, 10, 1), of which Amatius' movement[11] may serve as testimony. That is the fate of every statesman who walks the middle ground, and Mommsen indeed stressed Caesar's policy of compromise. Syme expressed it thus, 'A champion of the people, he had to curb the people's rights . . . to rule he needed the support of the *nobiles*, yet he had to curtail their privileges and repress their dangerous ambition (*RR*, pp. 51-52).

The results did not endure. Towards the end of his life the people's trust in Caesar vanished. He would have done better to follow the advice put so succinctly by a politician of a much later date, 'you can fool all the people some of the time, and some of the people all the time, but you cannot fool all the people all the time'. This would probably have sounded cynical to Caesar's admirers, but they had to admit that at an early date Aristotle recognized the fate of a middle-of-the-road statesman:

For the brave man appears rash relatively to the coward, and cowardly relatively to the rash man . . . Hence also the people at the extremes push the intermediate man each over to the other, and the brave man is called rash by the coward, cowardly by the rash man (*Eth. Nic.*, p. 1109 b, 19–26).

After reaching its pinnacle, Caesar's popularity began to dwindle. The senatorial aristocracy as well as the masses began to doubt him, for legislation alone was not enough to bolster popular opinion. Political conduct was just as important to such an image, and if we add this aspect to our interim statement, we can then understand the full significance of the Ides of March.

CHAPTER SIX

PUBLIC OPINION AND
THE IDES OF MARCH

The origin of the word *tyrannos* is unknown, but every Greek
knew what it meant, and the tyrants' courts were the subject of
many sagas and stories (Herodotus VI, 126-30). Herodotus
bitterly hated any form of arbitrary authority – 'a thing as
unrighteous and bloodthirsty as aught on this earth' (V, 92).
But he never put forward any theories on tyranny – he only
recorded stories, and illustrated the brutality with which the
tyrants treated the leading men of their cities. One of the most
famous tales told how Periander of Corinth sent a messenger
to consult his fellow-tyrant, Thrasybulos of Miletus. The
latter led the envoy through a corn-field and cut off the tallest
stalks. When this was reported to Periander, he readily understood the meaning of the message. The essence of the tale lay in
the description of the tyrant's treatment of leading citizens and
not in its historical truth, and when Plato and Aristotle set
themselves the task of classifying tyrants, they probably had
this story in mind.

Thucydides was the only writer to consider tyranny from an
economic viewpoint, 'As Hellas grew more powerful and
continued to acquire still more wealth than before, along with
the increase of their revenue, tyrannies began to be established
in most of the cities' (I, 13, 1). Socrates, Plato and Aristotle all
treated tyranny from a moral and political viewpoint, seeing in
it the degeneration of monarchy or the usurpation of legitimate government (see the account of Gyges: Herodotus I,
8-12; Plato, *Politeia* II, 359). In a famous passage (*Polit.* 1311 a;
1313 b–1315 b), Aristotle described the measures necessary for
a tyrant to establish his rule. Some may be enumerated here.[1]

The tyrant must do away with the nobility.[2] He must eliminate intellectuals, bar public banquets, and dissolve existing associations and cultural institutes. Discussion groups are to be forbidden. He must guard against close friendships and good relations between his subjects that might lead to mutual trust: such conditions might bolster their morale. He must supervise all activity on the part of his subjects; to this end they must appear at the gates of his palace, so that they remain in a state of servile subjection; above all, he must prevent their engaging in any political or public activity. He should not squander public money on his favourites, but present accounts outlining income and expenditure, so as to appear as his subjects' trustee, and not a despot. But at the same time he must develop an extensive network of secret police, spies must inform him of everything said and done. He must sow strife among the population, incite the masses against the nobility and the rich against one another.

He must reduce his subjects to poverty, cripple them with taxes, and, in order to keep them fully employed, build showpieces 'in order that they might have neither the wish nor the time to attend to public affairs' (Aristotle, *Const. Ath.* 16). From time to time he should wage a war, to make his subjects aware of his leadership. He should never trust his immediate entourage. He is anyway surrounded by flatterers, and they always have it in mind to overthrow him. He should rather associate with strangers (who are not citizens), before whom he does not have to exercise the same control. He should appear god-fearing and conscientiously observe all religious rites. His subjects will not dare mutiny against him so long as they think that the gods are on his side. Thus self-respecting persons of breeding and independent thought could not live peacefully with a tyrant. The despot who lives only for personal advancement and personal power is a danger to honourable citizens. He must also beware, for they are no less careful of their honour than the rich are of their wealth.

It is not difficult to think of Brutus and his associates in this context, but one must first examine what a Roman senator meant when he spoke of a tyrant. The Greek accounts of the various tyrants were well known to Roman annalists who described Tarquinius Superbus as being a typical one. He was a cruel and greedy, overweening and domineering person who disregarded the tradition of his forefathers, and went out of his way to treat the notables with brutality. Herodotus' account of the 'tall ears' was echoed practically word for word in Livy I,

54, and only the names of the people involved were changed. Sextus, Tarquinius' son, took control of the city of Gabii, and, on his father's advice, rid himself of the local aristocracy by this method. One is reminded of Herodotus' description of the tyrant who 'turns the laws of the land upside down, he rapes women and puts high and low to death' (III, 80, 4-5). This was how the Roman annalists depicted Tarquinius Superbus and, whatever the historical truth behind it, the Roman literary tradition was so unfavourable that Servius, the fourth-century commentator of Virgil, could say that the Romans made no distinction between king and tyrant (Servius, *Comm. Aen.* IV, 320). In the same breath Cicero spoke of enemies, traitors, thieves and tyrants (*In Pis*, 24), and the Romans knew that the Greeks honoured tyrannicides (*Pro Mil.* 80; *ad Brut.* I, 16, 6).[3] There is nothing more scandalous than subjection and servility in the face of the tyrant, nothing more shameful than the friendship extended towards him (*ad Att.* VII, 20, 2), and no more noble deed than his murder (*Phil.* II, 117).[4] 'Where there is a tyrant . . . it must be clearly said there is no commonwealth' (Ubi tyrannus est, ibi . . . dicendum est plane, nullam esse rempublicam; *de Rep.* III, 43).

The senatorial aristocracy, like every oligarchy, was not prepared to come to terms with a man who dared to appear as superior to his peers. They were very well aware of the danger that, to be successful, such a man had to go over their heads and appeal to the masses. The Romans were frequently reminded of Spurius Maelius, who attempted to bribe the masses with gifts of corn. He was murdered by C. Servilius Ahala in 439 BC, an incident Cicero made much of in the days of the Catilinarian conspiracy. In 384 BC, M. Manlius Capitolinus was executed after proposing the cancellation of debts, and for many years afterwards the Cassii bragged that Spurius Cassius, consul for the third time in 486 BC, was condemned to death by his own father because he aspired to kingship.[5] For centuries this attitude was a characteristic of Roman internal politics, and in 158 BC the censors ordered the removal of all the statues of former magistrates that ringed the forum except those which had been specifically decreed by the people or the Senate. The statue of Spurius Cassius 'qui regnum advectaverat' was even melted down by the censors (Plin., *NH* XXXIV, 30).

'Aiming at a kingdom' (*regnum*) cannot be taken literally:

during the political agitation at the end of the Republic it was
an almost routine expression of censure. Political opponents
made such accusations against Sulla and Cinna, Catiline and
Clodius, and even Cicero was not immune to the slanders;
when his enemies wanted to blame him for taking despotic
action during his consulship, they accused him of *regnum* and
tyrannis.[6] The passages in Cicero's writings in which he
alternately stigmatizes as tyrants Caesar and Pompey, Antony
and Dolabella, should be read only in this context.[7]

Hatred of the tyrant was a belief with ancient roots. It was
an integral component of the Roman tradition, and there is no
reason to suppose that such hatred was 'invented' only after
Caesar's murder, as a justification for it. It is, therefore,
credible that no sooner had Caesar fallen under the blows of
the dagger, than the people cried 'Down with tyranny' (Nic.
Dam. fr. 130, 96), and that Brutus and Cassius saw it as an
honour rather than a disgrace to be dubbed tyrannicides.

Nevertheless, it is doubtful whether men like Cicero and
Brutus were typical of the average Roman senator. Both were
steeped in Greek culture and knew, when they spoke of
tyrants, the difference between the moderate and enlightened
rule of an Athenian Peisistratus, for example, and the harsh
and arbitrary rule of Phalaris of Agrigentum (*ad Att.* VII, 20,
2). Cicero was an admirer of Plato,[8] and his letters were full
of quotations from Homer and the Greek tragedies. His education
was above average, the the many historical allusions in his
speeches and writings were never equalled by his contemporaries.

The average Roman senator did not bother to judge the
appearance and activity of a Roman politician from the point of
view of Greek political philosophy. He did not refer to
Aristotle's works in order to examine Caesar's conduct in the
light of the criteria cited above. He would not have defined
Caesar as a born tyrant with a character composed of 'brutality',
'desire for luxury', 'violence' and 'lust for power', particularly
as an objective assessment would also reveal redeeming traits of
character.[9] The rhetorician's average pupil would have judged
Caesar this way, but not a Roman senator, who had only one
criterion: loyalty or faithlessness to the Republican tradition. He
would have suspected every direct appeal to the popular
assembly over the heads of the Senate, every instance of
disregard of senatorial authority and every example of
disdainful conduct towards individual senators.

For instance, in 45 BC Servius Sulpicius complained that he had been robbed of his home, his position and his offices (*ad fam.* IV, 5, 2–3). To a Roman senator, the Republic was both a constitutional structure and a way of life.[10] His respect for *mos maiorum* was stronger than his sense of obligation to the formal law, even though obedience to the law was also a component of *mos maiorum*. Some Roman citizens had their doubts about this, and Cicero rightly suspected that moneylenders, wealthy merchants and small farmers (not to mention the city plebs) preferred even autocratic rule for the sake of peace and quiet (*ad Att.* VII, 7, 5). 'Pauci libertatem, magna pars iustos dominos volunt' became a platitude.

In times of crisis even Cicero was prepared to come to terms with a 'moderate ruler' who properly devoted himself to the people's interests, who curbed extreme elements and returned its dignity to the Senate. He had to justify his support of Pompey's *imperium infinitum* to Hortensius and Catulus and when, after Caesar's murder, he supported the young Octavian, he incurred the anger of Brutus, who said that 'Cicero would appear not to have shunned a master, but to have sought a friendlier master' (non dominum fugisse, sed amiciorem dominum quaesisse videberis: *ad Brut*, I, 16, 7). Cato, on the other hand, refused to renounce the traditional *libertas*, which was expressed, not in a just overlord, but in the lack of any form of overlordship (Cic., *de Rep*. II, 43), or, as it is even better formulated: 'that the state should be freed not merely of a monarch, but of monarchy (non rege solum sed regno liberari rem publicam: *ad Brut*. II, 5, 1). But Cato was the exception. Because he was ready to pay the full price for his principles, his suicide became the hallmark of protest against arbitrary authority (*ad Att*. XII, 4, 2; *de off*. I, 112), and he was more dangerous to Caesar in death than in life.

Yet, for ordinary mortals it was easier to admire principles than to live by them.[11] The majority of senators would have come to an understanding with Caesar had he treated them better and not made them the target of public scorn. These were the 'lovers of honour' (*philotimoi*), whom Aristotle advised should be treated with consideration: the tyrant should be especially cautious in his conduct towards those who love honour. For just as lovers of money (*philochrematoi*) are hurt when their property is touched, so are the lovers of honour and the virtuous, when their honour is in question

(Arist., *Polit.* 1315 a). And Caesar did wound the Senate's honour on numerous occasions, one of the chief reasons for the formation of the conspiracy. The conspirators saw Caesar as a tyrant, and tyrannicide[12] was their method of getting rid of him. His deeds and speeches made it easy for them to focus all their propaganda on one point – that he wanted a *regnum*.

It is not our intention to go into the detailed history and motives of the conspiracy yet again. Schmitthenner[13] has already referred to the difficulty of finding the truth. Nicholas Horsfall,[14] who has thoroughly examined every possible detail connected with the Ides of March is convincing when he suggests that the conspirators were working against the clock, because they feared discovery (Dio XLIV, 15, 1; Plut., *Caes.* 64 1), that Caesar was preparing to set out against Parthia on March 18, and that Brutus and Cassius were compelled to act as quickly as possible before that date (Dio XLIV, 15, 4).[15] None of the attempts to attribute more weight to one motive than to another has won general support from historians. F. D. Gräter,[16] for instance, called the whole affair a feud between families, while Balsdon[17] suggested that the role of Porcia, Brutus' wife, Cato's daughter and Bibulus' widow, should not be underestimated. The view that Brutus and Cassius initiated the conspiracy mainly for idealistic reasons met with as sceptical a reception as the idea that the conspirators were a gang, and that Cassius joined the plot only when Caesar refused to appoint him city prefect in 44 BC.[18] Although each individual probably had his own reasons for joining the conspiracy (Nic. Dam. fr. 130, 60), there is no doubt that the conspirators' real desire was to try any means that would eliminate a hated tyrant. One must agree with Horsfall's view that the fateful decision was probably not taken much before the end of February. Many plans were considered (Suet., *Div. Jul.* 80, 4), ranging from an attack on the Via Sacra to one at the gladiatorial games, before it was finally decided that the Curia would be the place, and that the time would be on the day when most of the proletariat was away from the city at the festival of Anna-Perenna (Ovid. *Fasti* III, 523).[19] Hermann Bengtson,[20] who emphasized the importance of contemporary sources, has warned against *post eventum* interpretation. The sources hardly permit a valid conclusion as to who was the *spiritus rector* of the conspiracy: M. Brutus, as is usually supposed, Decimus Brutus, as Nicolus Damascenus indicated, or Cassius, as Plutarch maintained. Even the origins of the conspiracy and the conspirators' plans are shrouded in a thick fog.[21]

The view that none of the conspirators had a clear plan for the restoration of the Republic finds a certain confirmation in the conduct of Brutus and Cassius in the period from March 16 44 BC until they left Rome on April 13 44 BC.[22] D. Junius Brutus Albinus, asked by M. Brutus directly after the murder what suggestions he now had to make, replied 'We must bow to Fortune' (dandus est locus fortunae: Cic., ad fam. XI, 1, 3); he further advised leaving Italy, living in exile, and returning to Rome when the hue and cry had died down. Or, if the worst came to the worst, a plea of self-defence as a last resort. The wealth of ideas suggested by the 'ultimus Romanus' is not exactly arresting, and one can only concur with Cicero, when he observed: 'the deed was done with manly courage but childish policy' (acta enim illa res est, animo virili, consilio pueruli: ad Att. XIV, 21, 3).

On the other hand, it is hard to believe that the conspirators' decision to murder Caesar, was made as a conscious act of self-destruction, and not in hope of victory. In this respect, Cicero's insight appeared to be based on subsequent knowledge of the facts. It is certain that he was not entrusted with the secret. This was either because the conspirators distrusted him (as Shakespeare characterized him: 'O name him not, for he will not follow anything that other men begin'), or because they knew that he was fundamentally a sceptic and a pessimist. The conspirators already knew how Cicero saw himself (ad fam. VI, 14, 1), 'If any man in the world is a coward in matters of importance involving any risk, and always more inclined to apprehend an unfavourable, than to hope for a favourable issue, I am that man' (46 BC). It must be added that the conspirators misjudged the political situation from the outset. How then, could experienced Roman senators make such childish mistakes?

The conspirators did not have a positive political plan; they simply believed that Caesar's standing in public opinion had reached an all-time low, that his murder would not cause a ripple of excitement, and that the Senate could easily manage the aftermath. The conspirators could count on the support of numerous senators, they could hope for an understanding with Antony and Lepidus, and even that they would ensure a favourable reaction in the army. Above all, they were convinced that the people had become disenchanted with Caesar.[23]

On March 16 they had to face the realization that their calculations were incorrect. Many years later Ovid would lament:

Naked swords were brought into the sacred curia; for no place in the whole city would do for this crime, this dreadful deed of blood, save only that . . . (*Metam.* XV, 800–803)

The people were cool to Brutus' justification of the assassination. When the praetor Cornelius Cinna called the murdered Caesar a tyrant, he was stoned. He fled to his house and barred the doors, but the crowd followed, piled firewood around the house and burned it down. Lepidus and the veterans were able to rescue him, but four days later Helvius Cinna the poet was murdered because the people mistook him for Cornelius Cinna.

If looked at superficially, the situation could have seemed to be different before the attempt on Caesar's life. The conspirators must have presumed that the masses were discontented as a result of cuts in the corn dole, that the handling of debts and rents was too slow, and because there was a ban on *collegia*. There were other indications, too, that encouraged the conspirators to act: the behaviour of the people at processions and in the circus, and their angry reaction to the reports of Caesar's claims to kingship. The crowd resented Caesar's habit of dictating letters during the games, and believed the rumours that he intended to move the capital from Rome to Alexandria, rumours that sounded plausible in the light of his relations with Cleopatra (Suet., *Div. Jul.* 79, 3; Nic. Dam. fr. 130, 68). After the affair at the Lupercalia and the clash between Caesar and the tribunes, the conspirators were wholly convinced that his bright star was waning.

The concept of 'image' in public opinion was not invented by modern journalists. The Romans called it *fama* or *existimatio*, (see Appendix, p. 214) and to them it had great significance, but modern researchers have paid insufficient attention to its importance. In the political arena, where a man's appearance as reflected by public opinion is more important than his real qualities, and his political stance is more impressive than the most progressive legislation, the *quomodo* is also more important than the *quod*. It must be assumed that, even in 46 BC, particularly at the time of Cicero's *Pro Marcello*, there was considerable expectation that Caesar would restore the Republic. Cicero was not the only one who nurtured this hope (*ad fam.* XIII, 68, 2, Sept. 46 BC; cf. IV, 4, 3). Before Munda many people were wary of the Pompeians, and even Cassius prayed for Caesar's victory (*ad fam.* XV, 19, 4). Afterwards the rumour reached Cicero that Brutus wished to count Caesar among the *boni viri* (*ad fam.* XIII, 40, 1).

There was no serious political significance in the attempt on Caesar's life in 46 BC. Caesar made a report on it in the Curia, and the incident disappeared into oblivion (*Phil.* II, 74, cf. *Pro Marcello* 21). But ever since the summer of 45 BC there had been rumours of steadily rising anger against the dictator (*ad Att.* XIII, 37, 2). That in itself does not explain the reason for the formation of the conspiracy, the details of which we shall never discover. It was a spontaneous decision that ripened into planned action shortly before March 15. It arose from a whole series of political dealings that poisoned the atmosphere and brought antagonisms to the surface, rather than as a result of the abundant *honores* heaped on Caesar by the Senate after Munda. I should like to suggest that the conspirators had sufficient reasons for believing that public opinion was behind them, but that they did not allow for its ambivalence.

Certain episodes can be used as illustrations. The Roman Optimates were never enthusiastic about the institution of the tribunate, but had nevertheless not gone to the lengths required to totally abolish it. They saw it as something of a compromise – a means of making their conservative policies palatable to the people. It was always possible to find one tribune among ten who was a traditionalist, and it was always much easier to take action against a Tiberius or a Gaius Gracchus when one could use the services of an Octavius or Livius Drusus the elder (Cic., *de leg* III, 24).

Not all of the tribunes were supporters of Caesar. His clashes with Metellus in 49 BC and with Flavus and Marullus in 44 BC stand out in stark contrast to the slogans published at the time of the crossing of the Rubicon, when Caesar castigated the Senate's conduct towards the tribunes as *crudelitas* (Caes., *Bell. Civ.* I, 32, 6). Finally, there must have been some people who were not prepared to accept the arbitrary dismissal of the tribunes without further argument.

Even though the masses remained loyal to Caesar's memory, the anti-Caesarian tribunes were still popular after the Ides of March (Dio XLIV, 11, 4; Suet., *Div. Jul.* 80, 3). Caesar was well aware of the tenseness between himself and the tribunes, as the following episode illustrates. In October 45 BC Caesar celebrated his Spanish victory. When his triumphal chariot passed the place where the tribunes stood, the tribune Aquila remained seated. Caesar angrily rebuked him, 'Come, then, Aquila, take back the Republic from me you mighty tribune', and for the next several days he would not make a promise to anyone without adding 'That is, if Pontius Aquila will allow me' (Suet., *Div. Jul.* 78, 2).

We have no clues as to why Aquila made such a public protest. Possibly he belonged to Pompey's camp and could not forgive Caesar for flouting tradition by celebrating a victory that had been gained in a civil war. The victory at Thapsus was camouflaged to appear as a triumph over the Numidian Juba, but after Munda Caesar was not so inhibited, and thereby aroused opposition.

It is possible that the reasons for the breach between Caesar and some of the tribunes went deeper. He sought full tribunician powers for himself, because he preferred to deal with the people directly and not through such middle-men, who did not always follow instructions. There were certainly some tribunes who were not prepared to put up with his disregard of the legal rights of the plebs, particularly as he was a patrician. On the other hand, these tribunes, the representatives of the people, proved very convenient for the Roman *nobilitas*, when they ate out of its hand. The appearance of *mancipia nobilium* (tribunes who served the *nobilitas*) was nothing new in Roman history (Livy X, 37, 11). The conspirators were encouraged by what they saw as a breach between Caesar on the one hand and the tribunes and the people on the other. An anonymous message was written on the statue of Lucius Brutus the liberator ' "Oh, that you were still alive" ', and another on Caesar's,

' "First of all was Brutus consul, since he drove the kings from Rome; Since this man drove out the consuls, he at last is made our king" '

(Suet., *Div. Jul.* 80, 2-3)

The conspirators were victims of their own propaganda. They

failed to understand that the discontent of a noisy minority could not be taken for the opinion of the silent majority, and that dissatisfaction with a dictatorial government did not necessarily endorse tyrannicide, especially as there was no possibility of preparing the ground by stirring up unrest. This false conclusion was born in the hope that Caesar's murder would see the 'end of tyranny'.

While it may be self-evident that not all the people respected Caesar, it is wrong to suppose that the Roman plebs as a group formed a monolithic structure. Tacitus knew the difference between the 'integra pars populi' – those connected as *clientes* with the great families of the *nobilitas* – and those who were loyal to the emperor, whom he dubbed *plebs sordida*, the rabble that was entertained with bread and circuses (*Hist.* I, 4).[24] This classification is also appropriate to the Republic: if we had a history of this period from the pen of one of Caesar's supporters, we would discover common people connected with the houses of Brutus, Cassius and Casca (and there were such) depicted as *plebs sordida*.

Another incident occurred soon. On December 31, 45 BC, a popular assembly (*comitia tributa*) met to elect the quaestors. After about two hours (around 8 am), it became known that the suffect consul (Quintus Fabius Maximus) had died suddenly. His term of office would have run out on that day, and the consuls for 44 BC, long since designated, were ready to take their places on January 1. But a man like Caesar was not inclined to leave Rome without a consul, not even for a single day. The *comitia centuriata* was hastily summoned, and C. Caninius Rebilus was elected to serve for those few hours. Rome mocked, and Cicero took the opportunity to make a bitter comment, 'Let us go quickly, lest the gentleman be out of office before we get there.' It was, in fact, customary to accompany a newly-elected consul to the Senate (Plut., *Caes.* 58, 1). In a letter to Curio, Cicero again ridiculed the affair, and wrote that Rebilus was a wonderfully wide-awake consul, for he had not closed an eye during his whole period of office (*ad fam.* VII, 30, 1).[25]

In this matter Caesar behaved precisely according to the law, but expressly against the legislator's original intention. By following the rules to the letter he mocked tradition, which prompted Cicero to write that 'If you were an eye-witness you could not keep back your tears' (*ibid.* 30, 2).

Caesar's powerful influence on the election of magistrates was well known, but some people were far from pleased that the election of a consul had become a laughing matter. When it was rumoured that Caesar had defined the Republic as nothing, a title without form and content (nihil esse rem publicam, appellationem modo sine corpore ac specie: Suet., *Div. Jul.* 77), or that he had required a carefully chosen form of address and his word to be regarded as law (*ibid.*), many people believed it (*ibid.* 76, for further examples). Mommsen wrote that Caesar was not only sole master, but also worked without partners, employing only henchmen.[26] Stefan Zweig's description of Napoleon comes to mind: the thoughtful psychologist made the most happy use of the rivalry between his ministers to spur them on the one hand, and at the same time keep them in check.

We have no definite clues about the teamwork in Caesar's camp, but his successes could not have been achieved by one man. Caesar had no time, and probably no patience, to bring every important matter before a full meeting of the Senate. Rather, he took advice from his confidants (*familiares*) and the Senate was powerless to prevent it. Senatorial decrees were drafted in Balbus' house and, when it suited his purpose, Caesar even used Cicero's name without his knowledge, as Cicero told Papirius Paetus in an angry letter in the late autumn of 46 BC.

Do you really think that there will be fewer decrees of the Senate, if I am at Naples? Here am I at Rome and in constant attendance at the Forum, and all the while decrees of the Senate are being drafted at the house of my dear friend who dotes upon you. Indeed, whenever it occurs to him, my name is put down as a witness to the drafting, and I am informed that some decree of the Senate alleged to have been passed in accordance with my vote has found its way to Armenia and Syria, before the matter has ever been mentioned at all. And pray don't think that this is merely a joke on my part; I would have you know that I have ere now received letters from kings in the uttermost parts of the world, in which they thank me for having given them by my vote the title of king, I being in ignorance not only of their having been so entitled, but of their ever having been born (*ad fam.* IX, 15, 4).

But Cicero did not confine his bitterness to private letters to friends. His sarcastic tongue was loose, and his witticisms circulated throughout Rome. When, on one occasion, Andron of Laodicaea came to Rome to request freedom for his city, Cicero, who defined the situation in Rome as *publica servitus*, said to him, 'If you are successful, put in a good word for us too' (Macrob., *Sat.* II, 3, 11).

This was a sore point. A Roman senator was not readily prepared to be a silent partner of state. If it was not considered necessary to consult him, at least his name should not be used without his knowledge. A consul who assailed the good name of a Roman senator could expect a sharp reaction, 'You are no consul in my book . . . since I am not even a senator in yours' (Val. Max. VI, 2, 2).

Caesar's way of handling matters hurt senators more than his election to four successive consulships. Since 49 BC, Caesar had made no attempt to conceal his unfathomable hatred of the Senate (*ad Att.* X, 4, 9), and even when power was firmly in his grasp, he did not change his attitude. He knew that he would not acquire many supporters in the Senate if they could gain access to him only through a distressful process of abasement (*ad fam.* VI, 14, 2), and had to wait for hours outside his door (*ad Att.* XIV, 1, 2; 2, 3). Nevertheless, he should have expected some understanding from a man like Cicero that a fully-loaded working day left him little time for pointless discussions.

On the other hand, it is difficult to explain why Caesar crossed senators unnecessarily. Did he have to tear down the Curia Hostilia in order to build a temple to Felicitas (Dio XLIV, 5, 1)? Was it absolutely essential to set up a bust of Cleopatra in the temple of Venus Genetrix (Dio LI, 22, 3; App., *BC* II, 102)? And how easily Caesar could have won Cicero's heart: when visiting the writer's estate (which was more in the nature of a billeting than a visit) did he take the time to discuss the political issues of the day? Caesar obviously tried to keep his literary friend in his place, and 'there was no serious talk, but plenty of literary discussion' (*ad Att.* XIII, 52). He left an embittered Cicero behind.

Eventually even Cicero wearied of Caesar, began to compare him with Alexander, and described his tactlessness, 'For there are countless cases of the same sort, and it would be more than I could bear, had I not taken refuge in the haven of philosophy' (*ad fam.* VII, 30, 2). But the majority of senators were not interested in philosophy, and their reactions were quite different. When Caesar was sitting in front of the temple of Venus Genetrix one day, a delegation from the Senate, led by consuls and praetors, came to inform him of a series of senatorial decrees – all to his honour and glory. 'He did not rise to receive them, but as if he were dealing with mere private persons, replied that his honours needed curtailment rather than enlargement' (Plut., *Caes.* 60, 3).

Many versions of this story spread throughout the city.[27] No doubt Caesar and his followers were anxious to circulate their own account: the dictator had not realized that the matter was of such special significance and he had been so preoccupied with very important problems that he had failed to rise from absent-mindedness and not from any intention to cause offence. There was another version, to the effect that Caesar was a good man, but had surrounded himself with a pack of advisers that led him astray. He had intended to rise and pay the senators the respect due to them, but Balbus had prevented him. Not that Caesar was a prisoner of his advisers outside the Senate, but responsibility for the incident was pushed on to the wealthy Balbus, who was considered a sort of privy councillor. In another version, those who hoped to blacken Caesar's reputation with the Senate reported that Trebatius had given him a signal to rise, but that Caesar had thrown him a hostile glance and remained seated. When Caesar attempted to justify this conduct, stating that he had had to stay seated on account of stomach pains, he merely added fuel to the flames, for shortly after the senators left he rose to his feet and walked home, hale and hearty (Dio XLIV, 8).

In enumerating the honours attributed to Caesar after the battle of Munda, Cassius Dio reported that the relevant senatorial decrees virtually created Caesar a monarch (XLIII, 45), yet he did not state that he had been crowned king. There were proposals to grant him the title, but when he learned of them Caesar threatened to refuse it on the ground that it was unwelcome in view of the curse that had been attached to it for generations (App., *BC* II, 107; Dio XLIV, 9, 2).

In January 44 BC, when he was returning from the *Feriae Latinae* there was a shout of 'Rex' at the city gate. He answered with a somewhat naïve play on words, 'Caesarem se non regem esse' ('he was Caesar, not king'), as though a mistake had been made about his name (App., *BC* II, 108; Suet., *Div. Jul.* 79, 2). Many saw hypocrisy in his refusal of the title. It remains an open question whether it was a spontaneous gesture, or, if not, who organized the shout from the crowd?

At all events, the story spread through the city like wildfire.

Can we come to the conclusion that Caesar really wanted to be king? Those who answer 'yes' can base their case on further examples. Not long after the incident at the city gate (the precise date is unknown), the statue of Caesar that stood on the *rostra* was crowned with a diadem. Cassius Dio (XLIV, 9, 2) said that it was done secretly by the conspirators. Plutarch also (*Caes*. 61, 4) said, rather vaguely, that 'Caesar's statues were adorned with crowns'. Suetonius (*Div. Jul.* 79, 1), who described the diadem as a laurel wreath interwoven with a white band, reported that the statue was adorned by 'someone from the crowd' ('quidam e turba'), and only Appian (*BC* II, 108) pointed out that this someone belonged to the group who wanted to spread the rumour about Caesar's attempts to become king. The truth behind the 'diadem affair' will never be clearly established. Were Caesar's opponents really behind it, with the object of dragging his name through the mud? Or did Caesar secretly give the instruction as a test of the people's reaction?

The affair became even more complicated. The tribunes of the people, C. Epidius Marullus and Lucius Caesetius Flavus, ordered the diadem to be removed and the person who put it there be thrown into chains. Caesar immediately dismissed the tribunes from office. Why? Because the attempt to put him forward as king had failed perhaps? Because its failure could make coronation more difficult? It is hard to believe that the crowning of a statue was seen as synonymous with coronation. Perhaps credit for his public refusal of the honour had eluded him? Or, finally, perhaps, because he thought the tribunes were responsible for the incident? According to Nicolaus Damascenus, Caesar blamed the tribunes for permitting the diadem to be put on the monument (*fr*. 130, 69). That Nicolaus was sympathetic to Caesar should not necessarily impugn his credibility.

Caesar's dispute with Flavus and Marullus after the Aquila affair must have led to a widening gulf with other tribunes too. The Senate was as pleased with this split as with the one between Tiberius Gracchus and Octavius, and many an eyebrow was raised among the Roman public when Caesar complained about the tribunes before the Senate in the Temple of Concordia and demanded their punishment. The man who had begun his career by the *via popularis* and had crossed the

Rubicon to protect the rights of the tribunes had come a long way. Now he faced a considerable dilemma: either he must act against his principles or watch his popularity decline (Vell. Pat. II, 68). Suetonius (*Div. Jul.* 79, 1) reported that Caesar removed the tribunes from office with violent insults. Even though some of his enthusiastic supporters (or, to use another term, sycophants) demanded the death penalty for the tribunes, Caesar did not deviate from his traditional *clementia* (Dio XLIV, 10, 2-3). His reputation, however, had been severely damaged, and he described the incident, in a speech before the Senate, as an attempt to stir up discord between himself and the people.

Chapters 60–62 of Plutarch's life of Caesar should be read with great caution, and from the point of view stated above (p. 197). There is no foundation to the report that the crowd (*hoi polloi*) turned to Brutus and Cassius as a result of the quarrel with the tribunes. A section of the people, however, did see in their removal the disparagement of the tribunate, but they belonged to the *clientelae* of the traditional aristocratic houses. A man who claimed a crown while infringing the tribunes' *sacrosanctitas* was also capable of aiming at royal status: hence the propaganda that Caesar was planning to crown himself did not fall on deaf ears.

Caesar was irritated, 'As a matter of fact, to one who aspires to power the poorest man is the most helpful . . .' (Sall., *Bell. Jug.* 86, 3), and, in spite of their small number and limited power, Caesar had to reckon with the fact that, in case of emergency, even a fly can do damage in politics (Sen., *de ira* I, 3, 2).

Three weeks later, on February 15, 44 BC, at the festival of the Lupercalia, Antony approached Caesar and presented him with a diadem. Caesar refused the gift, to the approbation of the crowd, and had it placed in the temple, since, as he said, Jupiter Optimus Maximus was the only king of the Romans (Dio XLIV, 11, 3). He had a record made in the *Fasti* to the effect that Antony had offered him the position of king in the name of the Roman people, but that he had refused it (Cic., *Phil.* II, 87).

Difficult questions arise at this point. Did Caesar want to be king? Did he want to test the reaction of the people, and was Antony's gesture made with Caesar's approval? Or did Antony perhaps offer him the crown to expose him publicly?

Was it not the case that in 45 BC, while still in Narbo, Antony had heard through Trebonius of the plan to murder Caesar, but had never uttered a word about it to his patron (Cic., *Phil.* II, 34; Plut., *Ant.* 13, 1)? Was Antony in the service of the conspirators on February 15, 44 BC? There are scholars who conclude from Nicolaus Damascenus (130, 72) that Antony co-operated with Casca and Cassius. Cicero's *Philippics* on the subject must be cautiously assessed, because he hoped to promote a split between Lepidus and Antony (*Phil.* V, 38; XIII, 17). Here, too, we shall never learn the truth.

Did Caesar really want the title so hated by the Roman people? In the last months before his murder, he was pre-occupied with plans for the Parthian campaign. At the same time (the exact date can no longer be determined, but probably about March 1), a rumour circulated that it was prophesied in the Sibylline Books that Parthia could be conquered only by a king: therefore Caesar ought to be granted the title (Suet., *Div. Jul.* 79, 3). But, when it became clear to him that the Romans would in no way agree to it (hence Plutarch's accounts, *Caes.* 60–61, of the negative reaction to the attempted coronation), Caesar resolved on a more moderate course: he would use the title only in the provinces and not in Rome. Cicero (*de div.* II, 110) explicitly said that this story was based on a false rumour ('falsa fama'). This is clearly corroborated by later sources. Suetonius (*Div. Jul.* 79, 3) spoke of a rumour circulating in the city ('fama percrebruit'), as did Appian (*BC* II, 110). Plutarch (*Caes.* 60, 1) maintained that the rumour was put about by those who wanted Caesar to have the status of king. Cassius Dio's version (XLIV, 15, 3-4) must be connected with this account: he reported that the story forced the conspirators to strike on March 15, or they would run out of time. Rumours based on the Sibylline Books and the prophecies of seers often had a receptive audience among the Roman public. Such was the case on this occasion.

The plot was organized at the end of February or, at the latest, the beginning of March. The malicious propaganda directed at Caesar reached its peak in the two weeks preceding the Ides of March.

The modern historian who dares to trace Caesar's red shoes, purple robe and laurel wreath to his vanity would give a sharp-tongued critic a marvellous opportunity to exercise his wit. Few of them take Suetonius seriously when he refers to

Caesar's vanity and passionate love of finery and ornament (*Div. Jul.* 45, 2-3), 'His baldness was a disfigurement which troubled him greatly . . . Because of it, he used to comb forward his scanty locks from the crown of his head, and of all the honours voted him by the Senate and people there was none which he received or made use of more gladly than the privilege of wearing a laurel wreath at all times.' Even if we adopt Brutus' view that the indulgent weakness and despairing mood of senators loyal to the Republic had enticed Caesar to make the attempt to become king (*Brutus to Cicero* I, 16, 3), this brings us no closer to an understanding of Caesar's intentions. It is wiser to leave the question open.

A detailed psychological analysis of the reasons for Caesar's nervous and irritable conduct is impossible, because there are no relevant references in the sources. Even if it were possible to prove that Caesar's conduct was nothing more than apolitical vanity, that would not have prevented the rumour spreading as part of a ruthless and venomous propaganda campaign; such was the prevailing political atmosphere. Brutus and Cassius were not interested in analysing Caesar's personality. They were, first and foremost, Roman senators, and Caesar was delivered up to the tongues of the crowd (*sermonibus volgi*, Cic., *de Rep.* VI, 25).

The fact remains that no one understood Caesar, and therefore it is idle to look for a formula that would clearly define so changeable a personality. One well-informed contemporary saw only motives of tyranny in all of Caesar's plans and deeds. Others could only observe how he always parted his hair in an artificial fashion, and how he scratched his head with only one finger (a particular sign of femininity in Rome), and it was unthinkable that 'this man would ever conceive of so great a crime as the overthrow of the Roman constitution' (Plut., *Caes.* 4, 4).

There was no let-up in scurrilous propaganda. Suetonius (*Div. Jul.* 79, 2) reported, 'But from that time on he could not rid himself of the odium of having aspired to the title of monarch.' That is probably the only accurate answer. We shall never be able to correctly interpret his own ambitions. We do know that he was never officially crowned, and never bore the title 'king'. And we also know that fresh rumours about his ambitions for the throne continually circulated, and various events were exploited by his opponents as proof of this ambition, an ambition that could have been fulfilled only by a regular and lawful coronation.

One of the rumours was that he planned to move the capital from Rome to Alexandria. The effect on the Roman public is not hard to imagine, especially when the rumour was accompanied by descriptions of what might happen: Caesar would depart, 'taking with him the resources of the state, draining Italy by levies, and leaving it and the charge of the city to his friends'. The affair with Cleopatra lent credibility to such gossip.[28]

Anyone attempting to solve the problem of Caesar's behaving as though he did not understand that his actions and speeches would provoke stubborn rumours must strive for a psychological interpretation. Shakespeare tried, and so did H. Nissen, O. E. Schmidt and J. H. Collins (if by different means), at a later date.

Caesar's degeneration first appeared in the last two years of his rule. Various illnesses and attacks of giddiness had already accentuated his tendencies towards anger, thoughtlessness and weakness of will. Those who accept Caesar's fantastic future plans as fact will be tempted to make use of psychology, but there is not sufficient evidence to make a medical diagnosis. In its absence we must take a more modest view. Caesar's contemporaries did not understand his psyche either, and judged him by his image, as reflected by public opinion. It is in this context that we, too, must try to understand the events of the year 44 BC.

The modern 'man in the street' reacts to rumour with 'no smoke without fire', and the reaction of the man in the street in Rome was no different. Street corners, especially the Solarium in the neighbourhood of the forum, the baths and the barbers' shops were centres of gossip. In Rome, malicious sarcasm was the order of the day and Horace spoke of Italian vinegar (*Italium acetum*). It is not without reason that satire ranks as one of Rome's original contributions to literature.

Cicero incurred a certain amount of hatred from the Roman nobility because of his unbridled tongue, and his conduct confirmed the suspicion expressed by Quintilian, that a Roman would rather lose a friend than an opportunity for a jest (*Inst. Or.* VI, 3, 28).

The most malevolent form of gossip was the spreading of a rumour and simultaneously contradicting it. A good example can be found in Cicero's defence of King Deiotarus. In his speech (33-34) he recounted, as if by accident, rumours current in Rome to the effect that many people hated Caesar, that they looked on him as a tyrant, that his statues were placed among those of the kings, and that such rumours had so incensed the crowd that there was no applause at his public appearances. Naturally, Cicero added, such rumours are without foundation. No sensible man would believe that Caesar actually beheaded and whipped to death countless persons and had allowed their houses to be destroyed. The rumour that the forum was occupied by the army did not correspond to the truth, and every child knew that Caesar was the most benevolent (*clementissimus*) of all rulers. Cicero said that the story about the statue was true, 'but what is a statue? Why should we refuse a man a statue when we have allowed him his triumphs and his spoils?' So far as the lack of applause was concerned, this story was also true, Cicero said, but it was quite wrongly interpreted. In the first place, the public was so thrilled at the sight of Caesar that it was stunned into speechlessness and could not applaud, and second, the people thought that Caesar was too great a man to be welcomed with a burst of applause. That was the usual way of greeting ordinary mortals, and to be so vulgarly acclaimed would be beneath Caesar's standing.

The irony is obvious. Cicero publicly repeated the most malicious rumours and then slyly added to them, smiling all the while: naturally, one cannot believe the rumours, for they are nothing but gossip . . . and the damage is done. Caesar's image suffered sorely – and no denial or counter-attack could stem the devastating allegations.

It makes no sense to examine the truth of rumours. Doubtless they circulated in Rome, suggesting that Caesar was attempting to get a crown for himself and to be treated as a god. Such rumours were the chief weapons of his opponents who were angered that he should be characterized (as earlier was Sulla as holding royal power, 'sine dubio habuit regalem potestatem' Cic., *Har. Resp.* 54). Apart from his titles, there was nothing objectionable in his activities from a legal point of view. For that reason the propaganda had to concentrate on events that could be seen as deviations from the old Republican tradition.

The many honours given to Caesar after the battle of Munda which, rightly or wrongly, were described as 'omnia simul divina atque humana' (see pp. 198–99), provided genuine material, to compromise Caesar in the eyes of the public. Here is one example. With Caesar's appointment as *dictator perpetuo*, many senators realized that a magistracy totally different from those common under the Republic had sprung into being before their very eyes. There were no limitations, such as annual tenure (*potestas ad tempus*) or collegiality (*par potestas*) – the office was lifelong and unshackled by the obligations of accountability. For the future conspirators, such a dictatorship was enough to make them want to be rid of Caesar.

But the appointment in itself was not enough to rouse the public to action. Caesar's partisans could give it the innocent character of an elective dictatorship, intended only to facilitate Caesar's appointment of officials for the years 42 BC and 41 BC in advance. Up to that time he could appoint officials only for one year; thus his claim that he would not march against the Parthians until affairs were settled in Rome ('se nisi constitutis rebus non iturum in Parthos')[29] ought to be understood and believed.

It was easier to stir up the masses by citing facts intelligible to them. If Rambaud (n. 372) is right, and Caesar himself believed that 'the better lie is one that contains a high proportion of truth', then his enemies, too, must have known the secret.

The number of his love affairs was proverbial (Suet., *Div. Jul.* 50–52) and his reputation for adultery clung fast. The people and the troops relished every detail of the gossip, which was part truth and part pure fantasy. In those circumstances, it was not difficult to make people believe the story that certain persons had proposed that Caesar should legally be allowed to associate with as many women as he wished (Dio XLIV, 7, 3) in order to provide for his succession. Suetonius' account was even more exact: the tribune of the people, Helvius Cinna, had personally arranged that the proposal be made law in Caesar's absence (Suet., *Div. Jul.* 52, 3). Such gossip was extraordinarily appropriate to the image of the tyrant (*Rex*), since *libido* is one of its distinguishing characteristics.

Psychologists and sociologists agree that rumours about a person spread within a group relative to the person's significance in the lives of the group members.[30] Gossip passes from mouth to mouth ('ut fama est'), and slanderers are always in a more favourable position, since the slandered are thrown on the defence from the outset, and can justify themselves only with difficulty. They can ignore the accusations, but then they risk the tide of rumour rising even higher and being taken as fact. They can switch to the attack, but in so doing put their reputation still further at stake. Caesar found himself in just such situations when he published *Anticato*,[31] and when Hirtius collected all Cato's 'vices', he ran the risk of only bolstering Cato's reputation still further. Thus it was not an easy matter to mount a defence against Cicero's and Brutus' pungent pens, for they never ceased to praise the dead Cato.

Spreading rumours by word of mouth is only one method of slander. In ancient Rome the publication of libellous pamphlets was also a favourite political weapon. When Livy (XXXVIII, 56, 12) described how Scipio Africanus rejected with disgust the title 'dictator for life' and refused to have his statue erected on the rostra, in the Curia or on the Capitol, his account was more suggestive of the libellous pamphlets written against Caesar, than of the history books of the second century BC. The descriptions were fairly transparent, but this was not the only pamphlet written against Caesar. Suetonius mentioned the malevolent writings of Aulus Caecina and the biting comic verse of Pitholaus (Suet., *Div. Jul.* 75, 5). There is no reason to doubt the correctness of this information, since the wave of rumours and slanders was reported by contemporary sources. One can imagine the reaction in the theatre when Laberius presented Publilius Syrus who, lashed with whips, shouted, 'Porro, Quirites, libertatem perdimus' (Macrob., *Sat.* II, 7, 4).

Caesar fumed, but did not retaliate. In his latter days 'he took no further notice of the conspiracies which were detected, and of meetings by night, than to make known by proclamation that he was aware of them; and he thought it enough to give public warning to those who spoke ill of him' (Suet. *ibid.*). Caesar's reaction in this instance is hard to explain. Perhaps, in point of fact, he was not impressed by set speeches.[32] Or perhaps he dealt according to Dante's: 'Set your course, and let people say what they will' (Segni il tuo corso e lascia dir le genti) because he believed a brilliant campaign against Parthia would once more refurbish his reputation in motion.

Or was the hero weary?[33] Did he prefer, after the unhappy

experience with his *Anticato*, to shun public debates and even to dismiss his Spanish bodyguard? This doubtless facilitated the conspirators' execution of their plans, for in the presence of the bodyguard they would probably not have dared to strike at all. We shall never discover the reasons for the dismissal of the bodyguard. Perhaps Caesar relied too much on the last *senatus consultum* and on the oath of loyalty that was sworn to him (Suet., *Div. Jul.* 86, 1).[34] Or, in the latter days of his life, could he have come to the conclusion that he would always be supported by the people? He blindly trusted his numerous enthusiastic supporters, he heaped scorn on his enemies, and was sure that only he and his well-being stood between the state and a civil war. Did it never occur to him that accidents can happen (*ibid.* 86, 2)? Or was he tired of life?

To these questions there are as many answers as there are scholars. One guess is as good as another. Using an analogy from our own times, examine the slurs that political candidates cast on their opponents via radio and television. Consider how an accidental comment made in the presence of journalists can ruin a politician's future, and how a wave of rumours can cause irreparable damage. There is nothing new under the sun.

In *ad Her.* II, 12, there is an almost scholarly analysis of rumours. Cicero knew quite well how much value should be set on them (*Pro Cluent.* 139). In Suetonius (*Div. Jul.* 76, 1) we discover the tyrannical atmosphere created by Caesar's behaviour and manner of speaking. As a writer Caesar knew how to avoid verbosity (Gell., *Noctes Atticae* I, 10, 4), but in conversation he did not take his own advice: he simply could not hold his tongue. His tactlessness made him more disliked than his measures. Every thoughtless bit of chatter at dinner, every chance conversation on the way to the Senate, every sarcastic remark made to a secretary, every good-humoured joke with a friend, was immediately broadcast through Rome, probably with some distortion, and ultimately to his ruin. When reproached about the quality of the men he had appointed to the Senate, he remarked that, 'if he had been helped in defending his honour by brigands and cut-throats, he would have requited even such men in the same way' (Suet., *Div. Jul.* 72). On another occasion he derided two tribunes in front of the people as 'Brutes and Cymaeans', celebrated for their stupidity (Plut. *Caesar* 61, 5).

His enemies lurked everywhere, on the watch for slips in his speeches, and exploited them to do untold damage. So long as he was in the field with his soldiers he fought against the tide of rumours with vigour – and successfully. When rumours were spreading about the size of Juba's army, he addressed his assembled troops, 'some of you may as well cease to ask further questions or make surmises, and may rather believe me, since I know all about it. Otherwise I shall surely have them shipped on some worn-out craft and carried off to whatever lands the wind may blow them' (Suet., *Div. Jul.* 66).

As he was getting on in years he gave in and his enemies won the day. His image was severely damaged and Suetonius appropriately described it as *existimatio lacerata* (*ibid.* 75, 5).

The conspirators fell into the trap. They let themselves be carried away by the 'public opinion polls' (to use the modern term). The true state of affairs came to light only after Caesar's death.

Under the Principate, people were aware of the vagueness of public opinion which was usually based on rumours. To Virgil, *Fama* was the most light-footed of all evils, 'Speed lends her strength, and she wins vigour as she goes'.[35] Public opinion was not always easy to interpret. At one time it might be *tacita existimatio* (Cic., *Verr.* II, 5, 176), at another *incerta* (*ad fam.* VIII, 2, 2; Livy IV, 15, 1). Seneca knew that it oscillated, but was always ambiguous, 'Existimatio hominum dubia semper est et in partem utramque dividitur' (*Ep.* 26. 6). Quintilian[36] offered a more thoughtful definition. Referring to *fama* and *rumores*, he said that one party called them the verdict of *publicum testimonium* (public opinion?) or the *consensus civitatis*; the other described them as vague gossip without proper foundation born of malevolence and related to credulity, an evil to which the most innocent person can be exposed if his enemies consciously spread lies about him.

Brutus and Cassius were not cautious enough. They believed the rumours about Caesar. They were wrong in assuming that the dictator's murder would solve their problem. After the assassination they rejoiced too soon, and were panic-stricken when they saw the people's real reaction.

This fits Ovid's allegory. *Fama* lives on a high mountaintop. The house has numerous entrances, but no doors to shut her out, and it is open night and day. The place is full of noise, and multiplies everything it hears. Inside there is no silence, no peace. And yet there is no shouting, only the suppressed noises of the waves of the sea heard from a distance. Crowds of people fill the hall, hundreds throng in and out, and everywhere thousands of rumours fly – lies mingled with truth and confused reports float around, 'mixtaque cum veris passim commenta vagantur milia rumorum confusaque verba volutant' *Fama*'s characteristics are first, *credulitas*, then *temerarius error*, later *vana laetitia* (empty rejoicing) and finally *consternati timores* (panic-stricken fear).[37]

No one who accepts this interpretation needs to give a definitive answer to the question, whether Caesar was a king, or a god or both, or to investigate whether his regime conformed with definitions used in political science. It is more important to answer the question whether some of his important contemporaries saw Caesar as a tyrant. This is not difficult: consensus may even be reached in modern scholarship.[38]

Brutus and Cassius and their supporters were not particularly troubled by the idea of the extraordinary authority of a single man for a limited period. In the last resort the Senate earlier had been prepared, in a time of crisis, to offer Pompey 'complete control of the corn-supply of the whole world for five years, control of the treasury, an army and a fleet and *maius imperium* in the provinces' (Cic., *ad Att*. IV, 1, 7).

Many senators regarded Caesar as superfluous after Munda: he had outlived his usefulness. They had their doubts about the honours heaped upon him, but when he was made dictator for life their doubts became certainty: it was no longer a Republican magistracy, and not just the temporary measure of an emergency. This is how the conspiracy against Caesar can be explained, without having to define whether he was aiming at a kingdom or at divinity. The moment he took up a lifelong dictatorship he was, in the eyes of the conspirators, *Rex*.

Was Caesar a charismatic ruler? Some time ago Carl Friedrich objected to the widespread use of the word,[39] but was ignored by the majority of sociologists and political scientists, who all seemed to designate prominent personalities in developing countries as charismatic (Nkrumah in his time, Sekou Toure, Sukarno in his heyday and Abdul Nasser).[40] The charismatic figure usually appears when the existing ruling class of a society has lost confidence, when the people begin to feel insecure about their laws and traditions and when the government seems unable to control them. Then a need for a strong man arises, one who promises political, social, economic or religious change, or all four at once. Little can be added to Max Weber's masterly generalization: the appearance of a charismatic leader brings about an almost irrational sense of security among his followers because charisma, he said, is a certain quality of an individual personality by virtue of which he is set apart from ordinary men and endowed with super-natural, superhuman or at least specifically exceptional powers or qualities.

The common denominator of all charismatic leaders is given that they do not want to turn their government into a reign of terror, they must continually demonstrate their qualities to the public. A charismatic leader would be forgiven for one mistake, but a leader in the traditional mould would not: a series of mistakes, one big blunder, or too long a wait for the fulfilment of promises leads to disappointment, and finally the pendulum swings against him. Charisma is usually shortlived and the swing is always extreme. As Metternich put it, 'la chute d'un grand homme est lourde!' Caesar's contemporary, Laberius, was already aware of that: 'When you have reached the highest rank of fame, you will find it hard to keep your place and you will fall more quickly than you could climb' (Macrob, *Sat.* II, 7, 9). Tacitus put the blame on the fickleness of the mob, 'Brevis et infaustos populi Romani amores'.

Simpy to hang the label 'charismatic leader' on a Hitler, Caesar, Churchill, Kennedy, Napoleon or a Nasser is not enough when trying to comprehend his personality. No real assessment can be made without taking into consideration that the ideal picture of a leader is often only created out of the fantasies and daydreams of his people. The leader and the led are two halves of a whole and should not be judged separately. They cannot be separated from a concrete historical context. This, too, is in keeping with Max Weber, 'How the quality in question [charisma] could ultimately be judged from any ethical, aesthetic or any other such point of view – is entirely indifferent for purposes of definition. What is alone important is how the individual is actually regarded by those subject to charismatic authority, by his followers or disciples.'

This should also be applied to Caesar. Whether his intel-lectual qualities made any impression on the people and the army is doubtful. Yet it was precisely because of them that he won over – for most of the time – Brutus and Cassius, Cicero and Varro; he fascinated the Roman intelligentsia with his personal style and with his penetrating knowledge of philosophy and history, grammar and rhetoric.[41] He was a devotee of the fine arts and an insatiable collector of objets d'art, gems, carvings, sculpture and paintings (Suet., *Div. Jul.* 42, 1; 47). He was also a first-class connoisseur of Cicero's wit, and even edited his *Apothegmata* (*ad fam.* IX, 16, 4), could quote Greek poetry by heart, and was at ease in the company of poets.[42] His appearance was certainly impressive. He surpassed his fellow-citizens in shapeliness (Vell. Pat. II, 41), and he could be compared to Alexander in beauty (App., *BC* II, 151), while his bisexuality emphasized the brilliance of his personality and his manliness yet further. He had considerable strength, which enabled him to undertake extremely strenuous tasks, and his endurance was almost incredible (Suet., *Div. Jul.* 57). He was a splendid swimmer, and such an expert rider that he could hold his arms behind his back at a full gallop (Plut., *Caes.* 17, 4). It is not difficult to imagine how such a commander looked to his soldiers. As an orator 'he is said to have delivered himself in a high-pitched voice with impassioned action and gestures, which were not without grace' (Suet., *Div. Jul.* 55, 3), and Cicero declared him 'master of an eloquence which is brilliant . . . and which in respect of voice, gesture, and the speaker's whole physique, possesses a certain noble and high-bred quality' (*Brut.* 261).

Nicolaus Damascenus (fr. 130, 64) reported the words of a contemporary, 'Rejoicing not unreasonably in his many splendid victories, thinking himself to be more than mortal, he evoked the wonder of the crowd'. Caesar knew how to make an impression on people. As far back as 65 BC, when he was aedile, his colleague Bibulus complained 'that his was the fate of Pollux, "For", said he, "just as the temple erected in the Forum to the twin brethren bears only the name of Castor, so the joint liberality of Caesar and myself is credited to Caesar alone" ' (Suet., *Div. Jul.* 10, 1, see above, p. 165).

But all that is not enough to ensure permanent affection. Caesar was a popular leader because the basic needs of the people were his primary consideration. He distributed land in Italy and in the colonies, provided for the corn supply, for the relief of debts and took care of rent problems. For the masses he organized entertainments, distributed gifts and benefits, provided conditions to ensure an increase in the birth-rate and his huge development projects produced an income for thousands. The widely-renowned general, the victor in many battles, took care to appear as a benevolent ruler whose *clementia* was praised by friend and foe alike.

By publicly humiliating the aristocrats and nobles, Caesar conquered the hearts of the crowd – a common device in Rome. In this light Livy described Terentius Varro, whom the people during the Hannibalic War saw as one of their own: he 'had endeared himself to the plebeians . . . by invectives against the leading men and the usual tricks of the demagogue. The blow he had struck at the influence and dictatorial authority of Fabius brought him the glory which is won by defaming others, and the rabble was now striving to raise him to the consulship' (Livy XX, 34, 2). Julius Caesar went far beyond his predecessors in providing for the masses, and we have shown that this is precisely what antagonized the senatorial aristocracy. At the same time, he appeared to his supporters as a benevolent ruler whose first care was the state and its citizens, and only they saw him as a charismatic ruler.

But others, among them ordinary citizens, who could not forgive him for the attacks on the tribunes, for dictating letters during the games, and for his indulgence to ex-Pompeians, saw him as obsessed with popularity, an ambitious show-off, to whom it was no coincidence that Euripides' verse, which Cicero translated, was applicable: 'If wrong may e'er be right, for a throne's sake were wrong most right' (Cic., *de off*. III, 82; cf. Suet., *Div. Jul*. 30, 5). Cicero could have had only these citizens in mind when he said that Caesar's murder was legitimate (*Phil*. II, 86). No wonder that Gibbon thought that Caesar had provoked his fate as much by the ostentation of his power as by the power itself.

To sum up, even those who reject the idea that Caesar tried to establish a monarchy and a divine cult must admit that he was much more than just a Roman dictator. They must also agree that his performance and achievements made restoration of the old Republic impossible once and for all. Whether all this was planned or brought about accidentally matters little.

Celeritas was distinctive of his style, impulsiveness led to his downfall. Many were enchanted by him, yet not a few felt repulsed. Since he neither wanted, nor could afford, to base his rule on a single class of society, he tried to curry favour with heterogeneous groups, at one and the same time. In his struggle for the support of the masses he overcame Pompey, but at the same time made considerable efforts to appease the *nobilitas*. He was called a benevolent ruler, but also a cruel despot (Luc., *Phars*. VIII, 835). He was on the whole a moderate statesman, who was nevertheless unable to avoid the impression that he put through his moderate policies by ruthless force.

In the future scholars may possibly discover other 'Caesars'. But admirers will continue to support Alföldi, 'For the most part the moderns follow the ancients in blaming Caesar for ruthlessly replacing the ancient structure of a village community by an efficient organization. The same moderns likewise follow the ancients in eulogizing Augustus, who constructed his monarchy on the firm foundations Caesar planted. In my opinion, one cannot condemn one and acquit the other of the same thing' (quod uno iustum, alteri aequum).[43]

I cannot argue with Alföldi about Caesar's greatness, but can establish that 'efficient organization' was never a slogan of the ancients, and in the Romans' opinion – the Senate as much as the plebs – the *quomodo* was equal in importance to the *quod*. It is wrong to put Caesar on a par with Sulla, just as it is wrong to put him on a par with Augustus.

Caesar did not have the gift of what the Romans called *humanitas*. Pliny the Younger defined it as the capacity to win the affections of lesser folk without impinging on greater (*Ep*. IX, 5). With his gifted intuition, Caesar ushered in a new epoch in Roman history. But he relied so much on his personal charm that he overlooked the need for tact, especially when he thought that he was in the right. Success lay open to a less brilliant and therefore more tolerant man – so when the Romans realized that there was no other choice than that of an autocracy, they preferred 'to take the bitter medicine from the hand of the most delicate of doctors'.[44]

APPENDIX

EXISTIMATIO
AND FAMA

This paper was delivered as a James C. Loeb Classical Lecture at Harvard University on
March 15, 1972, and published in HSCP 78 (1974), pp. 35–65.

I

Like frustration, alienation, ecology, and charisma – the
notions, 'image', and 'public opinion', have perhaps been too
frequently used, if not abused. Public opinion is as old as
political history, or, as Dicey put it: 'There exists at any given
time a body of beliefs, convictions, sentiments, accepted
principles, or firmly rooted prejudices, which taken together
make up the public opinion of a particular era or what we may
call the reigning or predominating current opinion.'[1]

Machiavelli thought that a wise man should not ignore
public opinion[2] and David Hume, using the term 'opinion',
wrote: 'The Sultan of Egypt or the Emperor of Rome might
drive his harmless subjects like beasts, but he, at least, must
lead his Mamelukes or praetorian bands by their opinion.'[3]

In traditional societies this opinion is formed according to
the guidance of the accepted military or religious leaders.
Sudden deviation from these principles or crimes against them
will cause a crisis. Modern sociologists believe that public
opinion can become an active factor in society when the
authority of the traditional leadership is upset, when new
values (not sanctioned by tradition or religion) show up and
when, within the structure of a society, social and cultural
cracks of disintegration appear. The late Roman Republic
would fit such a framework.

When I wrote *Plebs and Princeps* I was aware of the problem,
but touched it only *en passant* in two footnotes: 'This modern
expression is not found in classical sources but may perhaps be

conveyed by *consensus hominum* (Sen. *Polyb.* 6, 1) or *fama* (e.g.
Tac. *Ann.* IV, 40)'; and indeed *fama* is not included in the
index.[4] Under the Republic, *existimatio* is the relevant term.[5]

Christian Meier in his *Respublica amissa* is fully aware of the
important role of public opinion and rightly stresses the fact
(also in a footnote) that 'Im allgemeinen wird die Rolle der
Existimatio unterschätzt.'[6] He makes some short but very
valuable remarks on *existimatio*[7] which is much more frequent
in republican sources, especially in Cicero's writings. I shall
therefore deal with *existimatio* first.

Nations, cities, social groups, and institutions each have
their own reputation. Rome was no exception. Gradually her
public image became stereotyped, and her representatives
were expected to act accordingly. Cicero marched his army
against Pindenissus because the town harbored fugitives and
looked forward to the coming of the Parthians. He considered
of importance *ad existimationem imperi* to stop their audacity
(Cic. *Fam.* XV, 4, 10). When Verres robbed a young Syrian
prince (one of King Antiochus's sons who happened to come
to Syracuse), he caused injury to the reputation and prestige
of Rome (*existimatio atque auctoritas nomini populi Romani
imminuta*) (Cic. *Verr.* II, 4, 60). News spread around quickly
among foreign nations and in Cicero's usual exaggerations:
usque ad ultimas terras pervagatum est (*ibid.* II, 4, 64).

A sensational evening paper in our own days would probably have the following headline: 'Rome's image severely
damaged' and, as will be seen later, the term *existimationem
lacerare, violare, perdere* is often used in Latin as well.[8]

Cities can build up their reputation, and this is occasionally
useful. When pirates set fire to a Roman fleet, an angry crowd
demonstrated in front of Verres' house, but was restrained by
remembering that the situation was critical and by having
regard for the *existimatio* of Syracuse (Cic. *Verr.* II, 5, 94).[9]

Not all cities had a good reputation. Alabanda was famous
for its luxury (Strab. XIV, 661), Abdera, proverbially a city of
fools. The mathematician Licymnius said that the inhabitants
of Tralles had the reputation for being stupid and by unsuitable
disposition of statues they added a blemish to the city in public
estimation: Vitr. VII, 5, 6: *Ita indecens inter locorum proprietates,
status signorum publice civitati vitium existimationis adiecit.*

Social orders have their public image too, and the *existimatio*
of the *ordo senatorius* or *ordo equester* is often at stake (e.g. Cic.

Verr. I, 42; II, 1, 5; II, 2, 117; II, 2, 28). The good name
(*existimatio*) of the law courts can be lost or restored (Cic. *Verr.*
I, 2; II, 1, 22; II, 4, 113; *Div. Caec.* 48), and a group of people
serving on a jury can be made well disposed by revealing to
them what esteem (*existimatio*) they enjoy and with what
interest their decision is awaited (*Rhet. Her.* I, 5, 8; cf. Cic. *Inv.
Rhet.* I, 22).[10] This paper, however, will be focused on
existimatio of an individual.[11]

It seems (*prima facie*) as if the reputation of an individual is
based upon merit, provided he acts and behaves according to
the expectations of his peer group. The reputation (*existimatio*)
for better or worse of a private citizen could be deeply affected
by his behaviour as a trustee, a guardian, or a partner (Cic.
QRosc. 16; cf. *Quinct.* 53).[12] Nothing could be more disgraceful than to be unable to help a friend (*nihil ad existimationem turpius,* Cic. *De Or.* II, 200)[13] or to damage the
reputation of one's friend (Cic. *Planc.* 6). A father's *existimatio*
depended upon his care toward his son (Cic. *Att.* 14, 16, 4),
and a business man like Atticus never wearied of an enterprise
which he had once undertaken for the thought that his own
existimatio was involved: *suam enim existimationem in ea re agi
putabat.* (Nep. *Att.* 15, 2). A man with an *existimatio* of *gravitas*
is not expected to dance naked at a banquet (Cic. *Deiot.* 27).[14]
and a lawyer may lose his reputation by accepting the defense
of a notorious scoundrel (*existimationem amittere* Cic. *Verr.* II,
2, 192). If Cicero would defend Teucris (perhaps an agent of
Antonius) he would lose *existimatio* among both – *populares*
and *optimates* (here in the sense of public opinion, Cic. *Att.* I,
12, 1), but if he had kept quiet and not prosecuted Verres for
his crimes, his own *existimatio* would have been in danger (Cic.
Verr. I, 27).

In a case in which *existimatio* of a man is in danger (*quod
videtur ad summam illius existimationem hoc iudicium pertinere*)
(Cic. *Caecin.* 6), decisions should not be taken in a hurry (*Quia
existimationis periculum est tardissime iudicatur*) (*ibid.* 7, 9) because
such a verdict could ruin one's life. Some individuals, of
course, couldn't care less – but those who disregard *existimatio*
(their own reputation, as well as public opinion) are in the
same category with those who consider an oath as a joke and a
testimony as a game (*Cic. Flac.* 12; cf. *Clu.* 39; *Rhet. Her.* IV,
13, 19; *In Pis.* 65; *Verr.* II, 4, 102; II, 1, 87: *Te hominum
existimatio non movebat*).[15]

This being so in private life, a public figure had even more to submit to the judgment of the public not only statements or speeches made openly (Pliny *Ep.* II, 5, 3) but also his daily behavior.

Little was demanded and expected from lower clerks and magistrates. Loyalty toward their superiors and decency in performing their duties were, of course, essential. The *existimatio* of P. Terentius Hispo, deputy manager of a company which collected grazing dues (*scriptura*), mainly depended upon his settling of contracts with the rest of the states (Cic. *Fam.* 13, 65, 1).[16] In order to earn a reputation (*existimatio*) in the eyes of all the citizens in a city or province, like Sthenius in the eyes of all Sicilians (Cic. *Verr.* II, 2, 111), this was not enough. Birth (*genus*), official position (*honos*), and wealth (*copiae*) played an important role.

Existimatio as reputation or public opinion is generally of neutral connotation from a moral point of view. The *existimatio* can be *bona* (as in most cases) or *turpis* (e.g. Cic. *Caecin.* 8), but expressions like these have no absolute value. The author of the statement and the peer group should always be kept in mind. *Boni* and *Mali* in the late Republic had their own views about good and bad.

From a social and political point of view, *existimatio cuiusque* is best translated as one's standing in society; that is, a man must have reached a certain status or rank to be worthy of *existimatio*. There were people with no standing at all in political life, but they do not concern us here.

It is true that to a certain extent wealth and *existimatio* are intimately related (Suet. *Nero* 12); and this is precisely what Cicero had to say about Murena and his province: *L. Murenae provincia multas bonas gratias cum optima existimatione attulit* (*Mur.* 42). On the other hand, Maeandrius (to whom the people of Tralles entrusted their case) was an individual of low caste, without distinction. He was poverty-stricken, without property – and, of course, without *existimatio: Homo egens, sordidus, sine honore sine censu sine existimatione* (Cic. *Flac.* 52).

When Cicero wanted to discredit Asclepiades as a witness, he depicted him as a low-lived person: *Fortuna egens, vita turpis, existimatione damnatus* (*Flac.* 35). Yet more idealistic statements may be found: *existimatio* may remain '*integra*' even if one is deprived of money (Cic. *Quinct.* 49). *Bona existimatio divitiis praestat*, says the moralist (Cic. *De Or.* II, 172), and Agesilaus is praised because '*opulentissimo regno praeposuit bonam existima-tionem* (Nep. *Ages.* 4, 3). A good man should think very little of money but consider his reputation to be most sacred: *Pecunia levissima – existimatio sanctissima* (Cic. *QRosc.* 15).[17]

To sum up: in Roman daily life, origin and wealth were very important components of *existimatio*, but not the only ones.

II

In our own day, when mass media prevail, an image-conscious leader will develop a sophisticated network of public relations. Gifted public-relations men are essential in a modern election campaign, and good advisers are well paid. The author of the *Commentariolum Petitionis*[18] did not do it for money. His main advice was basic and elementary.

The main problem is not the candidate's personality. It is how he is thought of by others. It is not enough to be a good man, it is essential to appear like one. This is what Cicero had in mind when he advised his brother 'how to win friends and influence people,' using innumerable times the term *videri* (e.g. *QFr.* I, 1, 10; I, 1, 46, etc.).

Loyalty of (influential) friends is important but the feelings of (common) people should not be underestimated (16)*. As far as *voluntas popularis* is concerned, tribesmen, neighbors, clients, freedmen, and even slaves should not be neglected, for nearly all the talk which forms one's public reputation emanates from domestic sources. This is how the *fama forensis* (17) is formed, and a series of practical suggestions as to the behavior of the candidate follows:

A man who wants to attach people to himself should remember their proper names (28), pay them constant attention, show his liberality toward them, and behave tactfully (41-42). If nature had denied the candidate a certain quality, he should make up his mind to assume it so as to appear to be acting naturally. Clear distinction is made between a good man, *bonus vir*, and a good candidate, *bonus petitor* (45).

Flattery may be a discreditable fault in other transactions of life, but it is necessary during a candidateship. One should be accessible to all by day and by night (44) and not only by the doors of one's house, but in one's expression – which is the door of the mind (*vultu ac fronte quae est animi ianua*). It is not enough to make promises (although without them no candi-

*Numbered references in brackets on pp. 218–19 are to *Comm. Pet.*

dacy could get started); they must be made in a liberal and complimentary manner[19] because people are more taken by looks and words than by actual services.[20]

Many years later Seneca put it neatly: *Idem est quod datur – sed interest quomodo detur* (Sen. *Ben.* 2, 6, 1-2). The thing that is given may be just the same. The manner of the giving is all-important.[21] Indeed, all candidates distributed largesse, but the plebs preferred one bestower of largesse to another, and it was the *quomodo* that played an important role in winning the *fama popularis* (49). Observations which people make in one's favor will eventually spread around (50), and the candidate has a chance only when his activities are talked about and reach the people. A candidate has a house full of callers long before daybreak. They belong to every class, and it is his duty to give satisfaction to all – by looks and speeches, hard work, skill, and attention. In short, a lot of make-believe and window-dressing, humbug, and hypocrisy. Knowledge of the particulars of one's audience was a necessary condition for persuasion, or as Brunt once aptly put it, 'men do not appeal to standards that no one observes, and hypocrisy serves no purpose where virtue is not to be found.'[22]

III

A Roman governor or magistrate considered his *existimatio* to be above all else, and Cicero, once asking Q. Marcius Philippus – a governor of Asia – to do him a favor, stressed that this should be done unless it involved an outrage upon Philippus' reputation '*nisi quid existimas in ea re violari existimationem tuam*'; (Cic. *Fam.* XIII, 73, 2).

From this point of view Verres was no exception, at least during the first stages of his governorship (*Div. Caec.* 57). At a meeting of revenue contractors, a resolution was passed that all records damaging the reputation (*existimatio*) of C. Verres should be expunged (*Verr.* II, 2, 173).[23]

The reputation (*existimatio*) of a magistrate or of a provincial governor depended not only upon his own (good or bad) behavior – (Suet. *Vit.* 5) but also upon the behavior of his staff (Cic. *Verr.* II, 2, 28; II, 2, 58). This is why Cicero advises his brother not to entrust a fraction of his reputation to a suspicious subordinate (*nullam partem existimationis tuae commiseris*) (*QFr.* I, 1, 14), and when he himself wants to praise his own staff (on his journey to Greece) he emphasizes that they did everything to maintain his good name: *Plane serviunt existimationi meae* (*Att.* V, 11, 5, cf. *Quinct.* 66).

This leads us to the conclusion that *existimatio* is based not only and not always upon actual merit. A man can acquire his reputation wrongly (*falso venire in eam existimationem*; Cic. *Inv. Rhet.* II, 37), and in 59 BC Cicero is saddened when he hears of the high reputation (*existimatio*) of the governors of Sicily and Macedonia (Vergilius and C. Octavius). True, they did not excel his beloved brother Quintus (then Governor of Asia) in purity of conduct, but they surpassed him in the art of winning friends – *vincunt tamen artificio benevolentiae colligendae* (*QFr.* I, 2, 7).

In our own day an image of a public figure can be built up or destroyed by the mass media and public relations. Propaganda means in antiquity were basically similar, only less sophisticated.[24] There were always poets and writers who were able to enhance the reputation of their hero. Not in vain did Alexander envy Achilles, who found in Homer the herald of his valor (Cic. *Arch Poet.* 24). *O Fortunate, inquit adolescens, qui tuae virtutis Homerum praeconem inveneris!*

Some leaders employed court historians. Others wrote their memoirs themselves, but common people hardly read history books or political pamphlets.[25] The influence of such writings was indirect. Their content must have been spread by literate people, and it is for this reason that the value of written propaganda has been recognized by modern scholars. The hostile writings of Tanusius Geminus (Plut. *Caes.* 22; Suet. *Jul.* 9, 2), Marcus Actorius Naso (Suet. *Jul.* 9, 3; 52, 1) and Titus Ampius (Suet. *Jul.* 77) did harm to Caesar. Brutus attacked Pompey's dictatorship in a pamphlet (Quint. *Inst.* IX, 3, 95), and Metellus Scipio slandered Cato's activities in Cyprus (Plin. *NH*, 8, 196. Sen. *Controv.* X, 1, 8).[26] It seems that Caesar used the latter's material in his *Anticato*. The limited impact of poems with political allusions (Catull., 29, 54, 93) is not to be denied, but short and vulgar songs by soldiers and civilians (*vulgus*) (Suet. *Jul.* 49; 80) had far more influence on the masses. Malicious allusions in the theatre – e.g. *Miseria nostra magnus es* (*Att.* 2, 19, 3; Val. Max. 6, 2, 9)[27] and witty but short inscriptions (Suet. *Jul.* 80, 2-3) had a far stronger impact than speeches which were never delivered but only published (like Cicero's *Pro Milone* or the second *Philippic*). It is for this reason that other than written propaganda will now be dwelt upon.

The role of influential friends was decisive, and a man who was without them was *inops et ab amicis et existimatione* (Cic. *Att.* I, 1, 2). It was therefore possible to place one's reputation in the hands of other people (*existimationem committere, Quinct.* 98). Cicero is not only voting for the *supplicatio* in honor of P. Sulpicius Rufus; he also promises that on no occasion in the future will he fail to support his interests' *dignitas* and *existimatio* (*Fam.* XIII, 77, 1). This is precisely what Cicero would expect from Marcellus on behalf of himself (*Fam.* XV, 10, 2), and to L. Aemilius Paulus (cos. 50) he says explicitly: 'I should be glad if you would undertake to look after all my other interests, and most especially my reputation:' *maximeque existimationis meae procurationem susceptam velim* (*Fam.* XV, 13, 3).

In short, one's *existimatio* depended for better or for worse mainly upon what other people were doing and especially saying about him, and Cicero once assured Caelius that he had never done or said a single thing with the intention of disparaging the reputation of Appius Claudius Pulcher, his predecessor in Cilicia: '*Nihil autem feci umquam neque dixi, quod contra illius existimationem esse vellem*' (*Fam.* II, 13, 2, cf. *Fam.* V, 20, 1).

Words can do a lot of damage to one's public image (*existimationem violare* (*Quinct.* 73), and bad tongues could easily scoff at the reputation even of an excellent man (*illudere viri optimi existimationi, QRosc.* 39). Examples can be found in abundance.

When it was intended to besmirch Catilina, it was said that he compelled the participants in a *contio domestica* to take an oath, and passed around bowls of human blood mixed with wine. Even Sallust (*Cat.* XXII, 2-3) admits that details of that kind might have been invented by men who believed that the hostility which afterward arose against Cicero would be moderated by exaggerating the guilt of the conspirators whom he put to death. Sallust had no evidence to prove the point, but there is no doubt that these kinds of rumors severely damaged Catilina's reputation.

On another occasion, two respectable senators, Quintus Catulus and C. Piso, had vainly tried to induce Cicero by entreaties, influence, and bribery to have a false accusation brought against Caesar. They could not persuade the Consul and therefore took the matter into their own hands. They circulated falsehoods which they pretended to have heard from Volturcius or the Allobroges and stirred up hostility to Caesar (Sall. *Cat.* 49): *ipsi singillatim circumeundo atque ementiundo*.[28]

For this reason Roman politicians expended considerable effort in order to make people speak favorably of them and even organized the dissemination of rumors in order to enhance their reputations. Once rumor spread that Cicero stood in the way of a deputation which was about to go to Rome in order to eulogize the former governor of Cilicia, Appius Claudius Pulcher. The latter expressed immediately his suspicions concerning Cicero's loyalty toward him, and Cicero was quick to promise that he was by no means going to assail Appius's reputation in the province (*existimationem oppugnare, Fam.* III, 10, 8).

A good public-relations agent in our own day would organize a series of publications in newspapers and magazines, arrange interviews on television for his employer. The younger Cicero once asked Tiro to fulfil his promise and become with unshaken confidence the trumpeter of his reputation: *te buccinatorem fore existimationis meae (Fam.* XVI, 21, 2).

One had to work hard in order to become the subject of good news. In this respect the commoners were quite skeptical and were not satisfied with mere rumors. In order to become popular one had to prove oneself not only in words but in deeds.[29] It was much easier to denounce and degrade a public figure, and the Romans did it with much relish. Many vicious and stinging witticisms were tossed about in the capital.[30] And Horace rightly spoke of *Italum acetum (Sat.* I, 7, 32). Not in vain does satire pass for one of the original contributions of Rome to culture (Quint, *Inst.* X, 1, 93); Roman jokes were for the most part coarse and vulgar, and they were aimed especially at people's physical defects.[31]

Lucilius coined the term *concelebrare* – which means to spread report of *diffamare*, and he spoke of situations in which the folk split their sides with laughter (Lucil. 1121-1122 W). And we know that Cicero made himself hateful to the *nobilitas* to no small extent because of his unrestrained tongue, and his conduct bears out Quintilian's fears that a Roman would rather lose a friend than a jest – *potius amicum quam dictum perdendi* (Quint. *Inst.* VI, 3, 28, cf. Sen. *Controv.* II, 4, 13).

People were afraid of dismal sayings at least as much as of dire doings (*ibid.* 1084 W), and Lucilius used the verb *exultare*, which meant to do harm by physical act or words: *gestu vel dictu iniuriam facere*.

Vicious remarks made in public and then spread could do great harm to one's reputation (*existimationem offendere, Fam.* III, 8, 7).[32] People could be torn to pieces by gossip (Lucil. 149 W), but gossiping was almost a national sport in Rome (Cic. *Att.* VI, 1, 25). It was enough to send a series of letters to a few good friends in Rome (Macr. *Sat.* II, 7, 3). In no time the story was out and had become common property (*audita res erat et pervulgata*) (Cic, *ad Brut.* II, 4, 5). The *subrostrani* did their job quickly and efficiently (*Fam.* VIII, 1, 5). They carried the news to the Solarium (*Quinct.* 59; *Rhet. Her.* VI, 14), to the public baths, and the barber shops (Polyb. III, 20, 5; Hor. *Sat,* I, 7, 2). There were other means too. An influential patron had to be induced to express his opinion or disclose some news (not necessarily based on facts) to his clients, freedmen, and even slaves (Sen. *Controv.* V, 2, 1: *Tot servi sequuntur, ut quidquid dixerit rumor sit*).

And rumors, especially defamations, spread like fire. And only when the wave of rumors reached its crest did senators resort to the most devastating expedient. They repeated the gossip in public and denied it on the spot. Only then was the real damage caused (Hor. *Sat.* 1, 4, 96; 98).

When the news about Germanicus' death reached Rome, the *vulgus* spread the news like lightning, and before the magistrate could issue an order or the senate a decree, the people stopped all work, forsook the law courts, and shut their homes (Tac. *Ann.* 2, 82).

This is how *existimatio vulgi* was formed, and no political leader could underestimate it (Caes. *BGall.* I, 20, 3; cf. II, 1, 87; II, 4, 102). It was extremely powerful, and once a popular opinion was formed it was hard to evade (Sen. *Controv.* II, 7, 59). Prudent rulers had to be careful *'falsae imagines rerum insanos agitant'* (Sen. *Tranq.* 12, 5). Philosophers could ignore gossip of the foolish (Sen. *Ben.* IV, 21, 5.). Active politicians could not (*QFr.* II, 15B, 2).

Political leaders who contested for *favor populi* were characterized by their opponents as endowed with *levitas popularis*. This was discussed at some length elsewhere and does not need further elaboration.[33] Suffice it to say that consideration paid to *existimatio omnium* is not a bad thing if judged by its consequences. People holding positions had to live up to expectations. And a political figure is never freed of anxiety for his reputation (*liberatus existimationis metu – Verr.* II, 5, 175).[34]

Each one is sensitive to manifestations of feelings in the forum, in the theater, around the *rostra*. Few were indifferent to applause in public, and Cicero was happy when he could say, *Maximo clamore atque plausu in rostris collocatus sum* (*ad Brut.* I, 3, 2).[35] People had to compromise with custom and public opinion (*consuetudo et fama*) (Cic. *Tusc.* I, 109) and act accordingly.

In Rome no honorable man wanted to put a citizen to death. He preferred to be remembered as one who had spared when he could have destroyed. Cicero assures us that this is done for the sake of public opinion and the common feeling of humanity – '*hominum existimationis et humanitatis causa*' (*Quinct.* 51).

A Roman magistrate in a province would not dare to assail a Roman citizen. He would restrain his behaviour for fear of public opinion (*Verr.* II, 5, 167). A young lawyer like Cicero could keep his previous public image among his supporters only when he could prove to his countrymen that in the Verres case he had done his duty to the best of his power (*Div. Caec.* 72, cf. *Verr*, I, 27).

An influential patron is expected to do his utmost for his client. When Erucius is standing for office on Pliny's nomination, Pliny's *existimatio* is at stake (*Ep.* II, 9, 1). Substantial, not nominal, help was required.

A man could be convicted by public opinion before being expressly convicted by a court (*Clu.* 56), and judges could find it difficult to acquit a man condemned by *existimatio omnium* (*Rhet. Her.* IV, 14, 20, cf. *Verr*, II, 3, 146). People may fear a verdict (*metus*); but, as far as *existimatio* is concerned, one should rather think in terms of *pudor existimationis* (*Verr.* II, 2, 40).[36]

A little story may illustrate the point: In a fierce battle, two illustrious Roman centurions, Titus Pullo and Lucius Vorenus, found themselves dislodged with volleys of stones from all directions. Their tower was set on fire, and none of them dared to move. Both were competing for promotion; therefore Pullo suddenly remarked: 'Come on, Vorenus, what are you waiting for? We'll finish the argument today.' He immediately left the shelter of the rampart and made a dash for the thickest point he could find in the enemy ranks. Vorenus, of course, was after him in a moment. His reputation was publicly challenged: *Omnium veritus existimationem – subsequitur* (Caes.*BGall.* 5, 44).

A famous man's image (*omnium existimatione ornatissimus*) once destroyed in public (e.g. *Verr.* II, 2, 102) could not live with his *existimatio lacerata* (Suet. *Jul.* 75), or *existimatio laesa* (Suet. *Tib.* 58).

IV

I do not know what the results would have been if this present study had been rewritten with the concept of *fama* replacing that of *existimatio*. This is not an impossible undertaking. We could easily speak of the *fama* of nations, cities, social groups, and institutions – e.g. *fama populi Romani* (Cic. *Arch.* 23); or *fama nominis Romani* (Liv. 38, 58, 5); of Athens (Luc. *Phar.* 5, 52); cf. Sen. *Controv.* X, 5, 13: One man's misdeed cannot corrupt the reputation of a city – *Numquam unius malefacto, publica fama corrumpitur*; of a country (e.g. Arabia, Pliny *NH* XII, 56); of an island (Tenedos – Verg. *Aen.* II, 21, or Cyprus Flor. III, 9, 3); of an army (Tac. *Hist.* I, 30 *magna per provincias Germanici exercitus fama*); of a legion (Tac. *Hist.* III, 1); of a clan (*fama generis*- Cic. *Inv. Rhet.* I, 19); or of a tribe (Tac. *Germ.* 37).

Examples of the *fama* of individuals (especially of military leaders) are innumerable. Would it be correct to assume that *fama* is mainly based on rumor and hearsay and not on real merit?

The Macedonian kingdom rested on reputation and not on strength – *fama stetisse non viribus Macedoniae regnum* (Liv. 33, 8, 5). The Gauls had a great reputation among the Greeks which was not justified either (Liv. 38, 17, 19). Such a principle would not work, because it was possible (as we have seen) *falso venire in existimationem* (p. 220 above), and in Frontinus (*Strat.* I, 1, 10) an *existimatio* is formed on the basis of false rumors.[37]

It is therefore tempting to find another specific and clearcut interpretation for *fama* and *existimatio*. Hellegouarch has tried it,[38] and although he admitted that 'fama se présente comme un terme très proche d'existimatio,' he suggests that '*existimatio* désigne la réputation qui résulte d'un jugement personnel fondé sur l'opinion que *l'on a d'un individu.*' *Fama*, on the other hand, 'implique une opinion collective provoquée par les actions importantes, éclatantes.'

A quick look at the usage of this term in the sources will show that Hellegouarch's definition is true only to a certain extent. In 51 BC Caelius writes to Cicero about the consular elections: *De comitiis consularibus incertissima est existimatio* (*Fam.* VIII, 2, 2). The definition does not fit. '*Fama*', Hellegouarch continued, 'révèle une plus nette tendance à se colorer d'une nuance politique' (p. 365), whereas *existimatio* is 'un terme très vague et peu specialisé dans le vocabulaire politique.' This statement is also true only to a certain extent. *Fama* is at least as vague as *existimatio* and is used not only in a political context. One can speak in Latin about *fama* of a statue (Pliny *NH* 34, 83; 7, 34); of a ship (Liv. 35, 26, 5; Val. Max. 4, 6. Ext. 3); of a poem (Tac. *Ann.* 15, 49); of a day (Luc. *Phars.* X, 533); of a wine (Pliny *NH* 14, 72); of a river (Ovid. *Am.* 3, 6, 90); and of a temple (Liv. 29, 18, 3).

These remarks are made not to belittle the general value of Hellegouarch's important dictionary. I would like only to draw attention to the fact that rigid definitions, as far as Roman political terminology is concerned, do not always work. Ancient historians were not as careful as modern philologists and jurists in using political terms. They tried to avoid frequent repetition of the same word and occasionally used *fama* and *existimatio* as synonyms. A few examples:

Tac. *Hist.* IV, 6: *Suffragia et existimationem senatus reperta ut cuiusque vitam famamque penetrarent.*

Pliny *Pan.* 62, 9: *Persta Caesar, in ista ratione propositi, talesque nos crede qualis fama cuiusque est. Huic aures, huic oculos, intente! ne respexeris clandestinas existinationes.*[39]

Thus the two terms could be used interchangeably. When Cicero accused the judges in Clodius's trial, he was tempted to use a witty play on words: *fames magis quam fama commoverit* (*Att.* I, 16, 5). He could just as easily have used *existimatio*.

It is true that when Cicero is trying to undermine the credibility of the witness, Indutiomarus, in the Fonteius trial, he says (*Font.* 29): *Verebatur* (*Indutiomarus*) *enim videlicet, ne quod apud vos populumque Romanum de existimatione sua deperderet, ne qua fama consequetur eius modi* . . . (For he was afraid lest he should forfeit some of his reputation in your eyes [the judges] and those of the Roman people, afraid of the tale going around).

It might seem at first glance that there is still a difference between *fama* and *existimatio*. *Fama* is much more vague – based on rumors and hearsay – while *existimatio* is clearly one's good name or reputation among a certain group of people. But this definition also fails to bring us very far. In *Verr*. I, 17, *fama* is simply interchangeable with *existimatio*: *Eaedemque vestrae famae fortunisque omnium insidiae per eosdem homines comparantur.* The same insidious attacks are being organized by the same agents upon your good name . . . and upon the well-being of the community at large. The same is true when Verres is accused of having defiled the fair name of the Roman government in the eyes of all foreign nations: *cum apud externas nationes imperii nominisque nostria famam tuis probris flagitiisque violaris* (*Verr*. I, 82). We have seen above that Cicero also speaks of *existimatio imperii* (*Fam*. XI, 4, 10), but there seems to be little difference between this *existimatio* and the *fama* in Liv. 24, 19, 7.

The *loci classici* for interchangeability would be *Verr*. II, 2, 28: (a) *Pertinet hoc ad summam rempublicam et existimationem ordinis salutemque sociorum.* (b) *Primum omnium opera danda est ut eos nobiscum educamus qui nostrae famae capitique consultant.* And in a letter (*Fam*. XIII, 73, 2): . . . *Nisi quid existimas in ea re violari existimationem tuam. Quod ego si arbitrer numquam te rogarem mihique tua* fama *multo antiquior esset, quam illa necessitudo est.*[40]

The interchangeability of *fama* and *existimatio* can also be proved by the similar usage of verbs in connection with the two nouns:

Famam defendere (*Quinct*. 8; *QRosc*. 15; *Verr*. II, 1, 76); but also *existimationem defendere* (Caes. *BCiv*. I, 7, 7, Cic. *Fam*. III, 10, 8).

Famam conservare (*QRosc*. 25. *Div*. *Caec*. 71) or *famam tueri* (Att. XI, 2, 1. Fam. XII, 22, 2, XIII, 5, 1); but also *existimationem tueri* (Caes. *Bell*. *Civ*. III, 1, 3). The Thesaurus teaches us that the same is correct for *violare* or *perdere, amittere* or *lacerare*.[41]

All this leads us to an unimaginative but perhaps the only reasonable solution: the context determines the sense, and no other principle is valid.

ABBREVIATIONS

Abbot-Johnson — F. F. Abbot – A. Ch. Johnson, *Municipal Administration in the Roman Empire*, Princeton 1926.

A. N. R. W. — *Aufstieg und Niedergang der römischen Welt* (Hrsg. H. Temporini), Berlin–New York 1972.

A. R. S. P. — *Annali della R. Scuola Normale Superiore di Pisa*

C. A. H. — *Cambridge Ancient History*

C. I. L. — *Corpus Inscriptionum Latinarum*

E. S. A. R. — T. Frank (ed.), *An Economic Survey of Ancient Rome*, Paterson, N. J. 1959.

F. A. S. — *Frankfurter althistorische Studien*

F. G. H. — F. Jacoby (Hrsg.), *Fragmente der griechischen Historiker*

FIRA (Riccobono) — S. Riccobono, *Fontes Iuris Romani Antejustiniani*

G. W. U. — *Geschichte in Wissenschaft und Unterricht*

I. G. R. R. — *Inscriptiones Graecae ad res Romanas pertinentes*

I. L. S. — *Inscriptiones Latinae Selectae*

M. G. W. J. — *Monatsschrift für Geschichte und Wissenschaft des Judentums*

M. R. R. — T. R. S. Broughton, *The Magistrates of the Roman Republic*, New York 1951.

N. J. A. B. — *Neue Jahrbücher für Antike und deutsche Bildung.*

R. E. — *Paulys Realencyclopädie der classischen Altertumswissenschaft*

R. G. — Th. Mommsen, *Römische Geschichte.*

Rotondi — G. Rotondi, *Leges Publicae Populi Romani.*

R. R. (Syme) — Sir Ronald Syme, *The Roman Revolution*, Oxford 1939.

R. R. (Varro) — M. Terentius Varro, *de re rustica.*

S. I. G. — W. Dittenberger (Hrsg.), *Sylloge Inscriptionum Graecarum.*

WdF — *Wege der Forschung*, (Wissenschaftliche Buchgesellschaft, Darmstadt).

All other abbreviations (names of series, periodicals etc.) correspond to the ones used in *l'Année Philolgique.*

NOTES

Chapter 1

1 This chapter is in no way designed to be exhaustive. It is intended as a general survey for the educated reader, not for the specialist. In addition, the interested reader might like to read further in G. Walter, *César*, Paris 1947; M. Rambaud, *L'art de déformation historique dans les commentaries de César*, Paris 1966; *id.*, 'Rapport sur César', Ass. G. Budé, *Actes Congr. Lyons 1958*, Paris 1960, pp. 205-38; J. H. Collins, 'A Selective Survey of Caesar Scholarship since 1935', *Class. World* 57 (1963/64), pp. 46-51 and pp. 81-88; H. Opperman, 'Probleme und heutiger Stand der Caesarforschung', ed. D. Rasmussen, *Caesar*, *WdF*. XLIII, Darmstadt 1976, pp. 485-522.

While the present book was in preparation it was too late for me to take into account Helga Gesche, *Caesar, Erträge, der Forschung*, vol. LI, Darmstadt 1976. In this work Helga Gesche has collected and arranged chronologically and by subject some 2,000 titles selected from the academic literature published between 1918 and 1972-73. More important is the fact that she succeeded in overcoming an almost insurmountable task in producing not merely a survey of the literature but an accompanying critique of outstanding quality that immediately makes all other surveys of research seem out of date. In the not too distant future her work will rank as an essential component of every Caesarian scholar's library, and in the course of time the comprehensive bibliography can be cited, quite simply, by a brief reference, 'see Gesche, No. 620' etc. Nor was E. Wistrand's excellent study, *Caesar and contemporary Roman society*. Göteborg 1978, taken into account.

2 H. Stasburger, 'Caesar im Urteil der Zeitgenossen', *Hist. Zeitschrift* 175 (1953), pp. 225-64, Darmstadt 1968.

3 On the concept of 'image' in classical antiquity, see Appendix, p. 214.

4 Plut., *Caes.* 32; App., *BC* II, 35.

5 H. Strasburger, *Caesars Eintritt in die Geschichte*, Munich 1938; L. R. Taylor, 'The Rise of Julius Caesar', *Greece and Rome* IV (1957), pp. 10-18; 'Caesar's Early Career', *Classical Philology* XXXVI (1941), pp. 421 ff.

6 Suet., *Div. Jul.* 9, 2.

7 R. Syme, *The Roman Revolution*, Oxford 1939, p. 47, cf. J. Carcopino, *Les Etapes de l'impérialisme Romain*, Paris 1961, pp. 118 ff.; *id.*, *Julius César*, Paris 1968.

8 See the recently published study of Kurt Raaflaub, 'Dignitatis contentio', *Vestigia*, vol. 20, Munich 1974.

9 Caes., *BC*. III, 57, 4.

Similarly, too, U. Knoche in his article 'Die geistige Vorbereitung der augustäischen Epoche', in *Das neue Bild der Antike* (1942), p. 213: 'But actually it is astonishing and shocking (*sic*!) how small a role the idea of empire plays at all here. And it is extraordinary that Caesar, the master of propaganda, allowed this role to escape him.' Naturally Knoche particularly underlines Caesar's notions of leadership and following. This volume appeared at the time of the Nazi regime in Germany, and was edited by H. Berve.

10 *BC*. I, 32, 7. It is noteworthy that Strasburger does not quote the second part of Caesar's suggestion, I, 32, 7, 'But if they shrink through fear he will not burden them, and will administer the state himself.' That is simultaneously an invitation and a threat, and it is scarcely to be supposed that the Senate was overjoyed about it. See J. H. Collins, 'Caesar and the Corruption of Power', *Historia* IV (1955), p. 445.

11 W. den Boer, 'Caesar zweitausend Jahre nach seinem Tod', *WdF* XLIII, p. 436.

12 M. Gelzer, 'War Caesar ein Staatsmann?', *Hist. Zeitschrift* 178 (1954), pp. 449-70 (= *Kleine Schriften*, Wiesbaden 1963, vol. II, pp. 286 ff.).

13 *Id.*, *Kleine Schriften*, vol. III, p. 190.

14 *Ibid.* vol. II, p. 301.

15 A. Heuss, *HZ CLXXXII* (1956), p. 28 (see also A. Heuss, 'Matius als Zeuge von Caesar's staatsmännischer Größe', *Historia* XI (1962), p. 118.

16 M. Gelzer, *Caesar*[1], Stuttgart 1921[1]. See also his article, 'Caesars weltgeschichtliche Leistung', *Vorträge und Schriften*, *Preuss. Akademie d. Wiss.*, Heft 6, Berlin 1941 (= *Vom römischen Staat* II, pp. 147 ff.).

17 *Das neue Bild der Antike*, vol. II, p. 199. But otherwise Gelzer preserved his academic integrity during the Nazi period. Only in a lecture 'Caesars weltgeschichtliche Leistung', Berlin 1941 (De Gruyter), p. 4, was there the hint that it was not easy for him in every respect. He compared Caesar with Frederick the Great, with Napoleon, Richelieu and Bismarck, 'not to mention those who are still alive'. Is this irony or evasion? Yet there is no doubt about his general attitude. In 1928 he took up a critical position towards F. Münzer's *Entstehung des römischen Prinzipats*, Münster 1927, and made comments against the enthusiasm for the rule of the individual, 'Because we have conceived of a period of history as necessary, must we also hail it as salutary?'

18 M. Gelzer, *Caesar: Politician and Statesman*, tr. P. Needham, Oxford 1968, pp. 329-30 (= *Caesar*[2], Wiesbaden 1960, p. 306).

19 Cic., *de off.* II, 84.

20 Plin., *NH* VII, 91-2.

21 O. Seel, 'Zur Problematik der Grösse', *Caesarstudien*, Stuttgart 1967, pp. 43-92, especially p. 57.

22 Th. Mommsen, *Römische Geschichte*, vol. III, Berlin 1909 edition, p. 479 (*History of Rome,* vol. IV, tr. W. Dickson, London 1894 edition, p. 440.

23 J. Geiger, 'Zum Bild Caesars in der römischen Kaiserzeit', *Historia* XXIV (1975), p. 444.

24 R. Herbig, 'Neue Studien zur Ikonographie des Julius Caesar', *Kölner Jahrbücher für Vor und Frühgeschichte* IV (1959), p. 7 = *Gymnasium* LXXII (1965), p. 161 = *WdF* XLIII (1967), p. 69. Cf. also J. M. C. Toynbee, 'Portraits of Julius Caesar', *Greece and Rome* IV (1957), p. 2; Erika Simon, 'Neue Literatur zum Caesarporträt', *Gymnasium* XXVI (1954), p. 527.

25 J. H. Collins, *Gnomon* XXVI (1954), p. 527.

26 W. Roscher, *Politik, Geschichtliche Naturlehre der Monarchie, Aristokratie*, Stuttgart 1893, p. 588.

27 *Mémoires de Mme de Remusat* III, p. 349.

28 A.J.P. Taylor, *From Napoleon to Lenin. Historical Essays*, New York 1966, pp, 12-20.

29 Two additional passages of Cicero are worth mentioning in this connection, *ad fam.* XII, 18, 2, 'for the issues of civil war are invariably such that it is not only the victor's wishes that are carried out, but those also have to be humoured by whose assistance the victory was won', and *ibid.* 4, 9, 3, 'For there are many things a victor is obliged to do even against his will at the caprice of those who helped him to victory.'

30 L. Wickert, 'Zu Caesars Reichspolitik', *Klio* XXX (1937), pp. 232-53.

31 Presumably in 1895 Roscher was not yet aware of the then sensational articles of Dessau in *Hermes* XXIV (1889), pp. 337-92; XXVII (1892), pp. 561-605, on the historical value of the *SHA*. In any case the passage cited above can serve only by way of illustration.

32 Cf. A. Momigliano, 'Per un riesame della storia dell' idea di Cesarismo', *RSI* LXVIII (1956), p. 220-29, and 'Burckhardt e la parola Cesarismo', *ibid.* LXXIV (1962), pp. 369-71, and, in Hebrew, C. Wirszubski, 'The domination of Julius Caesar', *Molad* (Sept. 1957), pp. 348 ff., with similar conclusions.

33 L. Hartmann, *Theodor Mommsen*, Gotha 1908, pp. 66-77. Napoleon III himself wrote a book about Caesar, but his German tutor (Froehner) was under no illusions about Napoleon's philological and historical knowledge. In his memoirs he remarked that Napoleon muddled *Grammatici* with *Gromatici*, and was absolutely convinced that he had read Livy Book XI (!).

34 I assume that, in speaking of the vulgar sense, Mommsen would have had in mind such sentences as 'Roman history in general, viewed in the proper light, is and remains the most trustworthy guide, not only for our time, but for all times'. This sentence comes from Hitler's *Mein Kampf* (1939), p. 470.

35 Th. Mommsen, *Römische Geschichte*, vol. III, p. 477 f. (= Eng. tr. in Everyman's Lib., Vol. IV, pp. 439–440.

36 W. Roscher, 'Umrisse zur Naturlehre des Caesarismus', *Abh. der Sächs. Gesellschaft der Wissenschaften*, vol. X (1888), p. 641; F. Ruestow, *Der Caesarismus, sein Wesen and Schaffen*, Zürich 1879.

37 R. v. Pöhlmann, 'Entstehung des Caesarismus', *Altertum und Gegenwart*, Munich 1895, p. 245.

38 A. Gramsci, 'Note sul Machiavelli, sulla politica e sullo stato moderno', Einaudi-Jovino (1949), pp. 58-60 especially stresses the 'conciliatory character of Caesarism'.

39 N. A. Maškin, *Printsipat Avgusta*, Moscow 1949 (pp. 47 ff. German edition).

40 Momigliano, see n. 32.

41 Th. Mommsen, *loc. cit.* p. 513.

42 It is perhaps noteworthy that Caesar's power appeared legitimate to Napoleon, 'because it was the result . . . of the people's wish' (whether Napoleon was familiar with App., *BC* I, 4, 16 is debatable).

43 C. Merivale, *The Fall of the Roman Republic,* London 1874; W. W. Fowler, *Julius Caesar and the Foundation of the Roman Imperial System,* London 1892, to mention but two English examples. L. Wickert (*loc. cit.* p. 232) believed that an idea of empire always develops when

the territory of the state grows beyond a certain limit. Caesar's plan was to reshape the Imperium Romanum, replacing the Republican state that was head of a community by a state ruled by a monarch that was head of an empire. A necessary factor in the fulfilment of this task is the absolute rule of the individual, for only the monarch who is superior to all his subjects can gain the requisite support, impossible for collegiate government in the Roman style, involving several principals.

44 E. G. Brandes, *Caesar*, 2 vols, Copenhagen 1918-21; or, E. Kornemann, *Weltgeschichte des Mittelmeerraumes*, Munich 1948, 'The crime of March 15th effaced forever the empire planned by the powerful Julius.'

45 E.g. G. A. v. Mess, *Caesar*, Leipzig 1913, pp. 162-66, 'His aim was legalized monarchy. He was not only an innovator, but stirred into growth and strengthened what remained strong and healthy in the old roots; he was above party politics, and was the man to put new content into the old form.' Mess considered that Caesar's election as Pontifex Maximus ('head of the state church'), was a 'preparation for popular monarchy' (p. 41).

46 G. W. F. Hegel, *Vorlesungen über die Philosophie der Geschichte* (ed. Brunstäd), Leipzig 1907 (Reclam Verlag), pp. 400-1 (= English translation by J. Sibree, New York 1944, pp. 312-13).

Many nineteenth-century scholars who were not Hegelians shared this view, e.g. Droysen, who in 1834 wrote to Welcker that he had always preferred Alexander to Demosthenes and Caesar to Cato (G. Droysen, *Briefwechsel* (ed. R. Hübner), 1929, vol. I, p. 66.

47 F. Gundolf, *Caesar, Geschichte seines Ruhmes*, Berlin 1924, and *Caesar in 19. Jahnhundert*, Berlin 1926.

48 So, too, Jose Ortega y Gasset, *The Revolt of the Masses*, New York 1950, p. 118.

49 G. Ferrero, *The Life of Caesar*, London 1933, the second volume of his work *Grandezza edecadenza di Roma*, Turin 1904.

50 At first glance it may seem that there were no real anti–Caesarians before Ferrero, while devotees of Julius Caesar were to be found even among the founders of American democracy. Dumas Malone, *Jefferson and his Time*, Boston 1951, vol. II, p. 286, maintained that Hamilton was a great admirer of Caesar. In an article that has appeared recently Thomas P. Govan has proved precisely the opposite and has convincingly demonstrated that Hamilton, in fact, championed Ferrero's ideas even during the American Revolution. In his view, Caesar was not only an efficient general and despotic autocrat, he was also a Catiline – a demagogic conspirator – who flattered the people and destroyed their freedom. To warn Washington against people of this kind, Hamilton wrote, 'When a man unprincipled in private life, desperate in his fortune, . . . possessed of considerable talents, having the advantage of military habits, despotic in his ordinary demeanour . . . is seen to mount the hobby horse of popularity . . . it may justly be suspected that his object is to throw things into confusion, that he may 'ride the storm and direct the whirlwind.'

Hamilton hated those who fostered the folly and prejudices of the people and who played on their ambitions and fears. His comparison of Jefferson with Caesar in 1792 was no compliment. (Thomas P. Govan, 'Alexander Hamilton and Julius Caesar', *The William and Mary Quarterly*, July 1975, p. 477. I am grateful to my friend Prof. T. Draper for the reference to this article).

51 L. R. Taylor, 'Caesar and the Roman Nobility', *TAPA* LXXIII (1942), pp. 10–27; F. R. Cowell, *Cicero and the Roman Republic,* London 1948, pp. 203-4. This anti-Caesarian attitude is also not a new one. Since the time of Machiavelli and up to the French Revolution, conspirators whose declared aim was to free their enslaved country were highly regarded. The argument has become more intense since the time of Napoleon.

52 The new direction of Italian research on Caesar after World

War II was instituted by G. Perotta with the article 'Cesare scrittore', *Maia* I (1948), pp. 5-32. Cf. also G. Funaioli, 'Giulio Cesare scrittore', *Studi Romani* V (1957), p. 136; E. Paratore, 'Cesare scrittore', *Cesare nel bimillianario della morte* (ed. Radio Italiana), Rome 1956, p. 23; A. La Penna, *Cesare – La guerra civile – Introduzione*, Turin 1954. See also the important works of G. Pacucci, G. Funaioli, E. Paratore, A. La Penna, L. Canali (*Personalità e stile di Cesare*, Rome 1963); F. Semi (*Il sentimento di Cesare*, Padua 1966), and the extremely useful synopsis by E. Paratore, 'Das Caesarbild des 20. Jahrhunderts in Italien', *Caesar, WdF.*, see n. 24. I have unfortunately been unable to obtain G. Costa, *Giulio Cesare*, Rome 1934. See now J. Kroymann, 'Caesar und das Corpus Caesarianum in der neueren Forschung, *ANRW* I, 3, 457.

53 As an example of Soviet literature see Maskin (n. 39). Western Marxists did not follow the path of their Soviet colleagues, and works of the Italian left (cf. n. 52) such as those of Canali and La Penna are stimulating and refreshing.

54 See also U. v. Wilamowitz, 'Th. Mommsen. Warum hat er den vierten Band der Römischen Geschichte nicht geschrieben?', *International Monatschrift* XII (1918), p. 205, and especially the fine article by A. Wucher, 'Mommsens unvolendete Römische Geschichte',

Saeculum IV (1953), pp. 414 ff.

55 J. H. Collins, *loc. cit.* (p. 12, n. 10).

56 This was also the view of E. Herzog, *Geschichte und System der römischen Staatsverfassung*, Leipzig 1884-91, II. 1, p. 44 (1887). He did not doubt that Caesar strove for sole rulership as a regular, permanent form of government, and in this connection the title never bothered him.

57 E.g., E. Kornemann, 'Ägyptische Einflüsse im römischen Kaiserreich', *N. Jahrb. f.d. kl. Altertumswissenschaft* 1889, p. 118; J. Kaerst, *Studien zur Entwicklung und theoretischen Begründung der Monarchie im Altertum*, Munich 1898, especially pp. 80 ff.; H. Willrich, 'Caligula', *Klio* III (1902), p. 89. A. V. Domaszewski, 'Kleine Beiträge zur Kaisergeschichte', *Philologus* XXI (1908), p. 1.

58 See his *Kleine Schriften*.

59 E. Meyer, *Spenglers Untergang des Abendlandes*, Berlin 1925.

60 O. Weippert, *Alexander Imitatio und römische Geschichte in republikanischer Zeit*, Augsburg 1972, pp. 56 ff.

61 Cf., however, Gelzer's review of the year 1918, reprinted in *Kleine Schriften*, vol. III, p. 190.

62 J. Carcopino, *César*, Paris 1935; cf. 'La Royauté de César et de l'Empire universel', *Les Etapes de l'impérialisme Romain*, Paris 1961, pp. 118 ff., with the important review of T. Gagé, 'De César à Auguste', *RH*

CLXXVII (1936), pp. 279–342. Also R. Etienne, *Les Ides de Mars*, Paris 1973, whose interpretation is similar to Carcopino's.
63 L. Cerfaux and J. Tondriau, *Le culte des souverains*, Tournay 1957.
64 C. N. Cochrane, *Christianity and Classical Culture*, Oxford 1940.
65 E. Kornemann, *Weltgeschichte des Mittelmeerraumes*, Munich 1948, vol. I, p. 478.
66 P. Strack, 'Zum Gottkönigtum Caesars, Probleme der augustäischen Erneuerung', *Gymnasium* IV (1938), p. 21; also C. Koch, *Gottheit und Mensch im Wandel der römischen Staatsform* (1942), now in 'Religio. Studien zu Kult und Glauben der Römer', *Erlanger Beiträge zur Sprache und Kunstwissenschaft*, vol. VII, Nuremberg 1960, p. 94.
67 L. Pareti, *Storia di Roma e del impero Romano*, 6 vols. Turin 1952–61.
68 Cf. E. Meyer, 'Kaiser Augustus', *Kl. Schriften*, and E. Burck, 'Staat, Volk and Dichtung im republikanischen Rom', *Hermes* LXXI (1936), p. 307. Burck maintained that Augustus retreated from Caesar's notion of the Hellenistic state, embraced the old Roman tradition, and made way for a blood (*blutmässig*) reformation. The expression *blutmässig* was apparently better conceived in 1936.
69 H. F. Pelham, *Essays in Roman History*. Oxford 1911, p. 27.
70 *CAH* IX, p. 724.

71 R. Syme, *The Roman Revolution*, Oxford 1939, p. 54.
72 R. Syme, 'Caesar, the Senate and Italy', *PBSR* XIV (1938), p. 2.
73 When Syme spoke of nonpolitical classes he meant tax farmers, wealthy merchants and great landowners who had no political ambitions and supported any regime that could guarantee them economic returns.
74 Cf., the outstanding small volume, unfortunately all too seldom cited, *Colonial Elites*, Oxford 1958, pp. 27, 52.
75 R. Syme, *The Roman Revolution* p. 346.
76 F. E. Adcock, *CAH* IX, p. 271, and also the important article by J. P. V. D. Balsdon, 'The Ides of March', *Historia* XII (1953), pp. 80–94. The most important review of Syme's work, long since recognized as 'classic', comes from A. Momigliano (*JRS* XXX (1940), p. 75). Momigliano applauded Syme's work as a masterpiece, but was critical of the one-sidedness of its prosopography, ('prosopography is not history'), and regretted that 'spiritual interests of people are considered much less than their marriages'. Numerous scholars have since associated themselves with Momigliano, including A. W. Sherwin-White (*JRS* LIX (1969), p. 287), whom Lintott praised 'for considering ideas and actions of contestants rather than their matrimonial bulletins'. Momigliano also regretted that Syme

had not attached enough importance to Roman law, and in another place he pointed out that it would have been desirable to enquire '. . . how the Romans knew and used law and constitutional practices as the tool for building an empire. The Romans did not rule the world by nepotism' (*Contributo alla storia degli Studi classici* I, Rome 1955, p. 399). From another marginal comment it might be concluded that Momigliano was haunted by the question of whether Syme had in mind the rise of Fascism when he wrote the *Roman Revolution*, 'A candid admission of the purpose of one's own study, a clear analysis of the implications of one's own bias helps to define the limits of one's own historical research' (*Contributo* I, p. 374). In fact, it is not altogether easy to discover the *Zeitgeist* from Syme's text. It was easier in the case of Niebuhr. But one thing is clear: Syme learned more from Münzer than from Namier, and there is no reason for supposing that he had eighteenth-century England in mind when he wrote his *Roman Revolution*. He believed in the role of Dynamis and Tyche in history rather than in established trends that can be predicted, and in a period such as that before World War II, when political ideology was awash in a wave of slogans, he was more interested in the actors on the stage of history than in their warnings, 'Bonum publicum simulantes pro sua quisque potentia certabant'.

77 The Spartan Agesilaus likewise most vigorously refused divine honours (Plut., *Mor.* 210 D). Thus he once enquired of the inhabitants of Thasus whether they were in a position to change a mortal into a god. When they assented, he suggested they first make themselves into gods, then he would believe that they could also deify him (Plut., *Agesilaus* 21, 5; *Mor.* 213 A).

78 W. Steidle, *Sueton und die antike Biographie*, Munich 1963, pp. 13 ff.

79 Cf., Syme, *Roman Revolution*, p. 54, 'Cic. Phil. II, 110, however, is a difficult passage'.

80 W. W. Fowler, *Roman Essays*, Oxford 1920, p. 268.

81 J. Vogt, 'Zum Herrscherkult bei Julius Caesar', *Studies presented to D. M. Robinson*, vol. II, St Louis 1953, p. 1138.

82 V. Ehrenberg, 'Caesar's Final Aims', *HSCP* LXVIII (1969), p. 149 = *Man, State and Deity* 1974, 127.

83 K. Kraft, 'Der goldene Kranz Caesars und der Kampf um die Entlarvung des Tyrannen', *Jahrbücher für Numismatik und Geldgeschichte* IV (1952), p. 7. Cf., also the critical article of D. Felber, 'Caesars Streben nach der Königswürde', *Untersuchungen zur römischen Geschichte* (ed. F. Altheim), vol. I, Frankfurt/M 1961, pp. 211 ff.

84 F. Gundolf, *Caesar im 19 Jahrhundert*, Berlin 1926, p. 79.

85 L. Wickert, 'Caesars Monarchie und der Prinzipat des Augustus', *NJAB* IV (1941), pp. 12-23.

86 F. Vittinghoff, *Römische Kolonisation und Bürgerrechtspolitik*, Mainz 1951.

87 H. Opperman, *Caesar – Wegbereiter Europas*, Göttingen 1958, especially pp. 96–97; 106–7.

88 F. Taeger, *Charisma*, Stuttgart 1960, vol. II, pp. 50 ff., 65, 68, 70, 72.

89 R. Klein, *Königtum und Königzeit bei Cicero* (diss.), Erlangen 1962, especially pp. 57–59, 67.

90 E. Meyer, *Caesars Monarchie*, p. 401. Cf. F. Altheim, *Römische Religionsgeschichte* II, Baden-Baden 1953, p. 63.

91 B. E. Giovanetti, *La religione di Cesare*, Milan 1937.

92 M. Pohlenz, 'Eine politische Tendenzschrift aus Caesars Zeit', *Hermes* LIX (1924), p. 157. Pohlenz's view was not shared by all scholars. Some attributed the passage of Dionysius to the Augustan period (e.g. Premerstein), others to the time of Sulla (e.g. E. Gabba, 'Studi su Dionigi da Alecarnasso', *Athenaeum* XXXVIII (1960), pp. 175 ff.

93 J. Dobesch, *Caesars Apotheose zu Lebzeiten und sein Ringen um den Königstitel*, Vienna 1966, reviewed in *JRS* LVII (1967), pp. 247–48 and E. Rawson, *JRS* LXV (1975), p. 148.

94 The review by J. P. V. D. Balsdon, *Gnomon* XXXIX (1967), pp. 150 ff. is important. See also K. W. Welwei, 'Das Angebot des Diadems an Caesar und das Luperkalienfest', *Historia* XVI (1967), p. 44.

95 *Correspondance de Napoléon I*, vol. 32, p. 86, cited by Alföldi in 'Der neue Romulus', *MH* VIII (1951), p. 208.

96 *Ibid.*

97 See the bibliography of A. Alföldi, *Antiquitas*, series 4, vol. III, 1966, XIII.

98 At the time of writing only vol. 2 of *Das Zeugnis der Münzen*, Bonn 1974 (*Antiquitas*, vol. XVII), was available to me.

99 *MH* VII (1950), pp. 1–13.

100 On the diadem as employed by the Persians and Alexander, see Hans-Werner Ritter, *Diadem und Königsherrschaft*, Munich 1965 (*Vestigia* 7).

101 *Phoenix* XXIV (1970), p. 166.

102 *Gnom.* XII (1975), p. 12.

103 *RN* XV, 1973, p. 126.

104 *Phoenix* XXIV (1970), p. 176.

105 E. Gruen, *The Last Generation of the Roman Republic*, Berkeley-Los Angeles-London 1974, p. 544.

106 Alföldi, *loc. cit.* p. 105.

107 *Staatsrecht* II³, p. 780.

108 S. Weinstock, *Divus Julius*, Oxford 1971, p. 200, n. 4. A. H. M. Jones, *JRS* XLI (1951), pp. 117, 119, contra, A. Alföldi, *Vater des Vaterlandes*, Darmstadt 1971.

109 E.g., R. Syme, 'Imperator Caesar. A Study in Nomenclature', *Historia* VII (1958), pp. 172–88. R. Combes, *Imperator*, Paris 1966. J. Deininger, 'Von der Republik zur Monarchi', *Aufstieg und Niedergang der römischen Welt* (ed. Temporini), vol. I (1972), p. 982, with the conclusion that neither the coins nor the epigraphic evidence offers any clear proof that Imperator was more than a title to Caesar.

110 A. Alföldi, 'Der macht-verheissende Traum des Sulla', *Jahrb. d. bernischen Hist. Museums in Bern* XLI-XLII (1961), p. 284.
111 Michael H. Crawford, *Roman Republican Coinage*, 2 vols, Cambridge 1974. To cite only a few examples: p. 83, n. 5: 'The arrangement proposed by A. Alföldi, *JNR* 1954 may safely be ignored'. Or p. 89, n. 2: 'The attempt of Alföldi to date this issue must be regarded as a failure'. Or, '. . . the unacceptable view of Alföldi', p. 488, n. 1.
112 *Ibid.* p. 601, n. 3; p. 733, n. 2.
113 C. M. Kraay, 'Caesar's Quattuorviri of 44 BC: The Arrangement of their Issue', *NC* XIV, Ser. 6 (1954), p. 18; R. A. G. Carson, *Gnomon* XXVIII (1956), pp. 181-86 and *Greece and Rome* IV (1957), pp. 46-53. H. Volkmann, 'Caesars letzte Pläne im Spiegel der Münzen', *Gymnasium* LXIV (1957), p. 299.
114 D. Felber, 'Caesars Streben nach der Königswürde' in *Untersuchungen zur römischen Geschichte* (ed. F. Altheim), Frankfurt/m. 1961, vol. I, pp. 211-84.
115 A. H. M. Jones, 'Numismatics and History', *Essays in Roman Coinage presented to H. Mattingly* (ed. R. A. G. Carson and C. H. V. Sutherland), Oxford 1956, p. 32.
116 S. Weinstock, *Divus Julius* loc. cit., reviewed by A. Alföldi, *Gnomon* XII (1975), pp. 154-79; R. E. Palmer, *Athenaeum* LI (1973), p. 201, and J. A. North, *JRS* LXV (1975), p. 171.
117 Weinstock, *loc. cit.* p. 3; Alföldi, *Gnomon, loc. cit.* p. 158.

118 E.g. R. Syme, .'Livy and Augustus', *HSCP* LXIV (1959), 80, no. 85: 'Dio's passage (LXIV, 4, 3) is a patent anachronism'.
119 *Staatsrecht* II³, p. 756, n. 1. Adcock. *CAHM* IX, 721.
120 *Gnomon* XXXIX (1967), p. 155.
121 *NC* VI, Ser. 6 (1947), pp. 127 ff.
122 *Gymnasium* LXX (1963), pp. 312 ff. especially p. 333.
123 E. J. Bickerman, 'Die römische Kaiserapotheose', *Archiv für Religionswissenschaft* XXVII (1930), p. 1.
124 *Id.*, 'Consecratio, Culte des Souverains', *Fondation Hardt, Entretiens* XIX, Geneva 1973, pp. 3-37, especially p. 7.
125 C. Habicht, *Gottmenschtum und griechische Städte*, Munich 1957 (Zetemata, no. 14) (cf. n. 121), pp. 41 ff. and most recently in 'Consecratio'.
126 R. Cohen, *La Grèce et l'Hellenisation du monde antique*, Paris 1939, p. 614.
127 Cerfaux and Tondriau, *loc. cit.* p. 77.
128 M. Liberanome, 'Alcune osservazioni su Cesare e Antonio', *RFIC* XVI (1968), pp. 407 ff.
129 Felber, *loc. cit.* p. 226.
130 Cf. n. 106. and n. 111.
131 G. Haber, *Untersuchungen zu Caesars Pontifikat*, Tübingen 1971.
132 H. Gesche, *Die Vergottung Caesars*, Frankfurt/M. 1968.
133 A. Alföldi, *Phoenix* XXIV (1970), p. 169.
134 M. Cary, 'The Municipal Legislation of Julius Caesar', *JRS* XXVII (1937), p. 49.

135 *Gnomon* XIII (1937), p. 191.
136 W. Schmitthenner, 'Das Attentat auf Caesar', *Gesch. i. Wiss. u. Unterr.* XIII (1962), pp. 685 ff., especially p. 694.
137 R. E. Smith, 'Conspiracy and the Conspirators', *Greece and Rome* IV (1957), p. 62.
138 C. Meier, *Entstehung des Begriffs 'Demokratie', vier Prolegomena zu einer historischen Theorie*, Frankfurt/M. 1970, pp. 131-35.
139 J. H. Collins, *Historia* IV (1955), p. 445.
140 In his thesis, unfortunately unpublished, *Propaganda, Ethics and Psychological Assumptions in Caesar's Writings* (diss.), Frankfurt/M. 1952.
141 Collins assumed that Cicero would have happily seen Caesar dead (*ad Att.* XII, 4; XIII, 40). Other scholars do not take these passages seriously.
142 J. Béranger, 'Tyrannus: Notes sur la notion de Tyrannie chez les Romains particulièrement à l'époque de César et de Cicéron', *REL* XIII (1935), p. 85; 'Cicéron précurseur politique', *Hermes* LXXXVII (1959), p. 103. W. Allen, 'Caesar's Regnum', *TAPA* LXXXIV (1953), p. 227.
143 Z. Yavetz, *Plebs and Princeps*, Oxford 1969, p. 38.
144 For the evidence, *ibid.* p. 50.
145 *Ibid.* p. 101. Idem est quod datur sed interest quomodo detur.
146 *Ibid.* p. 53.
147 *Ibid.* p. 99.
148 *Ibid.* p. 50, n. 7.
149 *Ibid.* pp. 114-16.
150 G. Schulte-Holtey, *Untersuchung zum Gallischen Widerstand gegen Caesar* (diss.), Münster 1968. Others are inclined to stress the interests of Gallic merchants under Roman occupation, e.g. N. J. De Witt, 'Toward Misunderstanding Caesar', *Studies in Honor of Ullman*, St Louis 1960, p. 137; and C. Jullian, *Vercingetorix*, Paris, 1911, who deplores Caesar's conquest of Gaul as a conquest that arrested the development of Celtic civilization:
151 This sceptical view has deep roots. The question had already been posed by Livy: whether it would have been better for the state for Caesar to be born or for him not to have been born ('in incerto esse utrum illum magis nasci an non nasci rei publicae profuerit', Sen. *Nat. Quaest.* 5, 18, 4). Seneca had no clear answer to this question.
152 D. Thompson, *The Aims of History*, London 1969.

Chapter 2

1 In *Dizionario Epigrafico di Antichità Romana*, ed. De Ruggiero, vol. IV (1957), pp. 701 ff.
2 In *Leges Publicae Populi Romani*, Milan 1912.
3 For further details, E. Meyer, *Caesars Monarchie und das Principat des Pompeius*, Stuttgart and Berlin 1922, pp. 617 ff.
4 Paavo Castrén, 'Ordo populusque Pompeianus', *Acta Instituti Romani Finlandiae* VIII

(Rome 1975), pp. 55 and 93, with the evidence. I am grateful to E. Gabba for this reference.
5 The most important of the more recent works are U. Ewins, 'The Enfranchisement of Cisalpine Gaul', *PBSR* XXIII (1955), pp. 73-98; M. W. Frederiksen: 'The Lex Rubria; Reconsiderations', *JRS* LIV (1964), p. 129; F. Bruna: '*The Lex Rubria*', Leiden 1972 (text and commentary with detailed explanations). Still fundamental are Th. Mommsen, *Jur. Schriften* I (1905), pp. 178 and 192; E. G. Hardy, *Six Roman Laws*, Oxford 1911, pp. 110 ff.; *id.*, *Some Problems in Roman History*, Oxford 1924; H. Rudolph, *Stadt und Staat im römischen Italien*, Leipzig 1935; G. E. F. Chilver, *Cisalpine Gaul*, Oxford 1941; A. N. Sherwin-White, *The Roman Citizenship*[2], Oxford 1973, especially p. 157; F. F. Abbott and A. C. Johnson, *Municipal Administration in the Roman Empire*, Princeton 1926, pp. 322-24 and F. Vittinghoff, *Römische Kolonisation und Bürgerrechtspolitik unter Caesar und Augustus*, Wiesbaden 1952.
6 C. Niccolini, *I fasti tribuni della plebe*, Milan 1934, p. 441.
7 C. H. V. Sutherland, *The Romans in Spain*, London 1939; M. I. Henderson, 'Julius Caesar and Latium in Spain', *JRS* XXXII (1942), pp. 1-13; F. Vittinghoff, *loc. cit.*; C. Saumagne, *Le droit latin et les cités romaines sous l'empire*, Paris 1965, pp. 71-76; G. Dipersia, 'Le concessione delle cita-

dinanza romana a Gades nel 49 a.C.', *Contributo dell'Istituto di Storia antica I* (Milan 1972), p. 108; A. N. Sherwin-White, *The Roman Citizenship*[2], Oxford 1973, pp. 188-89, 301-4, 340 ff.; H. Galsterer, *Untersuchungen zum römischen Städtewesen auf der iberischen Halbinsel*, Berlin 1971 and P. A. Brunt, *Italian Manpower*, Oxford 1971, pp. 584 ff.
8 Cf. Galsterer's explanations of the conjecture that Gades was already organized as a *municipium* in the time of Caesar, *op. cit.* 19. On the difficult passages in Pliny, *NH* III, 7; IV, 119, cf. Sherwin-White, *op. cit.* p. 340 and Brunt, *op. cit.* pp. 584 ff.
9 R. A. Bauman, *The Crimen Maiestatis in the Roman Republic and Augustan Principate*, Johannesburg 1967, pp. 161-68.
10 Th. Mommsen, *Strafrecht*, pp. 128-29 and p. 655; A. W. Zumpt, *Das Criminalrecht der römischen Republik*, Berlin 1868/9; A. W. Lintott, *Violence in Republican Rome*, Oxford 1968, pp. 107-24; E. Gruen, *The Last Generation of the Roman Republic*, Berkeley 1974; Bauman, *op. cit.* (reviewed in *Gnomon* XLI (1969), pp. 288-93; *JRS* LIX (1969), pp. 282-84; M. Wlassak, *Römische, Prozessgesetze*, 1888 91; M. Voigt, 'Über die leges Juliae iudiciorum privatorum und publicorum', *Abh. der sächs Akad. d. Wiss.*, Leipzig XIII (1893), pp. 471-526; P. F. Girard, 'Les Leges Juliae iudiciorum et privatorum', *ZRG* XXXIV (1913), pp. 295-372).

11 Th. Mommsen, *Strafrecht*; *op. cit.* R. A. Bauman, *op. cit.*; H. G. Gundel, 'Der Begriff maiestas im Denken der römischen Republik', *Historia* XII (1963), pp. 283-320; J. E. Allison and J. D. Cloud, 'The Lex Julia Maiestatis', *Latomus* XXI (1962), pp. 711-31; H. F. Jolowicz and B. Nicholas, *Historical Introduction to the Study of Roman Law*[3], Cambridge 1972, especially p. 320; H. Drexler, 'Maiestas', *Aevum* XXX (1956), pp. 195-212; C. H. Brecht, 'Perduellio: eine Studie zu ihrer begrifflichen Abgrenzung im römischen Strafrecht bis zum Ausgang der Republik', *Münchener Beiträge zur Papyrusforschung und antiken Rechtsgeschichte* XXIX (1938) and C. Meier, 'Pompeius' Rückkehr aus dem Mithridatischen Kriege und die Catilinarische Verschwörung', *Athenaeum* XL (1962), p. 103.

12 Th. Mommsen, *De collegiis et sodaliciis Romanorum*, Kiel 1843, pp. 78-79; P. Kayser, *Abhandlungen aus dem Prozess- und Strafrecht* (vol. II: *Die Strafgesetzgebung der Römer gegen die Vereine*), Berlin 1873, p. 178; M. Cohn, *Zum römischen Vereinsrecht*, Berlin 1873, pp. 70-73; W. Liebenam, *Zur Geschichte und Organisation des römischen Vereinswesens*, Leipzig 1890, pp. 27-30; O. Karlowa, *Römische Rechtsgeschichte*, Leipzig 1892; J. P. Waltzing, *Etude historique sur les corporations professionelles chez les Romains*, Louvain 1895, vol. I, pp. 112-13; F. M. de Robertis, *Il diritto associativo romano*, Bari 1938, pp. 176-86; *id.*, *Storia delle corporazioni e del regime associativo nel mondo Romano*, 2 vols, Bari 1971, especially vol. I, pp. 195-247; S. Accame, 'La legislazione romana ai collegi nel I. sec. a. C.', *Bull. del Museo dell'Imp. Rom.* 13 (1942), p. 38; J. Linderski, 'Cicero's Rede Pro Caelio und die Ambitus und Vereinsgesetzgebung der Republik', *Hermes* LXXXIX (1961), p. 106; *id.*, 'Suetons Bericht über die Vereinsgesetzgebung unter Caesar und Augustus', *ZRG* LXXIX (1962), pp. 322-28; *id.*, *Der Senat und die Vereine in Gesellschaft und Recht im grieschisch-römischen Altertum*, ed. M. N. Andreew et al., Berlin 1968, pp. 94-132; G. Schrot, *Das Handwerk im alten Rom socialökonomische Verhältnisse im alten Orient und klassischen Altertum*, Berlin, Akademieverlag 1961, p. 245; H. Kühne, 'Die stadtrömischen Sklaven in den Collegia des Clodius', *Helikon* VI (1966) p. 111; A. W. Lintott, *op. cit.* p. 78; S. Treggiari, *Roman Freedmen during the Late Republic*, Oxford 1969 and E. S. Gruen, *op. cit.*

13 Mommsen, *Römische Geschichte*, vol. I, p. 250 (= *History of Rome*, vol. 1, p. 193).

14 Lintott, *op. cit.* p. 78.

15 Z. Yavetz, 'The Failure of Catiline's Conspiracy', *Historia* XII (1963), pp. 496-97.

16 Hildebrandt, *Jahrbuch für Nationalökonomie*, V, 1866, p. 299.

17 De Robertis, *op. cit.*, vol. I, p. 236.

18 H. J. Mason, *Greek Terms for Roman Institutions*, Toronto 1974, pp. 158 ff.

19 Augustus acted on the same principle, see Philo of Alexandria, *Leg. ad Gaium* 311-12, 'The first is a letter which he sent to the governors of the provinces in Asia, as he had learnt that the sacred first fruits were treated with disrespect. He ordered that the Jews alone should be permitted by them to assemble in synagogues. These gatherings, he said, were not based on drunkenness and carousing to promote conspiracy and so to do grave injury to the cause of peace, but were schools of temperance and justice where men while practising virtue subscribed the annual first fruits to pay for the sacrifices they offered . . .'

20 On this and the two following passages, cf. E. Gabba, 'Cicerone e la falsificazione dei Senatoconsulti', *SCO* X (1961), p. 89.

Chapter 3

1 W. Judeich, *Caesar im Orient*. Leipzig 1885; M. Rostovtzeff, 'Geschichte der Staatspacht', *Philologus*, Suppl. IX, 3 (1902), especially p. 272; T. Rice Holmes, *The Roman Republic*, Oxford 1923, vol. III, pp. 507 ff.; P. Graindon; *La Guerre d'Alexandrie*, Cairo 1931; T. Frank (ed.), *Economic Survey of Ancient Rome*, Baltimore 1938,

vol. IV, p. 579; M. Rostovtzeff, *Social and Economic History of the Hellenistic World*, Oxford 1941, pp. 562-71; D. Magie, *Roman Rule in Asia Minor*, Princeton 1950; A. E. Raubitschek, 'Epigraphical Notes on Julius Caesar', *JRS* XLIV (1954), p. 65, and E. Badian, *Publicans and Sinners*, Ithaca 1972, especially pp. 113, 116 and 157, n. 163; H. Heinen, *Rom und Aegypten* (51-47 BC) (diss.), Tübingen 1966.

2 R. Syme, *The Roman Revolution*, Oxford 1939, p. 71.

3 But see J. M. Reynolds, 'Aphrodisias: A Free and Federate City', *Akten des VI. Int. Kongr. für gr. und lat. Epigraphie*, Munich 1972 (1973), p. 115, and *Aphrodisias and Rome*, London 1982.

4 F. Ritschl, 'Römische Senatusconsulta bei Josephus', *Rh.M.* XXIX (1874), p. 337; XXX (1875), p. 428; L. Mendelsohn, 'Senatus Consulta Romanorum quae sunt in Josephi Antiquitates', *Acta Societatis Philol. Lipsiensis* V (1875), pp. 87-288; Th. Mommsen, 'Der Senatsbeschluss Jos. Ant. XIV, 8, 5', *Hermes* IX (1875), pp. 281-91; B. Niese, 'Bemerkungen über die Urkunden bei Josephus', *Hermes* XI (1876), pp. 466-88; F. Rosenthal, 'Die Erlässe Caesars und die Senatus Consulta in Jos. Ant. XIV, 10', *MGWJ* XXIII (1879), pp. 176-83; E. Schürer, *The History of the Jewish People in the Age of Jesus Christ: A new English version revised and edited by G. Vermes and F. Millar*, vol.

I, Edinburgh 1973; esp. p. 272 E. Schürer, *Geschichte des jüdischen Volkes im Zeitalter Christi*[3] I, pp. 220-63; 344-48; III, pp. 67-69; W. Judeich, *Caesar im Orient*, Leipzig 1885, p. 119; H. Graetz, 'Die Stellung der kleinasiatischen Juden unter der Römerherrschaft', *MGWJ* XXX (1886), pp. 329-46; A. Büchler, 'Die priesterlichen Zehnten und die römischen Steuern in den Erlässen Caesars', *Festschr. Steinschneider* 1896, pp. 91- 109; E. Täubler, *Imperium Romanum*, Leipzig 1913, pp. 157-87; pp. 239-54; T. Rice Holmes, *The Roman Republic*, Oxford 1923, III, p. 507; M. Ginsburg, *Rome et la Judée* 1928; A. Momigliano, 'Ricerche sull' organizzazione della Giudea sotto il dominio Romano (63 AC–70 AD)', *ARSP* 1934, series II, vol. III, especially pp. 183-221; M. Brucklemeyer, *Beiträge zur rechtlichen Stellung der Juden im römischen Reich*, 1939; M. Stern (ed.), *Greek and Latin Authors on Jews and Judaism*, Jerusalem 1974, I, p. 214. Further bibliography in *Josephus*, vol. VII (Loeb Class. Library 1961, pp. 780 ff.).

5 Momigliano, *op. cit.*, p. 266.

6 G. Rotondi, *Leges populi Romani*, Milan 1912, p. 389.

7 Th. Mommsen, 'Zur Geschichte der caesarischen Zeit', *Hermes* XXVIII (1893), pp. 599-604.

8 S. Weinstock, *Divus Julius*, Oxford 1971, p. 33; G. Wissowa, *Religion und Kultus der Römer*, Munich 1912.

9 Th. Mommsen, *Die römische*

Chronologie bis auf Caesar, Berlin 1859; *id.*, 'Inscriptio Apamensis', *Ath. Mitt.* XVI (1891), pp. 235-39 = *Ges. Schriften* v (1908), p. 529; *id.*, 'Reformen des römischen Kalenders in den Jahren 45 und 8 vor Christi', *Philologus* 45 (1886), p. 414; G. Wissowa, *Religion und Kultus der Römer*, Munich 1912; P. V. Neugebauer, 'Der julianische Kalender und seine Entstehung', *Astronomische Nachrichten* 257, no. 6149 (1935), pp. 65 ff.; K. Geiger, *Der römische Kalender und seine Verbesserung durch Julius Caesar*, Munich 1936; E. Giovanetti, *Le religione di Cesare*, Milan 1937; C. Koch, *Der römische Jupiter*, Frankfurt 1937; L. R. Taylor, 'Caesar's Colleagues in the Pontifical College', *AJP* LXIV (1942), p. 385; *id.*, 'The Election of the Pontifex Maximus in the Late Republic', *CP* XXXVII (1942), p. 421; F. Altheim, *Römische Religionsgeschichte*, Baden-Baden 1951; A. Heltweg, *Die politische Bedeutung des römischen Oberpontifikates* (diss.), Cologne 1952; J. Bleicken, 'Oberpontifex und Pontifikalkollegium', *Hermes* 85, (1957), p. 345; G. Radke, 'Die falsche Schaltung nach Caesars Tode', *Rh.M. NF* CIII (1960), p. 178; J. Bayet, *Histoire politique et psychologique de la religion romaine*, Paris 1957; K. Latte, *Römische Religionsgeschichte*, Munich 1960; A. K. Michels, *The Calendar of the Roman Republic*, Princeton 1967; V. Laffi, *Le iscrizioni relative all' introduzione nel 9 a.c.*

del nuovo calendario della provincia Asia, Pisa 1967; E. J. Bickerman, *Chronology of the Ancient World*,[2] London 1980, and G. Huber, *Untersuchungen zu Caesars Oberpontifikat* (diss.), Tübingen 1971.
10 Th. Mommsen, *Röm. Chron*, p. 278.
11 Introduced by G. B. Giglioni in *Lavori publici e occupazione nell' antichità classica*, Bologna 1973, p. 129, as *Lex Julia de urbe augenda*. See also M. W. Frederiksen; 'The Republican Municipal Laws. Errors and Drafts', *JRS* LV (1965), p. 321.
12 Little is known of Curio's proposals with reference to a *lex viaria* (Cic., *ad fam.* VIII, 6, 5; App., *BC* II, 27).
13 In detail see B. Cohen, *The Roman Ordines* (Hebrew diss.), Tel-Aviv 1972, and E. Herzog, *Geschichte und System der röm. Staatsverwaltung*, Leipzig 1884-91, p. 19, n. 2.
14 F. C. v. Savigny, 'Uber den römischen Volksbeschluss der Tafel von Heraclea', *Zeitschr. f. gesch. Rechtswissenschaft* IX (1838), 300 = *Verm. Schriften* III (1850), p. 279; H. Nissen, 'Zu den römischen Stadtrechten' *Rh. M.* XLV (1890), pp. 100 ff.; H. Hackel; 'Die Hypothesen über die sogenannte *Lex Julia municipalis*', *Wiener Studien* XXIV (1902), pp. 552 ff.; Th. Mommsen, *Juristische Schriften* I (1905), p. 146; H. Legras, *La table d'Héraclée*, Paris 1907; J. S. Reid, 'The so-called *Lex Julia municipalis*', *JRS* V (1915), pp. 207-48; A. v. Premerstein, 'Die

Tafel von Heraclea und die Acta Caesaris', *RG* XLIII (1922), p. 45; E. G. Hardy, *Some Problems in Roman History*, Oxford 1914, p. 239; K. J. Beloch, *Römische Geschichte*, Berlin-Leipzig 1926, p. 500; F. F. Abbot and A. C. Johnson, *Municipal Administration in the Roman Empire*, Princeton 1926; M. Cary, 'Notes on the Legislation of Julius Caesar', *JRS* XIX (1929), p. 113; H. Rudolph, *Stadt und Staat in römischen Italien*, Leipzig 1935, reviewed by H. Stuart Jones in *JRS* XXVI (1936), p. 268 f., also by H. Strasburger in *Gnomon* XIII (1937), p. 177 f.; F. Sartori, *Problemi di storia constituzionale italiota*, Rome 1953; E. Schönbauer, 'Die Inschrift von Heraclea – ein Rätsel'. *RIDA* I (1954), p. 373 (with a survey of earlier views); E. Sereni, *Communità rurali nell'Italia antica*, Rome 1955; B. Barbieri and G. Tibiletti, 'Lex', *Dizionario Epigrafico di Antichità Romane* IV (1957), pp. 725-27; L. R. Taylor, *The Voting Districts of the Roman Republic*, Rome 1960; A. Degrassi, 'Quattuorviri in colonie romane e in municipi retti da duoviri', *Scritti vari di antichità* I, Rome 1962, pp. 99-177; M. W. Frederiksen, 'The Republican Municipal Laws. Errors and Drafts', *JRS* LV (1965), pp. 183-98; F. De Martino, *Storia della constituzione Romana* III, Naples 1966; D. Adamesteanu and M. Torelli, 'Il nuovo framento della Tabula Bantina', *Arch. Class.* XXI (1969), pp.

2-17; F. T. Hinrichs, 'Das legale Landversprechen im Bellum Civile', *Historia* XVIII (1969), p. 521; R. K. Sherk, *The Municipal Decrees of the Roman West*, Arethusa Monograph II, Buffalo 1970; H. Galsterer, 'Die Lex Osca Tabulae Bantinae', *Chiron* I (1971), p. 191; P. A. Brunt, *Italian Manpower*, Oxford 1971, p. 524-35; J. P. Wiseman, *New Men in the Roman Senate*, Oxford 1971, especially pp. 90 ff.; E. Gabba, 'Mario e Silla', *ANRW* I (1972), p. 792; *id.*, 'Urbanizzatione e rinovamenti urbanistici nell' Italia centro-meridionale del I. sec. a.c.', *SCO* XXI (1972), pp. 73-112; *id.*, review of A. J. Toynbee, *Hannibal's Legacy* in *Esercito e società*, Florence 1973, pp. 553 ff. = *Republican Rome, The Army and The Allies*, tr. by P. J. Cuff (Oxford 1976), pp. 154 ff. U. Laffi, 'Sull' Organizzazione amministrativa dell'Italia dopo la guerra sociale', *Akten des VI. Int. Kongr. für griech. u. lat. Epigraphik*, Munich 1972 (1973), pp. 37-53; A. N. Sherwin-White, *The Roman Citizenship*², Oxford 1973 and E. Gabba, 'Considerazioni politiche ed economiche sullo sviluppo urbano in Italia nelle secoli II e I a.c.', *Hellenismus und Mittelalter* (ed. P. Zanker), *Abb. d. Akademie Göttingen* 1974, pp. 315-26. C. Nicolet: *Le métier de citoyen dans la Rome républicaine,* Paris, 1976, esp. p. 183 with the date 75-70 BC (Eng. trans., *The World of the Citizen in the Roman Republic,* London 1980, p. 136).

15 Th. Mommsen, *Staatsrecht* I³, pp. 367, 383, 664, 668; II, pp. 162, 480, 503, 557, 575; G. Vitucci, *Ricerche sulla praefectura urbi in età imperiale*, Rome 1956, reviewed by J. F. Cadoux in *JRS* XLIX (1959), p. 152 and A. Alföldi, 'Les prefecti urbi de César', *Mélanges d'histoire ancienne offerts à William Seston*, Paris-Boccard 1974, p. 1.
16 F. Millar, *The Emperor in the Roman World*, London 1977, pp. 292-94.
17 P. Willems, *Le sénat de la république romaine I-II*, Louvain 1878-83; H. F. Stobbe, 'Die candidati Caesaris', *Philologus* XXVII (1858), p. 88; I. W. Botsford, *The Roman Assemblies*, New York 1909, reprint 1968; G. Tibiletti, 'The comitia during the decline of the Roman Republic', *SDHI* (1959), pp. 94-127; L. R. Taylor, *The Voting Districts of the Roman Republic*, American Acad. in Rome 1960; W. K. Lacey, 'Nominatio and the Elections under Tiberius', *Historia* XII (1963), p. 167; L. R. Taylor, *Roman Voting Assemblies*, Ann Arbor 1966; B. M. Levick, 'Imperial Control of the Elections in the Early Principate', *Historia* XVI (1967), p. 209; R. Frei-Stolba, *Untersuchungen zu den Wahlen in der römischen Kaiserzeit*, Zürich 1967; S. Treggiari, *Roman Freedmen during the Late Republic*, Oxford 1964; E. S. Staveley, *Greek and Roman Voting and Elections*, London 1972, and C. Nicolet, *op. cit.*

Chapter 4

1 E. Fraenkel, 'Zur Geschichte des Wortes Fides', *Rh. M.* LXXI (1916), pp. 187-99; E. Meyer, *Caesars Monarchie und das Prinzipat des Pompeius*, Stuttgart 1919, p. 366 (especially n. 4); M. Polignano, 'P. Cornelio Dolabella uomo politico', *Atti Acc. Naz. Lincei cl. sc. mor.* S. VIII. 1 (1946), pp. 240 ff.; M. Gelzer, *Caesar*, Wiesbaden, 1960, pp. 203 ff.; M. W. Frederiksen, 'Caesar, Cicero and the Problem of Debt', *JRS* LVI (1966), p. 128; Z. Yavetz, 'Fluctuations monétaires et condition de la plèbe', *Recherches sur les structures sociales dans l'antiquité classique*, Paris 1970, pp. 133-57; P. Pinna-Parpaglia, 'La Lex Julia de pecuniis mutuis e la opposizione di Celio', *Labeo* XXII (1976), p. 30, and G. Crifò, *Studi sul quasi usufrutto Romano* I, Padua 1977.
2 J. Kromayer, 'Die Militär-kolonien Octavians und Caesars in Gallia Narbonensis', *Hermes* XXXI (1896), pp. 1-18; E. Meyer, *Caesars Monarchie und das Prinzipat des Pompeius, Stuttgart,* 1919, pp. 413-15; P. A. Brunt, *Italian Manpower,* Oxford 1971, pp. 319-26; id., 'The Army and the land in the Roman Revolution', *JRS* LII (1962), 69-86; F. T. Hinrichs, 'Das legale Landversprechen im Bellum Civile', *Historia* XVIII (1969), p. 521; E. Gabba, 'Urbanizazione e rinovimenti urbanistici nell' Italia centro meridionale del I. Secolo A.C.',

SCO XXI (1972), pp. 73-112; E. S. Gruen, *The Last Generation of the Roman Republic*, Berkeley and Los Angeles 1974, pp. 397-404.
3 E. Herzog, *Geschichte und System der römischen Staatsver-fassung*, vol. II (1), Leipzig 1887; M. I. Henderson, 'Caesar and Latium in Spain', *JRS* XXXII (1942), p. 13; F. Staehelin, *Die Schweiz in römischer Zeit*, Basle 1948, p. 100; F. Vittinghoff, *Römische Kolonisation und Bür gerrechtspolitik*, Wiesbaden 1952, especially pp. 64-91; M. Gelzer, *Caesar*, Wiesbaden 1960, pp. 275 ff.; L. Teutsch, *Das römische Städtewesen in Nordafrika in der Zeit von C. Grachus bis zum Tode des Kaisers Augustus*, Berlin 1962; G. Alföldi, 'Caesarische und augustische Kolonien in der Provinz Dalmatien', *Acta Antiqua* X (1962), p. 35 f.; H. Bögli, *Studien zu den Kolo-niengründungen Caesars* (diss.), Basle 1966, supervised by Fuchs, Pflaum and Alföldi; B. H. Isaac, 'Colonia Munatia Triumphalis and Legio Nona Triumphalis', *Talanta* III (1971), p. 11; H. Galsterer; *Untersuchungen zum römischen Städtewesen auf der iberischen Halbinsel*, Berlin 1971; P. A. Brunt, *Italian Manpower,* Oxford 1971, pp. 589-609; A. J. N. Wilson, *Emigration from Italy in the Republican Age of Rome*, Manchester 1966; B. Levick, *Roman Colonies in Southern Asia Minor*, Oxford 1967, and S. Treggiari, *Roman*

Freedmen during the late Republic, Oxford 1969.

4 For a list of provincial *municipia* see Brunt, *op. cit.* Appendix 16, p. 602.

5 For background see Z. Yavetz, 'The Living Conditions of the Urban Plebs', *Latomus* XVII (1958), pp. 500–17.

6 H. Bolkenstein, *Wohltätigkeit und Armenpflege im vorchristlichen Altertum*, Utrecht 1929.

7 R. Cagnat, *Le Portorium*, Paris 1880; S. Y. de Laet, *Portorium*, Bruges 1949. For a different date see C. Nicolet, *Le métier de citoyen dans la Rome républicaine*, Paris 1976, esp. pp. 228 ff. and 239 ff.

8 *Journal of Economic History* 18 (1958), p. 17.

9 For a brief survey see Helmut Schneider, *Wirtschaft und Politik*, Erlangen 1974, pp. 185 ff., and his splendid collection of sources on consumption at table and stocks of wine, *ibid.*, p. 194. See also J. Sauerwein, *Die leges sumptuariae als römische Massnahme gegen den Sittenverfall* (diss.) Hamburg 1970 and D. Daube, *Roman law, linguistic, social and philosophical aspects*, Edinburgh 1969, esp. pp. 124–26, with the view that these laws were intended to protect the finances of the hosts.

10 E. Meyer, *Caesars Monarchie und das Prinzipat des Pompeius*, Stuttgart 1919; J. Elmore, 'The professiones of the Heraclean Tablet', *JRS* V (1915), p. 125; R. J. Rowland, 'Number of Grain Recipients in the Late Republic', *A. Ant. Hung.* XIII

(1965), p. 81; D. Van Berchem, *Les distributions de blé et d'argent à la plèbe romaine sous l'empire*, Geneva 1939; A. R. Hands, *Charities and social aid in Greece and Rome*, London 1965; J. P. Wiseman, 'The Census in the First Century', *JRS* LIX (1969), p. 59; P. A. Brunt, *Italian Manpower*, Oxford 1971; G. Rickman, *The Corn Supply of Ancient Rome*, Oxford 1980; and C. Nicolet, *Le métier de citoyen dans la Rome républicaine*, Paris 1976.

11 G. B. Giglioni, *Lavori publici e occupazione nell'antichità classica*, Bologna 1973, p. 129. It might be interesting to investigate if there is any connection between the extension of the *pomerium* mentioned in Dio XLIII, 50, 1; XLIV, 49, 2 and Gell. *Noctes Atticae* XIII, 14, 4.

12 Mart. IX. 22: Ut donem; Pastor et aedificem.

13 G. B. Giglioni, *Jules César*[2], 1968, p. 510.

Chapter 5

1 The most important works on the Roman army are: E. Gabba, 'Le origine dell'esercito professionale da Mario ad Augusto', now reprinted in *Esercito e società nella tarda Repubblica Romana*, Florence 1973, pp. 1-174 (= *Republican Rome, the Army and the Allies*, tr. P. J. Cuff, Oxford, 1976); J. Harmand, *'L'armée et le soldat à Rome'* (107-50 BC), Paris 1967, *Gnomon* XLIV (1975), pp. 260–

66; P. J. Cuff, 'Caesar the Soldier', *Greece & Rome* IV (1957), pp. 29–35; and E. H. Erdmann, *Die Rolle des Heeres in der Zeit von Marius bis Caesar* (diss.), Constance 1972. The following works remain classics: J. Vogt, 'Caesar und seine Soldaten', reprinted in *Orbis*, Freiburg 1960, pp. 89–109, with a wealth of bibliography and an examination of Caesar's achievements, not merely from the point of view of strategy and tactics, but as a commanding officer with deep understanding of his soldiers' feelings. In addition, there are some first-rate observations in W. Schmitthenner, 'Das Attentat auf Caesar', *GWU* (1962), p. 685; J. Suolahti, *The Junior Officers of the Roman Army in the Republican Period*, Helsinki 1955; M. J. V. Bell, 'Tactical Reform in the Roman Republican Army', *Historia* XIV (1965), pp. 404–22; Th. Steinwender, *Die römische Bürgerschaft in ihrem Verhaltnis zum Heere*, Danzig 1888; E. Meyer, 'Das römische Manipularheer', *Kleine Schriften* II², p. 226; L. Topa, 'La relazione tra la forma di governo e l'organizazione militare romana dai Gracchi ad Augusto', *Ephemera Dacoromana* IX (1940), p. 119, and H. Drexler, 'Parerga Caesariana', *Hermes* LXX (1935), p. 225.
2 On Caesar's control of finances see A. Alföldi: 'Der Einmarsch Oktavians in Rom', *Hermes* LXXXVI (1958), p.

480; Eduard Meyer: *Caesars Monarchie und das Prinzipat des Pompeius*, Stuttgart and Berlin 1922, pp. 502–3; E. Badian, *Roman Imperialism in the Late Republic*, Oxford 1968, p. 89, and for the most detailed account I. Shatzman: *Senatorial Wealth and Roman Politics*, Brussels 1975, pp. 342–46; 483–85.
3 L. Friedländer, *Darstellungen aus der römischen Sittengeschichte*, Leipzig 1922, II, p. 80; H. Berve, 'Liberalitas', *RE* XIII. 1 (1926), cols. 82–93; R. Syme, *The Roman Revolution*, Oxford 1939, p. 369; K. H. Heuer, *Comitas, facilitas, liberalitas* – Studien zur gesellschaftlichen der Kultur ciceronischen Zeit (diss.), Münster 1941; Z. Yavetz, *Plebs and Princeps*, Oxford 1969, especially pp. 38–57; H. Kloft, 'Liberalitas principis', *Kölner historische Abhandlungen*, Cologne 1970, p. 60, n. 102 (banquet for Caesar), and J. P. V. D. Balsdon, *Life and Leisure in Ancient Rome*, London 1969, pp. 244–339.
4 P. Willems, *Le sénat de la République romaine* (I. II), Louvain 1878/83; P. Ribbeck, *Senatus Romanus qui fuerit Idibus Martiis annui a.u.c.* 710 (diss.), Berlin 1899; M. Gelzer, *Die Nobilität der römischen Republik*, Leipzig 1912, p. 11; F. Münzer, *Römische Adelsparteien und Adelsfamilien*, Stuttgart 1920, p. 358; P. Stein, *Die Senatesitzungen der Ciceronischen Zeit* (diss.), Münster 1930; R. Syme, 'Who was Decidius Saxa?', *JRS*

XXVII (1937), p. 128; *id.*, 'Caesar, the Senate and Italy', *PBSR* XIV (1938), p. 13; *id.*, *The Roman Revolution*, Oxford 1939, pp. 78 ff.; *id.*, 'Sabinus the Muleteer', *Latomus* XVII (1958), pp. 73-80; H. Dessau, *Geschichte der römischen Kaiserzeit* I (1942), p. 94; D. R. Shackleton Bailey, 'The Roman Nobility in the Second Civil War', *CQ*, N. S. X (1960), p. 253; E. S. Staveley, *Greek and Roman Voting and Elections*, London 1972; H. Schneider, *Wirtschaft und Politik*, Erlangen 1974; I. Shatzman, *Senatorial Wealth and Roman Politics*, Brussels 1975; H. Bengtson, 'Die letzten Monate der römischen Senatscherrschaft', *ANRW*; C. Meier, Introduction to *Caesar: Der Bürgerkrieg*, tr. H. Simon, Bremen 1964; *id.*, 'Caesars Bürgerkrieg', *Entstehung des Begriffs Demokratie. Vier Prolegomena zu einer historischen Theorie*, Frankfurt 1970; K. Raaflaub, *Dignitatis Contentio*, Munich 1974, and F. Millar, *The Emperor in the Roman World*, London 1977, especially pp. 290-96. Shortly before it was printed the important dissertation by Hinnerk Bruhns, *Caesar und die römische Obersicht in den Jahren 49-44 v. Chr.*, was sent to me by the author.

5 Cf. also Plin. *NH* VII, p. 135; Val. Max. VI, 9, 9; Vell. Pat. H, 65, 3; Dio XLIII, 51, 4-5; Cic., *ad fam.* X, 18, 3.

6 G. Favaloro, *Delle fonti di Plutarco* (69-29 a.c.), Florence 1921, p. 85, with an unusual and original interpretation of Caesar's *clementia*; H. Dahlmann, 'Clementia Caesaris', *Neue Jahrb. f. Wissenschaft u. Jugendbildung* X (1934), p. 1726; L. Wickert, 'Zu Caesars Reichspolitik, *Klio* XXX (1937), p. 232; V. Pöschl, *Grundwerte römischer Staatsgesinnung in den Geschichtswerken des Sallust*, Berlin 1940, p. 984; M. Treu, 'Clementia Caesaris', *MH* V (1948), p. 197; M. Rambaud, *L'art de la déformation historique dans les commentaires de César*, Paris 1953, especially pp. 283-93; O. Leggewie, 'Clementia Caesaris', *Gymnasium* LXV (1958), p. 17; L. Canali, *La personalità e stile di Cesare*, Rome 1963, especially p. 15; J. Adam, *Clementia Principis*, Stuttgart 1970; S. Weinstock, *Divus Julius*, Oxford 1971, especially pp. 233 ff. and Z. Yavetz, 'Reflections on Titus and Josephus', *GRBS* XVI (1975), pp. 411-32.

7 H. Fuchs, 'Zur Verherrlichung Roms und der Römer in der Gedichte des Rutilius Namatianus', *BZG* (1943), p. 37 f.

8 E. Polay, 'Der Kodificationsplan des Pompeius,' *A. Ant. Hung.* 13 (1965) p. 85; *id.*, *Der Kodifikationsplan des J. Caesar*, Jura 16 (1865), 28.

9 E. Gruen, *The Last Generation of the Roman Republic*, p. 211.

10 E.g., Cic., *ad fam.* XIII, 8, 2; Suet., *Div. Jul.* 38, 1; Dio XLII, 54, 1; App., *BC* II, 94.

11 Z. Yavetz, *Plebs and Princeps*, Oxford 1969, pp. 60 ff.

Chapter 6

1 The sequence has been altered.

2 When asked what he thought of Mussolini's prospects, Al Capone replied, 'He'll be O.K. if he can keep the boys in line.'

3 H. Friedl, Der *Tyrannenmord in Gesetzgebung und Volksmeinung der Griechen*, Stuttgart 1937.

4 Cf. *de inv.* II, 144. For further references see M. Gelzer, *Cicero*, Wiesbaden 1968, pp. 360 ff.

5 Th. Mommsen, 'Sp. Cassius, M. Manlius, Sp. Maelius: Die drei Demagogen der älteren republikanischen Zeit', *Römische Forschungen* II, pp. 153–220.

6 For the evidence see C. Wirszubski, *Libertas*, Cambridge 1950, p. 60, n. 2.

7 J. Béranger, 'Cicéron précurseur politique', *Hermes* LXXXVII (1959), p. 101; W. Allen, 'Caesar's Regnum', *TAPA* LXXXIV (1953), p. 227; R. Dunkle, 'The Greek Tyrant and Roman Political Invective of the Late Republic', *TAPA* XCVIII (1967), p. 151; F. K. Springer, *Tyrannus, Untersuchungen zur politischen Ideologie der Römer*, (diss.), Cologne, 1952; and the comprehensive article by E. Rawson, 'Caesar's Heritage: Hellenistic Kings and their Roman Equals', *JRS* LXV (1975), pp. 148–59, in which the author convincingly handles the Romans' ambivalent relationship to kings. She holds that

Caesar actually rejected the title of king, but was not opposed to divine honours.

8 'Deus ille noster Plato' (*ad Att.* IV, 16, 3, cf. *ad Qu. fr.* I, 1, 28–29.

9 In the *Pro Ligario* Cicero discovered in Caesar *humanitas, clementia, misericordia* and *liberalitas*, obvious flattery, but with some elements of truth.

10 C. Wirszubski, 'Julius Caesar', *Molad* 1957, p. 353 (in Hebrew). *id., Libertas*, pp. 87–91, with the most important evidence.

11 'Praestate enim nemini imperare quam alicui servire. Sine illo vivere honeste licet, cum hoc vivendi nulla condicio est', Quint., *Inst. Or.* IX, 3, 95.

12 Malalas, who definitely characterized Caesar as a tyrant, can also be traced back to this tradition (IX, 214, 11; 215, 13, ed. von Stauffenberg, Stuttgart 1931).

13 W. Schmitthenner, 'Das Attentat auf Caesar', *GWU* XIII (1962), p. 685; R. Etienne, *Les ides de Mars*, Paris 1973, introducing the relevant sources, and emphasizing the negative programme of the conspirators, especially in the section 'Vingt quatre coniurés sans programme', pp. 167 ff.

14 N. Horsfall, 'The Ides of March. Some New Problems', *Greece & Rome* XXI (1974), p. 191.

15 J. Hubaux, 'La mort de Jules César', *L'académie royale de Belgique* XIII (1957), pp. 76–87.

16 F. D. Gräter, *Über Caesars*

Ermordung und Ciceros Ansicht derselben, Zürich 1820, p. 13.

17 J. P. V. D. Balsdon, 'The Ides of March', *Historia* VII (1958), p. 80.

18 M. Radin, *Marcus Brutus*, Oxford 1939, but cf. M. Rothstein, 'Caesar über Brutus', *Rh. M.* LXXXI (1932), p. 324, with an analysis of *ad Att.* XIV, 1 and 2 'sed quidquid volt, valde volt'.

19 R. Kassner, 'Die Iden des März', *Merkur* X (1956), p. 202.

20 H. Bengston, 'Zur Geschichte des Marcus Brutus', *ABAW* (1970), pp. 3-50.

21 *Ibid.* p. 18.

22 Cf. also Z. Yavetz, *Plebs and Princeps*, pp. 58 ff. with the same conclusion but different arguments.

23 Cicero calls such a mistake *ignoratio* and *error humanis*, *Pro Marcello* 13.

24 Z. Yavetz, 'Plebs Sordida', *Athenaeum*, NS XLIII (1965), pp. 295-311.

25 Cf. also Macr., *Saturnalia* II, 3, 6.

26 Th. Mommsen, *Römische Geschichte* III, p. 490 (= *History of Rome*, tr. W. P. Dickson, London 1894, V, p. 342).

27 Suet., *Div. Jul.* 78; Nic. Dam. fr. 130, 79; Livy, *Per.* 116; Eutrop., VI, 20, cf. Pl., *Caes.*, 60.

28 J. Carcopino, 'César et Cléopatre', Annales de l'Ecole des Hautes Etudes de Gand (AEHEG) I (1937), pp. 37-77; K. W. Meiklejohn, 'Alexander, Helios and Caesarion', *JRS* XXIV

(1934), p. 194; H. Volkmann, *Kleopatra: Politik und Propaganda*, Munich 1953, (Engl. transl. *Cleopatra*, 1958) with source material and survey of literature on the subject; H. Heinen, *Rom und Aegypten von 51–47 v. Chr.* (diss.), Tübingen 1966.

29 Cic., *ad Att.* XIII, 31, 3 (May 45); cf. XIII, 7, 1 (June 45); cf. Dio XLIII, 51, 2, and, in addition, J. Jahn, 'Interregnum und Wahldiktatur', *FAS* (1970), p. 187. It is doubtful whether hints of a *dictatura perpetua* are to be found at so early a date (May 45).

30 Gordon W. Allport and L. Postman, *The Basic Psychology of Rumour in Public Opinion and Propaganda*, New York 1954, p. 394.

31 A. Klotz, *Caesarstudien*, Leipzig 1910, especially p. 158, On Caesar's *Anticato* cf. Cic., *ad Att.* XIII, 50, 1; Tac., *Ann.* IV, 34; Plut., *Caes.* 54, 2; *Cic.* 39, 5; Juv. VI, 338.

32 Jokes made by soldiers about their commander constitute an exception. It was usual to make fun of successful generals on the occasion of their triumphs (Mart. I, 4, 3-4); jokes of this type were often a sign of the affection and popularity enjoyed by the general (cf. Suet., *Div. Jul.* 50-52).

33 On Caesar's world-weariness: A. Esser, *Caesar und die Julisch-Klaudischen Kaiser im biologischen/ärtzlichen Blickfeld*, Leiden 1958, p. 32.

34 The best investigation of this difficult subject is to be

found in P. Hermann, 'Der römische Kaisereid', *Hypomnemata* XX (1968), pp. 66–78. The author stressed that the scanty information about its contents permits the inference that it was an oath 'pro salute Caesaris', i.e., essentially a promise to protect his person and avenge attacks on him, and not a 'ius iurandum amicitiae'. Hermann found no suitable basis for Caesar's general patronage over the whole citizen population. Hermann's book was not available to me when my *Plebs and Princeps* went to press in 1969.
35 Virgil, *Aen.* IV, 174, 'Fama, malum qua non aliud velocius ullum.'
36 Quint., *Inst. Or.* V, 3.
37 Ovid, *Met.* XII, 39–63.
38 Especially in Balsdon, Smith, Strasburger and C. Meier.
39 Carl J. Friedrich, 'Political Leadership and Charismatic Power', *The Journal of Politics* XXIII (No. 2) (1961), p. 14.
40 Important is R. C. Tucker, 'The Theory of Charismatic Leadership', *Daedalus* 1968, p. 731.
41 Macr., *Saturnalia* I, 5, 1; Gell., *Noctes Atticae* I, 10 (*inter alia*).
42 J. W. Spaeth, 'Caesar's Friends and Enemies among the Poets', *CJ* XXXII (1936/7), p. 541.
43 *Mélanges d'histoire ancienne offerts à William Seston*, Paris 1974, p. 14.
44 Cf. Plut., *Caes.* 28, 5 (with

reference to Pompey); Suet., *Div. Aug.* 42, 1; Cass. Dio LVI, 39, 2.

Appendix

1 A. V. Dicey, *Law and Public Opinion in England* (London, 1920) 19. For another definition, see J. Schmoller: *Grundriss der Volkswirtschaftslehre* (7-10 Aufl. pt. I [1908]) 14: 'Die öffentliche Meinung ist die Antwort der zunächst mehr passiv sich verhaltenden Teile der Gesellschaft auf die Wirkungsweise des aktiven Teiles.' See also Pietro Chimienti. *La pubblica opinione nello stato moderno* (Annuario della Università di Cagliari 1909); W. Bauer: *Die öffentliche Meinung in der Weltgeschichte* (Berlin 1929).
For additional modern works, see A. Palmer, 'Concepts of Public Opinion in the History of Political Thought', unpubl. thesis, Harvard University 1933. For a summary treatment of the historical development of the concept, public opinion, see Harwood Childs, *Public Opinion* (New York, Van Nostrand, 1965) 26–38, with bibliography. J. Strayer, 'The Historian's Concept of Public Opinion', in M. Komarovsky, ed, *Common Frontiers of the Social Sciences* (Glencoe, Ill., Free Press 1957). L. Benson, 'An Approach to the Scientific

Study of the Past', *Public Opinion Quart.* 31 (1967) 522–567.

For public opinion in Eastern Europe; see Alex Inkeles, *Public Opinion in Soviet Russia*, Cambridge, Mass. (Harvard University Press 1950). I am indebted to Professor Z. Gitelman's lecture: 'Public Opinion and the Political System in Eastern Europe', delivered in 1970 to the American Political Science Association.

2 Machiavelli, *Discourses* (1950 ed.) 320.

3 David Hume, *Essays* I, 100.

4 Z. Yavetz, *Plebs and Princeps* (Oxford, 1969) 109 n. 9; 134 n. 1.

5 For *existimatio omnium*, see Cic. *Verr.* II, 3, 133; II, 1, 148; *existimatio hominum, ibid.*: II, 3, 137; II, 3, 210; *existimatio civium* (Sen. *Ep.* 76, 29); *existimatio Achaeorum* (Liv. 35, 49, 3). For the term *opinio publica* see Serv. *Comm, in Verg.* VI, 136.

6 Christian Meier, *Respublica amissa* (Wiesbaden 1966), 9 n. 15.

7 *Ibid.*, p. 8.

8 For *existimatio populi Romani*, see also Cic. *Verr.* I, 20; I, 44; II, 1, 21; II, 5, 143.

9 This passage (like many others) is quoted for the usage of language and not to establish the historical truth. Note also that in this context Cicero prefers the more neutral *multitudo* for crowd and refrains from the more derogatory *vulgus*; cf. Z. Yavetz, *Athenaeum* n.s. 63 (1965) 97.

10 For *existimatio* of the Senate (see Tac. *Hist.* IV, 7); of a jury Cic. *Rosc. Am.* 55.

11 E.g. Cic. *Sest.* 113: *Iam de C. Fannio quae sit existimatio videmus.*

12 On *fiducia, tutela, societas, see* J. Hellegouarch, *Le vocabulaire latin des relations et des partis politiques sous la République* (Paris, 1963) *ad loc.*

13 Or to defeat a friend in court, especially when his *existimatio* is at stake. (*Att.* I, 1, 4.)

14 Cf. Lucil. 1133 (Warmington), who, like a fool, went among the low debauchees to dance.

15 For similar expressions see Cic. *Verr.* II, 3, 210; II, 4, 54; *Phil.* II, 9.

16 On the *existimatio* of Philodamus of Lampsacus, Cic. *Verr.* II, 1, 64; on Amyntas of Apollonis, Cic. *Flac.* 72; on Cluentius Habitus of Larinum, *Clu,* 11; cf. the *existimatio* of Fonteius' family, *Font.* 41.

17 A more balanced statement, which is probably Cicero's own view, is to be found in *Inven. Rhet.* II, 157: *existimatio* holds a middle position between virtue and profit. People are attracted by virtue, knowledge, and truth, by their intrinsic merit – and by their own worth. Profit and advantage (*fructus et utilitas*) are derived from money. But there is something which unites qualities from both these classes: by its own merit and worth it entices us and leads us on, and also holds out to us a prospect of some advantage to

induce us to seek it more eagerly. Examples are friendship (*amicitia*) and *existimatio bona* (reputation).

18 Against authenticity: M. I. Henderson, 'De Commentariolo Petitionis', *JRS* 40 (1950) 8; R. G. M. Nisbet, 'The Commentariolum Petitionis,' *JRS* 51 (1961) 84, thinks that it is too cynical to have been published during an election campaign, see esp. §§5, 19, 35, 42, 45-47, 52. J. P. V. D. Balsdon, 'The Commentariolum Petitionis', *CQ* 56 (1963) 292. See, however, R. Syme, *The Roman Revolution* (Oxford 1939) 11 n. 5: The pamphlet reveals much of the truth about Cicero's candidature, though it is not necessarily written by Q. Cicero. Cf. *JRS* 37 (1947) 200; Chr. Meier: *Res publica amissa* (Wiesbaden 1966) passim. And recently, John S. Richardson, *The Commentariolum Petitionis, Historia* 20 (1971) 436. R. E. A. Palmer, Tre lettere in cerca di storico, *Riv, di fil.* Class 99 (1971) 385.

19 *Homines enim non modo promitti sibi, praesertim quod de candidato petant, sed etiam large et honorifice promitti volunt [Com. Pet. 44).*

20 *Sic homines fronte et oratione magis quam ipso beneficio capiuntur (Com. Pet. 46).*

21 Z. Yavetz, *Plebs and Princeps* 101 ff; cf. p. 43. Isoc. IV. 130, VIII, 72.

22 P. A. Brunt, '*Amicitia* in the Late Roman Republic', *Proceedings of the Cambridge Philological Society* 191, n.s. XI (1965) 19.

23 For other examples about Verres' eagerness to keep up his image (*existimatio*), see *Verr.* II, 3, 137; 139; 140; 154.

24 I dealt with the problems in *Plebs and Princeps.* 132 ff and will not discuss these points here.

25 M. Gelzer. *Kl. Schriften.* II, 312.

26 L. Piotrowicz, 'De Q. Caecilii Metelli Pii Scipionis in M. Porcium Uticensem invectiva', *Eos* 18 (1912) 129; F. Roger Dunkle, 'The Greek Tyrant and Roman Political Invective', *TAPA* 98 (1967) 155.

27 On crowd reactions in circuses and theatres, see Z. Yavetz, *Plebs and Princeps,* 18-24. I was not aware of Traugott Bollinger, *Theatralis Licentia* (Winterthur, 1969).

28 For rumors spread against Crassus, see Sall. *Cat.* 48.

29 Z. Yavetz, *Plebs and Princeps* 137. On propaganda and public opinion from 58 to 53 BC, see especially L. R. Taylor: *Party Politics in the Age of Caesar* (Berkeley, Calif. 1949) esp. 142 ff. J. H. Collins, 'Propaganda, Ethics, and Psychological Assumptions in Caesar's Writings', Frankfurt 1952 (unpubl.).

30 Cic. *Cael.* 16, 38.

31 U. E. Paoli, *Rome: Its People, Life and Customs* (1958; Eng. trans., 1963, p. 267 ff.).

32 Though such is not the case in this passage. For Cicero's wit see Maer *Sat.* II (1-15).

33 Z. Yavetz, *Plebs and Princeps* 51-53, 64, 98-100, 105.

34 When the younger Pliny was censured for having written licentious verses and for having read them in public, he said: *Nec vero moleste fero hanc esse de moribus meis existimationem* (*Ep.* 5, 3, 3). He was happy that people expected better things of him.

35 Cf. *QFr.* II, 15B, 2.

36 Cf. *Deum me sancit facere pietas, civium porcet pudor* (Ennius *Trag.* 338 W).

37 See also Cic. *Verr.* II 3, 190: *In hoc genere facilior est existimatio quam reprehensio* – It is easier to form one's opinion (in the

sense of the Greek *doxa*) than to make out a case for blame based on solid facts.

38 J. Hellegouarch, *Le Vocabulaire Latin*, 365.

39 For *existimatio* in the plural, see also Cic. *QFr.* I, 1, 43; cf. also *clandestina existimatio* with *tacita existimatio*, in Cic. *Font.* 28.

40 The use of the *fama* and *existimatio* in *Div. Caec.* 71–72 is also very instructive.

41 Cf. Hellegouarch, *Le Vocabulaire Latin*, 363.

INDEXES

INDEX OF SUBJECTS AND NAMES

INDEX OF SOURCES

INDEX OF AUTHORS